STUDIES IN IMPERIALISM

general editor John M. MacKenzie

Established in the belief that imperialism as a cultural phenomenon had as significant an effect on the dominant as on the subordinate societies, Studies in Imperialism seeks to develop the new socio-cultural approach which has emerged through cross-disciplinary work on popular culture, media studies, art history, the study of education and religion, sports history, and children's literature. The cultural emphasis embraces studies of migration and race, while the older political, and constitutional, economic and military concerns will never be far away. It will incorporate comparative work on European and American empire-building, with the chronological focus primarily, though not exclusively, on the nineteenth and twentieth centuries, when these cultural exchanges were most powerfully at work.

Travellers in Africa

This book shows how the writings of travellers in Africa during the era of Victorian exploration tell us more about nineteenth-century Britain than about Africa.

The author places the narratives in their historical and cultural context, and examines how racial images may be affected by social change and literary form.

Through detailed considerations of accounts of Africans' eating habits, of the reported effects of Africa upon the objects the travellers carried with them, and of Stanley's controversial Emin Pasha Relief Expedition, deep anxieties over British social change and cultural identity are exposed. The author argues that such concerns have to be recognised in any discussion on the construction and transmission of racial stereotypes. The book closes with a consideration of Conrad's *Heart of Darkness* as a travel narrative and contrasts Marlow's Congo with Stanley's.

Tim Youngs is Lecturer in English at the Nottingham Trent University.

STUDIES IN IMPERIALISM

Propaganda and empire
The manipulation of British public opinion, 1880–1960 John M. MacKenzie

Imperialism and popular culture
ed. John M. MacKenzie

Ephemeral vistas
The Expositions Universelles, Great Exhibitions
and World's Fairs, 1851–1939 Paul Greenhalgh

'At duty's call'
A study in obsolete patriotism W. J. Reader

Images of the army
The military in British art, 1815–1914 J. W. M. Hichberger

The empire of nature
Hunting, conservation and British imperialism John M. MacKenzie

Imperial medicine and indigenous societies
ed. David Arnold

Imperialism and juvenile literature
ed. Jeffrey Richards

Asia in western fiction
ed. Robin W. Winks and James R. Rush

Making imperial mentalities
Socialisation and British imperialism ed. J. A. Mangan

Empire and sexuality
The British experience Ronald M. Hyam

Imperialism and the natural world
ed. John M. MacKenzie

Emigrants and empire
British settlement in the dominions between the wars ed. Stephen Constantine

Revolution and empire
English politics and the American colonies in the seventeenth century Robert M. Bliss

Air power and colonial control
The Royal Air Force 1919–39 David E. Omissi

Acts of supremacy
The British Empire and the stage, 1790–1930 J. S. Bratton et al.

Policing the Empire
Government, authority and control, 1830–1940 ed. David Anderson, David Killingray

Policing and decolonisation
Nationalism, politics and the police, 1917–65 ed. David Anderson, David Killingray

Popular imperialism and the military, 1850–1950
ed. John M. MacKenzie

The language of empire
Myths and metaphors of popular imperialism, 1880–1918 Robert H. MacDonald

Travellers in Africa

BRITISH TRAVELOGUES, 1850–1900

Tim Youngs

MANCHESTER UNIVERSITY PRESS
Manchester and New York

Distributed exclusively in the USA and Canada by
ST. MARTIN'S PRESS

Published by Manchester University Press
Oxford Road, Manchester M13 9NR, UK
and Room 400, 175 Fifth Avenue, New York, NY 10010, USA

Distributed exclusively in the USA and Canada
by St. Martin's Press, Inc.,
175 Fifth Avenue, New York, NY 10010, USA

Extracts from *Heart of Darkness* by Joseph Conrad, A Norton Critical
Edition, edited by Robert Kimbrough, are reprinted by permission of
W. W. Norton & Company, Inc. © 1988, 1981, 1963 by W. W. Norton
& Company, Inc. Copyright renewed 1991 by Robert A. Kimbrough.

British Library Cataloguing-in-Publication Data
A catalogue record for this book is available from the British Library

Library of Congress Cataloging-in-Publication Data
   Youngs, Tim.
      Travellers in Africa : British travelogues, 1850–1900 / Tim
   Youngs.
        p.   cm.
   Includes bibliographical references.
   ISBN 0–7190–3969–X
      1. British travellers—History—19th century. 2. Africa–
   –Description and travel. 3. Travellers—Africa. I. Title.
   G240.Y69   1994
   916.04'23—dc20   94–12624

ISBN 0 7190 3969 X *hardback*

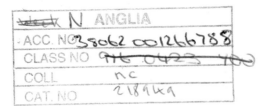
Photoset in Trump Medieval by
Northern Phototypesetting Co. Ltd., Bolton
Printed in Great Britain by
Biddles Ltd, Guildford and King's Lynn

CONTENTS

List of figures — page vii
General introduction — ix
Author's acknowledgements — x

Introduction   1

1 Adventures in Abyssinia   14
The terrain   14
Mansfield Parkyns: the black diamond   15
The hostage crisis   24
The reporter   29
The capitalist   37
The emissary   39
The outcome   48

2 Victorian writing; African eating: digesting Africa   54
Food and the town   54
Raw states   58
Eating and writing   72
Food, commodity, and identity   75

3 Beads and cords of love   81
The context   81
Speke's cords of love   84
Grant's modesty and the cooking pot   93
Burton's baubles   95
Cameron: the umbrella and the loin cloth   99
The white man with the open hand   105

4 'Gone the cry of "Forward, forward" ': crisis and narrative   113
Get Emin   113
The crisis of authority   118
Troup and damages   121
Barttelot: the true English nature   122
Jameson and the good name   127
Jephson's class   131
The doctor   135
Ward: the adventurer   137
Stanley and the book   140

CONTENTS

5 **Consuming Stanley**   151
   The press   151
   Public opinion and the sham explorer   167
   Stanley and the market   173

6 **Vaporising Bula Matari: Conrad's *Heart of Darkness***   182

Conclusion—208
Bibliography—215
Index—231

FIGURES

1 King Theodore's House at Magdala 1869.
By kind permission of the Royal Geographical Society   *page* 27

2 G. H. Portal in Abyssinian Costume.
From Gerald H. Portal, *My Mission to Abyssinia*
(London: Edward Arnold, 1892)   40

3 'An Abyssinian Devouring Raw Beef'.
From John Camden Hotten, ed., *Abyssinia and Its
People; or, Life in the Land of Prester John* (London:
John Camden Hotten, 1868)   60

4 African celebratory feast in Boma, Zaire. Dr Falkenstein 1876.
By kind permission of the Royal Geographical Society   63

5 Speke with copy of *Blackwood's Magazine* 1864.
By kind permission of the Royal Geographical Society   86

6 'Stanley's Hot Goal'. *Rare Bits*, 15 November 1890.
By kind permission of the Royal Geographical Society   164

7 John Bull and Stanley. *John Bull*, 22 November 1890.
By kind permission of the Royal Geographical Society   166

8 First house built by Stanley, showing railway material.
Photographed by Moore in the 1880s.
By kind permission of the Royal Geographical Society   188

9 Congo railway material. Photographed by Moore in the 1880s.
By kind permission of the Royal Geographical Society   190

GENERAL EDITOR'S INTRODUCTION

Non-fictional publishing in the nineteenth century was sustained by accounts of exploration and travel. Publishers' lists abounded with such works which became the major means by which representations of other geographies and other cultures were transmitted to a western public. By the last few decades of the century, these publications had become a significant arena for the discussion and dissemination of some of the key issues of the imperial project. Those produced by dominant figures like David Livingstone and some of those relating to *causes célèbres* such as the Emin Pasha Relief Expedition or the death of Gordon were among the greatest best-sellers of the age. If most of the purchasers of the originals were members of the middle and upper classes, material from them inevitably percolated downwards through popular summaries, juvenile literature and articles in periodicals.

Such works of travel have been the subject of increasingly sophisticated studies in recent years, for they are capable of delivering insights into the attitudes and psychology of their originators, the discourses of power and intellectual hegemony through which they represented other peoples and cultures and the demands of the growing market which they satisfied. They are in other words a prime location for the myths, metaphors and tropes of imperial hegemony as well as of the doubts and ambiguities that characterised the extension of empire.

They were not of course produced in a vacuum. As Tim Youngs demonstrates in this study, they can be understood only within specific social and economic contexts, by careful reference to their attendant relationships of commerce and class. He also places them within the rapidly developing dynamic of Victorian imperialism. He introduces strikingly fresh criteria, for example diet and eating habits, into the discussion of the representation of cultural relativities and demonstrates the complexity of the 'struggles for meaning, control, and definition' together with questions of social and national identity which permeate these publications. In his extended discussion of the many accounts of the Emin Pasha Relief Expedition, he takes the analysis of that extraordinary sequence of events in important and stimulating new directions. I commend this work as a significant contribution to the post-structuralist debate about culture and imperialism.

John M. MacKenzie

AUTHOR'S ACKNOWLEDGEMENTS

The Ph.D. work on which this book is based was undertaken at The Nottingham Trent University and its former avatars, Nottingham Polytechnic and Trent Polytechnic, between 1987 and 1991. The idea for the project came from Elisabeth Joyce, and funding for the research post was provided by the institution. My department, under Sandra Harris, has an enlightened policy towards research activity and conference attendance, and I am glad of this chance to acknowledge the financial assistance I have been given over the past six years, first as a research assistant and latterly as a lecturer.

Many people have given generously of their time and ideas, during my postgraduate term and since, as I have carried the study on. Historians Roy Bridges, John MacKenzie, George Shepperson and Iain Smith, and historian of geography Felix Driver all lessened my anxieties about the interdisciplinary nature of my task, and I am grateful to them for the interest they showed and for the helpful suggestions they made. Dave Murray introduced me to work on colonial discourse and ethnography, which I found invaluable, and took the trouble to read one of my chapters in draft form. John Lucas taught me much about the nineteenth century and a great deal besides. For the inspiration and information he has provided, no acknowledgement is sufficient. I wish also to thank my colleagues John Davie for his encouragement and support, and for always finding time for a helping word; Dave Woods and Val Cliff for technical assistance; and Karen Roberts for coping with a multitude of inter-library loan requests.

I have profited from the presentation of work-in-progress at various conferences. The paper which eventually became chapter two of this book was presented at the Association of Cultural Studies conference at Sheffield in 1990, and I am grateful to Joseph Bristow for soliciting it. Before that, Mike Cole gave me the chance to try out my ideas at the History Workshop 22 Conference at Brighton Polytechnic in 1988. More recently, the European Society for the Study of English conferences at the University of East Anglia (1991) and at Université de Bordeaux II (1993), the 'Images of Empire' conference at Royal Holloway and Bedford New College (1992), the Sociology of Literature symposium on travel writing at Essex University (1992), the Interdisciplinary Nineteenth-Century Studies conference at Arizona State University (1993), and 'The End' conference at Universitat de Barcelona (1993), all produced useful feedback. To all those concerned, and to Peter Hulme too, my thanks.

For permission to quote from the letters of Mansfield Parkyns I am grateful to John Murray, London. I am likewise indebted to the Trustees of the National Library of Scotland for permission to quote from material in the Blackwood Papers; to the Royal Geographical Society for permission to quote from newspaper cuttings held in their files on the Emin Pasha Relief Expedition, for allowing me to reproduce cartoons therefrom, and for permission to reproduce

AUTHOR'S ACKNOWLEDGEMENTS

photographs in their possession (which Nicky Sherriff, Manager of the Picture Library, kindly helped arrange); to the Library at the School of Oriental and African Studies for permission to quote from the Mackinnon Papers; to the Pitt Rivers Museum, University of Oxford, for permission to consult and quote from the Jameson Papers; to the Trustee of the Wellcome Trust for permission to quote from Wellcome's correspondence; and to the Wellcome Foundation for allowing me to quote from the company's catalogue and price lists held in the Wellcome Group Archives, London.

Every effort has been made to trace the holders of copyright material, but anyone claiming copyright is invited to get in touch with the author.

For Gurminder,
with love

Introduction

It is probably as well that I had been working on this project for six years at what is now The Nottingham Trent University, and had my Ph.D. safely awarded, before I came across Graham Greene's remark on how 'you couldn't talk of darkest Africa with any conviction when you had known Nottingham well'.[1] At the risk of appearing to engage in a belated exercise in face-saving, however, I hope to turn Greene's statement to my advantage, for it is in part my purpose in this book to undermine the conviction with which nineteenth-century British writers talked about darkest Africa, however well they knew Nottingham, or any other British town for that matter. Indeed, it is my contention that these authors wrote about Africa in the way they did because of their growing, if sometimes subliminal, unease with changes in the Britain they thought they knew so well. Let me make it clear at the outset, then, that this study is not an examination of 'darkest Africa', but rather is one of representations of Africa.

In the years since the publication of Edward Said's *Orientalism*,[2] a massive amount of scholarly work on imperialism and colonial discourse has been produced.[3] This is not the place for a detailed discussion of Said's ideas, but it may be helpful if I spend just a moment outlining the principal matters in which I follow him, for it is from his work that much of the criticism on the representation of other cultures has derived. Said points to the importance of narrative features in representing the other,[4] summing up his claims thus: 'In any instance of at least written language, there is no such thing as a delivered presence, but a *re-presence*, or a representation'.[5] This issue of representations of encounters has also been well put by Anthony Fothergill, who reminds us of a truth which is so obvious that we are likely to overlook it:

> The means by which we come to know the unknown Other will always be determined by our own terms of reference, our own horizon of understanding. Even the absolutely alien is always our alien, the negation of *our*

normality. In this sense any writing of the Other, whether it acknowledges it or not, is a writing from within, a re-inscribing, via negation, of
the writer.[6]

Discussing this process as we see it in Conrad, one literary critic,
Jeremy Hawthorn, has described imperialism as 'the imposition of alien
meanings on an unwilling recipient'.[7] Of course, imperialism is a good
deal more than this, despite the notoriously cloudy usage of the term.[8]
And plenty of things which are not imperialism also involve the
coercive attribution of significance. Nevertheless, while I do not want
to use 'imperialism' as a loose metaphor for all kinds of cultural domination, neither do I wish to restrict myself in this particular study in
imperialism to a use of the word solely in its actual economic or
political manifestations. Rather, my interest is in the beliefs and perceptions which made possible the physical exercise of imperialism and
colonialism (and which, by implication, continue to make possible
neo-colonialism and military expressions of a reputed national will).

I have as my concern, then, the cultural and political context of the
formation and circulation of images of the other as they occur in one
particular mode – travel writing – in a particular part of the world – East
and Central Africa – at a particular time – the second half of the
nineteenth century, though I hope that my methodology, and some of
my observations and conclusions, will have relevance to studies of
encounters and representations in other regions and other periods.

Since my attention throughout is on the ideology of these texts and of
the authors and their readers, it would be as well to explain in what
sense I use the term. I shall do this very briefly as any discussion of the
theories of ideology would be self-generating, would take up space I need
to devote to case-studies, and is in any case to be found in many other
places. Although the meaning of my usage of 'ideology' should be clear
from the contexts in which I employ it, I am broadly in line with John
Thompson's definition:

> Ideology, broadly speaking, is meaning in the service of power. Hence the
> study of ideology requires us to investigate the ways in which meaning is
> constructed and conveyed by symbolic forms of various kinds, from every-
> day linguistic utterances to complex images and texts; it requires us to
> investigate the social contexts within which symbolic forms are
> employed and deployed; and it calls upon us to ask whether, and if so how,
> the meaning mobilized by symbolic forms serves, in specific contexts, to
> establish and sustain relations of domination.[9]

Edward Said has drawn attention to the fact that the 'relationship
between Occident and Orient is a relationship of power, of domination,
of varying degrees of a complex hegemony'.[10] While this is true of the

Orient, the question of power and domination is indisputably true too of Africa. However, Said dismisses any simplistic notion that accounts of the Orient are mere lies or myths which can easily be debunked. Instead, he emphasises the social context and material connections of the discourse to which they belong, highlighting the latter's: 'very close ties to the enabling socio-economic and political institutions, and its redoubtable durability'.[11]

Travel writers are at once establishing their cultural affinities with, and spatial, experiential difference from, their readers. Travel writing, especially in an imperial or colonial context, is an expression of identity based on sameness to and yet remoteness from the members of the home society. One of the concerns of the present study is to investigate the use of this textual, physical, and cultural space for an exploration and affirmation or reconstitution of identity. This process is made possible also by the use – at times unconsciously, at times playfully and ironically, at times modified – of the structures and conventions of travel writing. Travel writers, that is to say, play on the organisation and tropes of the genre with the effect of signalling their own characters and their lineage. Said has distinguished between:

> strategic location, which is a way of describing the author's position in a text with regard to the Oriental material he writes about, and *strategic formation*, which is a way of analyzing the relationship between texts and the way in which groups of texts, types of texts, even textual genres, acquire mass, density, and referential power among themselves and there-after in the culture at large.[12]

Broadly speaking, a concern with these strategies underlies the present discussion.

In the last twenty years or so, anthropological concerns with structures of cultural representation have offered a means to the understanding of implicit and encoded power structures both within texts and in the societies from which those texts emanated.[13] However, these critiques have sometimes been deficient in their awareness of the contemporary material culture and often lacking much sense of the contemporary literary conventions.[14] This is a weakness, I think, of much of the recent work on colonial discourse, particularly that which concentrates on offering particular post-structuralist or psychoanalytic readings. Although each school of criticism has valuable contributions to make, too often there is insufficient reference to contemporary material circumstances which, if known about, would have to modify the arguments being made. I do have some sympathy with Homi Bhabha's view of the ambivalence of the colonial stereotype which leads him to suggest that in readings of colonial discourse:

[3]

the point of intervention should shift from the *identification* of images as positive or negative, to an understanding of the *processes of subjectification* made possible (and plausible) through stereotypical discourse.[15]

But where I part company from Bhabha is with his wish to return the results of colonial discourse to the realm of the psychoanalytic. I accept that there is a psychological impulse to colonial activity and its discourse, and it is helpful of Bhabha to point out the contradictory nature of stereotypes (blacks as savage yet as obedient servants; as sexually rampant yet as innocent as children, and so on). I do believe, however, that there are limits to the usefulness of reading racial stereotypes in terms of fetishism. Bhabha's emphasis on the role of the split subject is helpful and I share some of his views on this, but there are great problems with particular psychoanalytic approaches. They often fail, for example, to take sufficient account of the roots of psychoanalytic theory in late nineteenth-century European culture,[16] in which they are so embedded that both conceptually and linguistically its terms share the images of polarity and affinity, of repulsion and desire, of culture and nature, civilisation and savagery, lightness and darkness, of order and disorder, that characterise contemporary discourses of race, class, and gender. Thus the structures and language of psychoanalysis often look more like symptoms than explanations. Besides this aspect, there is also the problem of accounting for the relation of the individual to the collective psychology. It is in this consideration especially that psychoanalytic theories of race often fall down. Of course I am simplifying this issue tremendously, and I know there are complex ways of answering these charges, but it is worth saying for the sake of the present study that the idea of a dramatised separation '*between* races, cultures, histories, *within* histories . . . that repeats obsessively the mythical moment of disjunction'[17] may be seen as tending toward the ahistorical and unhelpful.

I share the unease expressed by Peter Hulme in his appraisal of the post-structuralist position (or rather lack of position) on ideology; that:

In purely philosophical terms [it] . . . is difficult, perhaps impossible, to counter, and it has much to teach . . . about the rigour with which one's own conceptual framework must be examined. Politically, though, such a position can lead only to quietism, since no action at all can be validated from its theoretical endpoint, or to a false radicalism which engages in constant but ultimately meaningless transgression of all defended viewpoints.[18]

I want, then, to draw upon ideas and approaches from critics of ethnography and colonialist discourse but to use them within a more historicist view than they are often given. Conversely, there is the problem of historical and biographical studies which even now take for granted the words of the explorers whom they quote. Some scholars for whom I have great respect have, frankly, seemed unable or unwilling to acknowledge, let alone deal with, the problematical status of travellers' accounts.[19]

The importance of an examination of the explorers' narratives cannot be underestimated. Too often they have been taken as straightforward evidence of their authors' claims without any critical attention being paid to the conditions of their production, their literary and ideological constructions, or their reception. In an early essay, Roy Bridges, who has done more to consider the role of travel narratives than any other historian of British imperialism in East Africa I know of, wrote that:

> Their observations on East Africa's economic potential tended to create a notion that here was a field for investment. Explicitly or implicitly most of them recommended that East Africa should be ruled by Europeans. While such ideas had little effect until the late 1870's, they did create a 'frame of reference' within which later missionaries and administrators were to work.[20]

But this acknowledgement of part of the narratives' significance stops well short of studying their composition. However, in a more recent and somewhat more sophisticated discussion, Bridges made the following suggestion:

> Broadly speaking, the material an explorer produced as a record of his journey may be divided into three categories. There is the first-stage or 'raw' record made as he went along, the more considered and organised journal or perhaps letter written during intervals of greater leisure and finally the definitive account of the expedition, usually composed after his return to Europe with a view to publication.[21]

In some ways this is a useful division and it allows Bridges to make several pertinent points. His conclusions are that, generally, journals and letters tend not to differ significantly from published travel books and that, with a few reservations, one can 'regard the explorers' published accounts of their travels as reasonably accurate representations of the evidence they actually collected at first hand or the things they themselves actually did.'[22] Yet Bridges's approach is, I feel, too empiricist. His temptation to categorise might itself be a legacy of the nineteenth-century organisation of knowledge and, while he does admit that the categories may in practice become blurred and merge, his first category is not at all helpful, for it separates the traveller from the culture to which he or she belongs. In ideological terms the 'raw' record begins with the socialisation process before the subject has even

[5]

thought of travelling. The failure to realise this, even though Bridges does acknowledge the existence of prejudice prior to travel, means that cultural phenomena are seen as acts of personal volition or as expressions of an individual rather than political unconscious.

So far as the period of study, 1850–1900, is concerned, like any set of dates it can be open to challenge: some of what I have to say applies to some texts prior to 1850 and to some texts after 1900, yet the chosen time-span provides not only a frame, but one within which important developments can be traced. Scientific and technological progress and class tensions and shifts in Britain coincide with a change in attitude towards Africa and Africans. I suggest that the relationship is a causal one. And it is my judgement that what travellers describe in Africa is mainly Britain: that the portrayal of the wilderness contains an apprehension of the city; that accounts of feudal systems in Africa constitute a commentary on the changes in British society; that the traveller's report on his or her relation to companions and to Africans is displacement of or compensation for anxieties about one's position in the British class system. To talk therefore of a homogeneous, fixed centre is misleading and deflects from material processes. As one historian of geography, Felix Driver, has stated: 'attitudes towards both exploration and empire were far more diverse than has often been recognized'.[23]

It is of course true, as Gramsci has said, that 'A given socio-historical moment is never homogeneous; on the contrary, it is rich in contradictions'.[24] And I want to do all I can to emphasise these contradictions. In doing so I am not at all understating the complicity of all classes in imperialism. Nor am I seeking to talk up the opposition to imperialism or to exaggerate any anti-racist sentiment (particularly as the apparently more benign pronouncements on race involved their own currency of stereotypes no less racist in the assumptions they made). But what I am suggesting is that the way in which those who held or aspired to power in mid- to late-nineteenth-century Britain defined themselves in opposition to others depended upon a bracketing of undesirable features and groups within Britain with scorned peoples abroad. To put it plainly, the languages of class, gender, and race are often used interchangeably. Studies which assume an undifferentiated imperial centre consensually imposing linguistic, political, and economic rule on external societies are guilty of creating the very monolith they purport to condemn. In order to compensate for what I believe is the paucity of historically informed studies emphasising social tensions present in travel writing, I have concentrated principally on the conjoining of race and class, though I do raise issues of gender and regionalism explicitly at a number of points and implicitly most of the way through.[25]

My method of criticism is aimed at recovering some sense of the struggles for meaning, control, and definition during Victoria's reign. I hope to show how, by projection and displacement, profoundly troublesome questions of national identity and self-identity were addressed obliquely, sometimes even unconsciously, as questions of authority and order, of purpose and direction, were mapped on to another landscape.

When I talk about the role of stereotypes in this process, I am in some agreement with Jan Nederveen Pieterse, who is also keen to avoid any notion of stereotypes as fixed throughout time:

> Social representations arise out of a multiplicity of historical configurations, and therefore cannot be reduced to a few simple schemas. . . . I emphasize in this study [of images of blacks in western popular culture] not their durability but their changeability, the historical relativity of social representations, and the fact that images of blacks, like ideologies of 'race', are social constructions.[26]

In short, 'Social representation is a process and to this process there is no end'.[27] There can be no overstating this message. The habit of collapsing all the changes and contradictions of the nineteenth century into an undifferentiated view of 'the Victorian age' is invidious.

My framework for the literary criticism is strongly indebted to Raymond Williams's idea that:

> any historical analysis, when it centres on a date, has to begin by recognizing that though all dates are fixed, all time is in movement. At any particular point there are complex relations between what can be called dominant, residual, and emergent institutions and practices. Then the key to an analysis is investigation and identification of the specific places these occupy within an always dynamic field.[28]

Williams is writing of 1847–48, of the year which saw – three years before the Great Exhibition at Crystal Palace heralded an idea of a feeling of calm and equipoise after Chartism and the hungry forties – the publication of *Wuthering Heights* (among other novels). In that novel the dark force is Heathcliff, with 'his black countenance . . . and his sharp cannibal teeth'.[29]

I have looked in some chapters at tropes and in others at specific deployments of them. A part of my purpose is to discern any movement in the forms and structures of representations as socio-historical conditions within my chosen period shift.

I focus on East and Central Africa both for the sake of a clear focus and because to write on West or South Africa would have required an examination of earlier periods beyond the scope of my study and would have diminished the strength of the frame. This is probably the place to

[7]

say, too, that, although I have read Livingstone and read about him, I have said little about him in this book. Much has already been written on him, and to discuss him in full would have had him take over the book completely. Much of what I say about the other travellers applies to Livingstone, and his call for commerce to accompany Christianity is felt throughout my third chapter. I have written exclusively on British narratives since to introduce those of other European countries would not leave space for a consideration of the factors internal to and the relations between those nations that had a bearing on the discourse produced, though of course (as with narratives on other regions of Africa) I have read a considerable amount of the material. Again, I hope that what I have to say about my field will have some applicability to others. It will become evident, so I may as well say it here, that I am not especially interested in attempting a definition or sweeping description of the travel narrative as a genre.[30] Travel writing feeds from and back into other forms of literature. To try to identify boundaries between various forms would be impossible and I would be deeply suspicious of any attempt at the task. It is more important to look at how travel writing works and at what functions it performs. I have many things to say about the characteristics of the narratives but my aim is to do so in terms of their purpose and effects.

My first chapter deals with Abyssinia and with how I think images of that country and the means of communicating those images changed in response to social developments in Britain. I look in particular at the 1867 military expedition against that country, and at the cultural significance of some of its narratives.

The second chapter considers accounts of food and eating habits. My theory, in a nutshell, as it were, is that as bourgeois values became increasingly important in the nineteenth century and technology advanced, so the rituals of civilised behaviour and the distance between the producer and the consumer, between even the consumer and the product, were justified by the scorn of African ways of eating.

My third chapter picks out a range of objects and commodities mentioned in narratives. I argue that the ambiguities and ambivalence of the travellers are revealed in their relation to those objects. The artefacts are used to introduce to Africa capitalist values but at the same time reflect great unease in the westerners' own social positions.

The fourth and fifth chapters have as their subject Stanley's expedition to relieve Emin Pasha. An analysis of the production and consumption of its narratives allows me quite specifically to place them in the social and intellectual context of the time, and thus to see how racial images are affected by their historical situation. I have read little on the expedition that does this. In the grand tradition of English historiography, biography, and criticism, the deep divisions over the outcome and conduct of the expedition have been personalised.[31] Any idea that these are profoundly symptomatic of the age disappear, like Emin Pasha himself, from the window. My comments on class, the relationship of the writers to their product, the commoditisation of experience and of person, and on the relationship between the literature and its society afford the opportunity for an implicit contrast with ideas of travel and heroism earlier in the century, and prove, I hope beyond any doubt, that racial representations are in large part determined by the cultural conditions of the traveller's society; that these therefore change as the nature of that society changes; that one has to understand the literary forms and their determinants before one can appreciate the ideology of representations; and that although the images may change the motivation and purpose for their construction does not.

My final chapter, on Conrad's *Heart of Darkness*, argues that the text is best read as what it purports to be: a kind of travel narrative. Only when it is seen as such and is regarded in the context of the *fin de siècle* can one begin to appreciate both the extent and the limitations of Conrad's innovativeness.

I hope this project will do something to dispel some of the myths about the myths of the so-called 'dark continent'. A much-cited work on nineteenth-century images of Africa, so much so, in fact, that its statements have quickly become accepted orthodoxy, is Patrick Brantlinger's chapter on 'The genealogy of the myth of the "dark continent"'.[32] Whatever the merits of his piece, Brantlinger is, I think, guilty of not distinguishing between different parts of Africa or between different 'tribes', a distinction which in actuality was made by contemporary commentators to a much greater extent than is commonly realised. It may well be that the basis of those distinctions was false and certainly self-serving, but to ignore them is to perpetuate a myth about the myth of the 'dark continent'. There were quite different representations of West, East and Central, North, and South Africa, according to different geographical and historical relationships. Brantlinger is by no means alone in eliding differences in this way.

Brantlinger's more general readings of explorers' narratives relies on a simplified view, though again he is not untypical in this:

> The great explorers' writings are nonfictional quest romances in which the hero-authors struggle through enchanted, bedeviled lands toward an ostensible goal . . . The humble but heroic authors move from adventure to adventure against a dark, infernal backdrop where there are no other characters of equal stature, only bewitched or demonic savages.[33]

To call these texts non-fictional is to erect a barrier needlessly and misleadingly between fiction and non-fiction. They may be quest romances based on journeys actually undertaken, but the parallels with fictional accounts of adventure are too close for there to be such a rigid distinction. The sense of the land as enchanted and bedevilled is far less pervasive than Brantlinger would have us believe.

Brantlinger understates the various movements within and across British society that helped intensify and shape the image of others. He writes that 'For middle- and upper-class Victorians, dominant over a vast working-class majority at home and increasing millions of "uncivilized" peoples of "inferior races" abroad, power was self-validating'.[34] The fact of the matter is that the dominance was being challenged; the very composition of the middle class and its relation to those above and below it was in flux. It was this fluidity and uncertainty that gave much of the charge to representations of the other. Brantlinger's model does not permit him the flexibility necessary to realise this. When, discussing the problems of writing (or not writing) about miscegenation, he refers to Joseph Thomson's *Ulu* as 'ludicrously inconsistent',[35] he inadvertently reveals a strange expectation of consistency in texts generally. There are plenty of inconsistencies in all these texts. A lot of them are ludicrous, but some are just more apparent than others.

To talk of the myth of the dark continent, then, itself assumes a more unified view than was actually the case. If anything, it would be more accurate to write of the *myths* of the dark continent, or at least to acknowledge the extent of the range of figures within the canon of the myth. One impulse behind the present study is the conviction that one cannot begin to combat continuing racism without acknowledging and examining the full range of stereotypes involved.

In his latest book, Edward Said has written of the (not always obvious) importance of empire in literature and other cultural productions. Adopting the phrase 'structures of attitude and reference', he aims to modify Raymond Williams's idea of 'structures of feeling' and apply it to, for example, the allusions to empire found in nineteenth – and early twentieth – century British and French culture, but especially in the British novel. He refers to:

> the way in which structures of location and geographical reference appear in the cultural languages of literature, history, or ethnography, sometimes allusively and sometimes carefully plotted, across several individual works that are not otherwise connected to one another or to an official ideology of 'empire'.[36]

Travel narratives are one of the primary media for the circulation, if not the formation, of structures of attitude and reference. Passing references in novels and other cultural forms to places and peoples of empire would evoke feelings and images that lengthier treatment in the writings of travellers and explorers would have instilled in their audience:

> one must connect the structures of a narrative to the ideas, concepts, experiences from which it draws support. Conrad's Africans, for example, come from a huge library of *Africanism*, so to speak, as well as from Conrad's personal experiences.[37]

The present study is, I hope, in keeping with Said's dictum that 'The job facing the cultural intellectual is . . . not to accept the politics of identity as given, but to show how all representations are constructed, for what purpose, by whom, and with what components'.[38] In making some suggestions as to the connections between image, power, social context, and narrative form, and in tracing some of the representations of Africans in the second half of the nineteenth century, I by no means intend to imply that the topic ceases to have relevance after 1900. On the contrary, the processes continue and the images are recycled and adapted, just as the direct consequences of European activity continue to be felt.[39]

Notes

1 Graham Greene, *Journey Without Maps* (London: Pan Books, 1957), p. 101.
2 Edward W. Said, *Orientalism* (Harmondsworth: Peregrine, 1985). The book was first published in 1978.
3 For an overview of some this work see Benita Parry, 'Problems in current theories of colonial discourse', *The Oxford Literary Review* 9, 1–2 (1987), 27–58.
4 Where I have used the term 'other' I have generally used lower case so as to avoid confusion with any particular psychoanalytic or philosophical usage. I use the word in the broad sense of a culture or representative of a culture perceived to be different from the self, and upon the basis of whose differences from the self the identity of the self and the society it normally inhabits is constructed or reaffirmed. Any variation on this usage will be clear from the context in which it occurs.
5 Said, *Orientalism*, p. 21.
6 Anthony Fothergill, 'Of Conrad, cannibals, and kin', in *Representing Others: White Views of Indigenous Peoples*, ed. Mick Gidley (Exeter: The University of Exeter Press, 1992), pp. 38–9.
7 Jeremy Hawthorn, *Joseph Conrad: Language and Fictional Self-Consciousness* (London: Edward Arnold, 1979), p. 24.
8 On this see, for example, Raymond Williams, *Keywords: A Vocabulary of Culture and Society* (London: Fontana Press, 1988), pp. 159–60.
9 John B. Thompson, *Ideology and Modern Culture: Critical Social Theory in the Era of Mass Communication* (Oxford: Polity Press, 1990), p. 7.
10 Said, *Orientalism*, p. 5.
11 Said, *Orientalism*, p. 6.
12 Said, *Orientalism*, p. 20.
13 See for example, James Clifford and George E. Marcus, eds, *Writing Culture: The Poetics and Politics of Ethnography* (Berkeley: University of California Press, 1986).
14 I am thinking particularly of Clifford Geertz's *Works and Lives: The Anthropologist as Author* (Oxford: Polity Press, 1988). See my review-essay on this book in *Theory*

   and Society 19 (1990), 382–6.

15 Homi K. Bhabha, 'The other question: difference, discrimination and the discourse of colonialism', in *Literature, Politics and Theory: Papers from the Essex Conference,* eds Francis Barker, Peter Hulme, Margaret Iversen, Diana Loxley (London: Methuen, 1986), p. 149.

16 Dennis Porter makes a similar point, arguing that, whatever their insights, 'Freud's observations on travel need themselves to be located in the cultural and historical context of late-nineteenth-and-early-twentieth-century Austria'. Dennis Porter, *Haunted Journeys: Desire and Transgression in European Travel Writing* (Princeton, N.J.: Princeton University Press, 1991), p. 14.

17 Bhabha, 'The other question', p. 170.

18 Peter Hulme, *Colonial Encounters: Europe and the Native Caribbean, 1492–1797* (London: Methuen, 1986), p. 6.

19 See for example: Christine Bolt, *Victorian Attitudes to Race* (London: Routledge & Kegan Paul, 1971); H. Alan C. Cairns, *Prelude to Imperialism: British Reactions to Central African Society 1840–1890* (London: Routledge & Kegan Paul, 1965); Philip D. Curtin, *The Image of Africa: British Ideas and Action, 1780–1850* (London: Macmillan, 1965); Douglas Lorimer, *Colour, Class and the Victorians: English Attitudes to the Negro in the Mid-Nineteenth Century* (Leicester: Leicester University Press, 1978). The books by Cairns and Lorimer are particularly fine and incredibly detailed, but even they suffer from a lack of literary awareness.

20 R. C. Bridges, 'Explorers and East African history', *Proceedings of the East African Academy* 1 (1963), 69.

21 Roy C. Bridges, 'Nineteenth-Century East African travel records with an appendix on "armchair geographers" and cartography', in *European Sources for Sub-Saharan Africa Before 1900: Use and Abuse*, eds. Beatrix Heintze and Adam Jones, *Paideuma* 33 (1987), 180.

22 Bridges, 'Nineteenth-century travel records', 190.

23 Felix Driver, 'Henry Morton Stanley and his critics: geography, exploration and empire', *Past & Present: A Journal of Historical Studies* 133 (November 1991), 136.

24 David Forgacs, ed., *A Gramsci Reader: Selected Writings 1916–1935* (London: Lawrence & Wishart, 1988), p. 393.

25 One recent full-length study of women's travel writing is Sara Mills's *Discourses of Difference: An Analysis of Women's Travel Writing and Colonialism* (London: Routledge, 1991). A great deal of work is now being produced on women travellers. I have tried to apply some of my ideas from the present inquiry to women's travel texts in my essay, 'Buttons and souls: some thoughts on nineteenth-century women travellers to Africa', paper given at the 1992 Sociology of Literature Symposium, 'Writing Travels', University of Essex. See also Susan L. Blake, 'A woman's trek: what difference does gender make?', in *Western Women and Imperialism*, eds. N. Chaudhuri and M. Strobel (Bloomington: Indiana University Press, 1992), pp. 19–34. Criticism on women travellers tends to look particularly at how women's subordinate position at home may be reflected in possibly more sympathetic attention to the domestic and personal activities of the people they encounter than may be shown by male travellers. Much of the criticism also focuses on the nature of textual authority in women's texts. This involves matters of tone, imagery, and the manipulation of established structures and conventions. Attitudes towards gender roles, which a number of critics feel are objectified by the distancing gained through travel (i.e. women travellers find a physical and textual space in which to perceive more clearly, and perhaps comment on, culturally specific ideas of gender, thereby leading to a new sense of subjectivity) are also receiving an increasing amount of attention. One of the most persuasive approaches to these ideas is provided by Erin O'Connor, '"A pleasure to be indulged with caution": gender and prophylaxis in Mary Kingsley's *Travels in West Africa*' (a paper delivered to the 1993 INCS Conference at Arizona State University).

26 Jan Nederveen Pieterse, *White on Black: Images of Africa and Blacks in Western Popular Culture* (New Haven: Yale University Press, 1992), p. 12.

27 Jan Nederveen Pieterse, *White on Black*, p. 15.
28 Raymond Williams, 'Forms of English Fiction in 1848', in *Writing in Society* (London: Verso, [n.d.]), p. 150.
29 Emily Brontë, *Wuthering Heights*, ed. David Daiches (Harmondsworth: Penguin Books, 1965), p. 212.
30 A recent book which does concern itself more with the generic structures and images of travel narratives in the colonial context is Mary Louise Pratt's *Imperial Eyes: Travel Writing and Transculturation* (London: Routledge, 1992).
31 Felix Driver has made a similar point about the treatment by explorers' biographers of disputes in which their subjects were caught up. See Driver, 'Henry Morton Stanley and his critics', 136.
32 See Patrick Brantlinger, *Rule of Darkness: British Literature and Imperialism, 1830–1914* (Ithaca: Cornell University Press, 1988), pp. 173–97. The chapter first appeared as an essay with the title 'Victorians and Africans: the genealogy of the myth of the dark continent' in *Critical Inquiry* 12, 1 (autumn 1985), 166–203. My page references are to *Rule of Darkness*.
33 Brantlinger, *Rule of Darkness*, pp. 180–1.
34 Brantlinger, *Rule of Darkness*, p. 173.
35 Brantlinger, *Rule of Darkness*, p. 190.
36 Edward W. Said, *Culture and Imperialism* (London: Chatto & Windus, 1993), p. 61.
37 Said, *Culture and Imperialism*, p. 79.
38 Said, *Culture and Imperialism*, p. 380.
39 Of course the recycling of images depends largely on language, so it needs to be clearly understood here that where this study uses such problematic terms as 'chief', 'king', and, though I have tried to avoid it, 'tribe', it is only in paraphrasing nineteenth-century accounts of Africa. Another problematic term . . . is 'nature' which, for the sake of consistency, I have used in lower case throughout, hoping that the distinction between the physical and metaphysical will be clear from the context.

CHAPTER ONE

Adventures in Abyssinia

The terrain

It is my belief, as I have suggested in my Introduction, that post-structuralist criticism has tended to ignore changes in the material and social conditions of production and that historians have tended to concentrate on the influence of specific events upon racial images without paying sufficient attention to the forms and structures of the expression of ideology and racial stereotyping in literature. Both approaches lose sight of important processes in the construction and consumption of such images.

The present chapter will consider some British visitors to Abyssinia during the latter half of the nineteenth century. I focus on one traveller from mid-century, narratives of a military campaign in the late 1860s, and the mission of a government representative in the late 1880s.

In the first case we see a survival of the romantic idea of the Noble Savage, suggested by a playful, often detached narrative voice. In the examples from the second period we find a hardening of attitudes expressed by more aggressive narrators who aim and compete for a complete community of interest with their audience. And in the final section we witness a nostalgic if laboured reconstruction of earlier images, only for them to be wistfully dismissed. Each type of narrative I have chosen is characteristic of a certain kind of travel writing and all of them attracted some notice when they appeared. Examined in relation to one another they reveal significant connections between racial ideology, literary form and structure, and socio-political developments.

Since my framework is provided by the years from 1850 to 1900, this is not the place for a discussion of the literature on Abyssinia prior to the mid nineteenth century, and I shall save my comments on James Bruce, who travelled there between 1769 and 1772, but whose descriptions of the country were referred to throughout the nineteenth century, for my next chapter, where I shall focus on his famous accounts of the people's dietary habits. But it may be worth noting here that among the attractions of that country were its long history of Christianity, the rumours that it contained the sources of the Nile, and tales of its fabulous treasure. From ancient Greece to Renaissance times there had gathered around Homer's claim in the *Odyssey* ideas of two Ethiopias: one, of admirable people, in the east; the other, of bestial savages, in the west:

> Homer's division, nourished by a European propensity towards binary thinking, continued to develop into the most powerful of European myths about Africa, growing over the centuries into the elaborate meliorative mythologies of a 'terrestrial paradise' at the sources of the Nile or in the south, beyond the Mountains of the Moon; into the legends associated with Prester John and Abyssinia; of Monomotapa; of Sofala or Zimbabwe as King Solomon's Ophir – all these as transformational extensions of the Meroitic Ethiopia [the powerful Kushite empire of Meroe on the Nubian Nile] of the east and all set variously and at different times against a recidivist mythology of the west: the 'white man's grave', the locale of the slave trade, and the barbarities eventually so readily associated with Dahomey, Asiante and Benin in West Africa.[1]

The medieval Christian church produced allegorical images on its maps, and this 'move to a map as icon rather than as chart'[2] was consolidated by the Vandal and then the Muslim conquest of North Africa which closed the interior of Africa off from Europe for nearly a thousand years.

The Nile continued to fascinate because of the idea of a huge river flowing from a desert, its unknown sources, the empires on its upper reaches, and the stories of fabled kingdoms at its headwaters. All these notions helped create the myth of the Nile as the Gihon, one of the four rivers of Paradise. This, briefly, is something of the background against which one commentator wrote in 1868:

> It seems that there has always been something in the land which prevented a truthful estimate being formed of it. Nor have the narratives of modern travellers enlightened to any great extent the public mind upon this mysterious country.[3]

Mansfield Parkyns: the black diamond

In the 1850s Britain was by far the richest country in the world and was experiencing a period of acclaimed calm after the 'hungry forties' and the radical thirties.[4] The year 1851 had seen the Great Exhibition at the Crystal Palace. Fears of working-class protests and of mob disturbances at the opening proved unfounded and, in the words of one historian: 'The sun of social harmony seemed to rise bright in an unclouded heaven'.[5] By the close of the exhibition more than six million tickets had been sold to members of all classes. The role of railways in carrying people to the event had helped promote the idea of London as the centre of a cohesive nation, whilst the organisation of exhibits enshrined the principle of hierarchy with Britain at the international apex.[6] It was only two years after the Great Exhibition that *Life in Abyssinia* by the gloriously named Mansfield Parkyns was published.[7]

Parkyns's father was from landed gentry and his mother from a rising commercial class in Nottinghamshire; a type of alliance of great importance in nineteenth-century Britain as the power structures and material interests of the two groups were negotiated.[8] Parkyns himself was sent down from Cambridge (for reasons now unknown), and his journey to Abyssinia via the Middle East seems to have been undertaken in the spirit of adventure. The ambiguity of Parkyns's social situation, illustrative of the growth in power and mobility of the commercial middle class and of its increasing encroachment on and accommodation by the upper and aristocratic classes, is reflected in his narrative and in the response of reviewers to his book (as I shall show below). Indeed, I believe that it is mirrored in the very structure and form of his work, which I take to be an indication of the changes in writing about 'race' that were to occur in the nineteenth century.

At the beginning of his book Parkyns writes:

> It was my original intention to write solely on the habits of the people, without bringing myself into notice in any part of the story; but from this I was dissuaded, by being told that without a little personal narrative the book would be unreadable. I have therefore divided the subject into two parts – Travel, and Manners and Customs. (I, 3–4)

The statement suggests a revealing conflict between the cultural or anthropological function and the literary convention of self-presentation. This unease over the relationship of the narrator to the content reflects the larger changes that were to occur from mid-century. The rise of the middle class posed a challenge to the idea of the gentleman amateur, while the professionalisation of science not only hardened racial attitudes but left little room for the kind of individual whimsy on which gentlemen like Parkyns traded. Discomfort over the growing sense of the changing situation is apparent throughout Parkyns's volumes, especially in his attempts to use humour to deflect it.

During the composition of his work Parkyns wrote to his publisher:

> I can I believe with truth assert that the part [sic] you have read & that I now send you are among the least interesting, further on in proportion to my stay in the country, you will find an increase of anecdote & adventure

though of the latter I have not put too much for fear of falling into the common fault of egotism.[9]

Parkyns's shyness of egotism owes more to a gentlemanly distaste for brash self-promotion than to a genuine urge for personal withdrawal. The precedents available to him encouraged the creation of a first-person narrator whose observations contributed to the construction of that character yet who could be viewed as distanced from the author himself. This unavoidably has consequences for the literary record of travels. If Parkyns can draw upon and cultivate a manner of writing which offers an apparent individuality of expression and combine it with a seemingly accurate account of places and people he has encountered then he can satisfy both his audience's demand and his own desire not to be immodest. (This, as will be seen below, fosters a characteristically British reading of him as an eccentric; a reading which eases the problem of class by evading it since he cannot, therefore, be readily classified.) Thus, again during the writing of his book, Parkyns told his publisher:

> As regards alterations I have always said that I yield everything to your superior judgement in these matters. Only two things I would suggest – 1st that I should not like my book to appear 'got up' but to remain as much as possible in my own style bad though it be – & 2nd that in some cases, passages & expressions which might appear superfluous to a good judge or critic might be the very ones which would take most with a large proportion of the less literary public & perhaps it might occasionally be as well to risk a little ill treatment from the critics, with the chance of pleasing the manyheaded.[10]

Parkyns is clearly hoping that an idiosyncrasy of expression will convey authenticity but also that it will have popular appeal. It is a patronising gesture, but he feels the need for it and that is interesting. In the same letter he explained that in the 'Manners & Customs' section he had inserted, on the advice of literary friends, 'several extraneous bits' to save his book from being judged little better than 'an Abyssinian Domestic Cookery'.

It is the recognition of the writer's voice that gives the work a distinctive flavour without distracting from its ostensible subject: the country which has been visited. On one level, then, Parkyns's narrative voice is a very self-conscious one and *Life in Abyssinia* proves to be one of the most 'literary' of African travel narratives, with references and allusions to such authors as Chaucer, Dickens, Cervantes, and Samuel Johnson (one chapter even picking up on the latter's story, first published in 1759, of the 'Prince of Abyssinia', *Rasselas*, in its title of 'The Happy Valley').

Parkyns's experiences become his readers' vicarious ones and they are read about after he has returned to England and to his cultural traditions. He may be expected to pass on to his audience lessons learned from his proximity to nature, the Abyssinians and their land being seen as lying closer to an original state of nature than does 'civilised society'. He draws such conclusions as the following: 'Nature is the founder of custom in savage countries; though we should scarcely opt to suppose it if we judge by what we see in civilised parts of the world, where custom is the great enemy of nature' (I, 12). That this sentiment is not really as subversive as it may seem is apparent from the fact that while it is 'civilised' society which receives adverse criticism in these comments, the opposing terms would not be altered for the reverse prejudice to be expressed. That is to say, later in the century aggressively racist statements would still be premised upon the opposition of nature to civilisation. What does make Parkyns distinctive, however, is his readiness to strip away, literally, his wrappings of civilisation (he assumes Abyssinian dress) and to adopt as preferable the customs of the people with whom he is temporarily residing. Parkyns distinguishes himself from other travellers by 'the fact of my having identified myself with the natives, perhaps more than any of my predecessors, not only in habits, but also in feelings' (I, 3).

In fact, Parkyns's approach is no less racist for all that. It depends upon a one-way movement which fixes the 'natives' in a timeless and changeless state.[11] In short, Parkyns is willing to 'go native' but not to have the 'natives' go civilised. He frees himself to enter their spatial and temporal domain but they must not invade his.

As indicators of his cultural shift Parkyns includes passages on his adopting the Abyssinians' modes of eating and dress. Told in an intimate and often humorous tone, these episodes create a degree of candidness which, together with his self-deprecating manner, solicits our confidence. But in fact this voice conceals as much as it discloses, most notably on the matter of sexual relations. Despite the presence of a voyeuristic eroticism in Parkyns's book, he does not reveal that he did take an Abyssinian wife, Tures, whom he describes as a 'friend whose sincerity and attachment and . . . a servant whose devotion and fidelity might well set aside the prejudices which vain Europeans have against a skin a little darker than their own'.[12]

The silence on the marriage to Tures must make us question Parkyns's openness with us and resist the disarming appeal of his narrative voice, especially since even a few years later, at the start of the British military campaign in Abyssinia (which I discuss below), marriages by Europeans to Abyssinian women were discussed with no great rancour, although it may be that in those cases such unions are safely distanced through a third voice.[13]

Parkyns does use Abyssinia to criticise the attitudes and customs of his home country, but we ought nevertheless to beware of assuming his complete abandonment of those values. His national and class identities are projected quite clearly if not consistently and it is note-worthy that, as well as his reticence about his marriage, he has little to say about Said, his black servant. We should not rush into believing that because of the extent of his apparent initiation into Abyssinian society Parkyns somehow transcends the dominant ideologies of his age. He has this to say about the black women:

> Though flowers of beauty nowhere bloom with more luxuriance than in Æthiopia, yet alas! there shines on them no mental sun. Passion, the species of affection borne by a faithful dog to its master, and childish gratitude for kindnesses, are the best qualities discernible in the physi-ognomy of an Eastern woman. (II, 5)

His entry into the other cultural world allows him a critical per-spective on troublesome features of his home society, the better to work out, even if subconsciously, his own cultural and national position; to fix it, in other words, through the gaze of the other. When watching a troop of monkeys he remarks that 'their women are as noisy and fond of disputation as any fish-fag in Billingsgate' (I, 228), and he tells jokes against the Irish (disparaging references to whom are prevalent in the travel narratives of these years). Such remarks are born of deep unease at the domestic situation. It is as if in divesting himself of the trappings of civilisation Parkyns is concerned to find his own essential worth through his reflection in the eyes of the Abyssinians. And perhaps such an ostensibly liberal instruction as his call to: 'Remember that you should endeavour to adapt yourself to the customs and ideas of the people where you are travelling, and not expect them to fall into yours' (I, 423) is merely a device to facilitate this particular kind of self-discovery. If blacks are closer to nature, then they can better appreciate the natural worth of white visitors, a question important to the Europe of increasing industrialisation and of developing technology.

Although the use made by Parkyns of the Abyssinians in having them confirm his essential self and his attitude to his home country is quite evident, he cannot depend upon any smooth unified literary structure for its expression. He attempts to enshrine his travels in one volume and a description of the people in another, and even then is unsure as to whereabouts in one of the volumes he should place the chapter on history. He wonders too about the length of the chapters. Informing his publisher of complaints he has heard from several people about this fault in other books, he asks:

[19]

could not the very long ones we have in this 2nd vol be broken into shorter ones – as for example chapt. – Religion – next chapter Religion (continued) & it looks better in a book & is more convenient for reading.[14]

And it is only in the appendix to the first volume of *Life in Abyssinia* that Parkyns feels it fit to declare:

> *Real* worth is not lost among savages; a great or good man, whether he be one of themselves or a stranger, is soon recognised; but titled nothingness is a luxury which, poor creatures! their unenlightened minds cannot well appreciate, however deserving of respect the possessor of it may be among civilized people, as the walking monument of some ancestor who *was* a great man, or of some ancestress who was a king's mistress. (I, 423)

Parkyns's dismissal of families' past glories belongs to the sentiments of those who saw the aristocratic Dedlocks in Dickens's *Bleak House* (published in book form in the same year) in a similar light, and is in keeping with the growing nineteenth-century emphasis on individual merit, though in this case that merit is determined by intrinsic qualities rather than particular achievements; a kind of natural aristocracy to replace the decaying socially constructed one.

But once more there is no real dialogue here. We do not have a direct report from the 'savages' on their estimate of the 'real worth' of white travellers. The former are used only to objectify the narrator's own prejudices and outlook.

My point about the relationship between cultural and social changes and literary form and structure may be illustrated by the fact that in Parkyns's book the romantic perspective sits uneasily with the scientific one. Throughout the second volume, which purports to give an account of the geography, natural history and social customs of Abyssinia, we are actually offered little detailed and verifiable information. What we are given is primarily anecdotal. The chapter entitled 'Births and Marriages' introduces the master of the house at his birth, and moves on to relate in voyeuristic terms early sexual encounters and young marriages, a licentious wedding feast and the marriage of a twelve-year-old girl to a man in his mid-fifties.

Nevertheless, despite the division of the work into two volumes, Parkyns undermines the readers' expectations of what to find in the second. Later in the century, as anthropology developed as a professionalised scientific discipline, this would become more difficult for writers to do, but here Parkyns appears in part to be subversive and in part to play tricks in order to underline his character and individuality. He commences the chapter 'Anecdotes Illustrative of Character, etc.' by warning travellers against attributing to 'an entire population traits which they may have observed in the townspeople, or even in their own immediate followers' (II, 180), and warning readers against 'attributing to character what may belong only to custom' (II, 181). He then recites tales of bloodthirsty cruelty and afterwards remarks that the earlier admonishment was given so that we wouldn't see the whole nation as barbaric, but at the end of the chapter he shockingly exposes his audience to itself, forcing upon it some amount of self-reflexiveness. He explains that 'I have only told a few striking occurrences of the worst possible nature' because: 'anecdotes of benevolence, justice, fidelity, etc., are rarely interesting enough either to become topics of conversation where they happen, or to amuse an English public' (II, 222). Of course, Parkyns is attempting to have it both ways: to reinforce the stereotype while making a show of dissecting it. This is perhaps why he places the English and Abyssinian public on common ground by implying that a taste for horror and scandal characterises them both. Indeed, the implication is that this is a universal trait as the phrase 'where they happen' would indicate. As the movement towards imperialism gathered pace in later years such mocking tones grew rare – at least in the narratives of male travellers – and with it the constant subversion and teasing of the literary structures employed to express certain racist views. This is not to claim that the romantic view of the savage, for example, was free from racism, but it may be that there was greater scope for flexibility and therefore for strategies of questioning than later science and professionalisation, with their encoding of hierarchies, permitted.

Parkyns also delivers a remarkable passage in which he readily acknowledges the problems of writing on his subject, of trying to transmit a just idea of the country and its people to someone who has never been there. With great astuteness and an astonishingly frank self-awareness, he notes that:

> a description of things so totally different from what we are accustomed to, as everything in those romantic countries is, cannot help losing its African feeling and becoming Anglicized, first by an English description, secondly and mainly by passing through the English imagination of the reader. (II, 317–18)

There can be no denying the fact that behind this utterance is a desire to fix the other in its place, to keep the exotic at a distance, but equally it must be conceded that Parkyns does raise here large and genuine questions of cultural translation and assimilation.

Yet the book's final emphasis is on the way Parkyns has used Abyssinia and its peoples as the means of situating himself so that he can criticise aspects of Europe. As he prepares to return home Abyssinia has fulfilled its function for him:

[21]

Europe in general, but perhaps England in particular, has customs which, to a stranger, or even to a native who, like myself, has the power of closing an English mind's eye and opening a nigger one whenever he pleases, appear as wonderful and unaccountable as any that I have described or that could be found among the most barbarous nations in the world. (II, 329–30)

Parkyns does seem ostentatiously tactical in this posture. Pretending to see one's home and people through a black person's eyes is no less inaccurate and no less insidious than claiming to speak for the black person. All the same, Parkyns's stance does, I think it right to say, prefigure the dilemma facing the modern ethnographer outlined by Vincent Crapanzano, who writes that when the ethnographer arrives back in his first country:

In many ways the shock of return is more difficult than the initial encounter . . . His sense of self has been altered. At home he must be his old self again, must adopt the standpoint of those significant within his 'own' socio-historical horizon. He requires re-affirmation – reconstitution – and this he tries to accomplish in many ways, including most notably, the *writing* of ethnography.[15]

There are signs that Parkyns does not get over the shock of return. He brings with him an Abyssinian servant and names his home 'Abyssinia Cottage' (which causes us to giggle a good deal more than the naming of African lakes, mountains and waterfalls after British monarchs, aristocrats, and businessmen). More fundamentally, we find him acknowledging the effect of his travels upon his English sensibility, and the expression of this anxiety makes very clear the perceived problems of fitting a cultural journey into a stable form. Again, the admission is contained in a letter to his publisher:

I am rejoiced that we did not publish sooner for I find that the early part of my writing is not at all suited to my present taste, in fact I was then only half an Englishman – I wish you would look over pages 19 & 20 of the *MS Appendix* I now send & scratch out anything you may think too *liberal*.[16]

Parkyns's view of himself as having been 'half an Englishman' is a perfect illustration of Crapanzano's point. Of more interest than Parkyns's personal predicament, however, is his culture's response to it. The image of him as something less than an Englishman survived within and beyond his book. And it would seem either that his readership never recovered from its shock at the sense of self which emerged from his narrative or that it perpetuated this shock as a means of managing a potentially threatening position. (Even Cumming's recent biography of Parkyns was marketed on this perception, with its title of *The Gentleman Savage*.) It was recognised of Parkyns that 'He is a genuine traveller in spirit and in manners'.[17] The trouble for many was that he had travelled too far. In acquiring those Abyssinian habits his readers considered detrimental he had in their eyes alienated himself from European civilisation. There was a limit to how far his readers would be carried along with him. A complaint by the same anonymous reviewer in *The Athenæum* makes explicit the vital significance of literary structures in transmitting racial ideologies. The reviewer has this to say on the connection between the structure of Parkyns's journey and the organisation of his book:

> He seems to be perfectly indifferent as to time, and is never anxious to arrive anywhere. This indifferent state of mind is reflected in his narrative, in which he rarely takes the trouble to say where he is going or what is his motive for moving rather than staying still.[18]

Condemnation of Africans' alleged indifference to the passing of time was commonplace throughout the latter two-thirds of the nineteenth century and is closely associated with the capitalist quantification of time (and space) in the guise of the moral and spiritual worth of productivity.[19] Western impatience with alleged African indolence connoted a movement away from the envied pre-lapsarian leisure of the Noble Savage (which belonged to an earlier stage in the development of industrial society), and might therefore be said to mark the irreversible acceptance of the changes wrought by the growth of technology and the expansion of capital. But the reviewer's complaint relates socioeconomic unproductiveness to a literary irrationality and purposelessness in a manner that is not a simple call for further explanation and logical progress, but a demand for the kind of narrative in which the hero's physical and social journeys have recognisable validity and tangible benefits.

Parkyns at this time could not really be seen as useful and so for many of his contemporaries could be accommodated only as a pointed anachronism, endearing or otherwise. He was labelled an agreeable savage and an eccentric. The *Athenæum* review concludes with these words: 'We have quoted enough to show that here is, in its peculiar way, a genuine book, – a pleasant contribution from a traveller of the good old stamp to Christmas reading'.[20] The terminology of that sentence imbues Parkyns with an exoticism furnished by uniqueness of character and antiquated survival while the seasonal recommendation aims to contain any threat he may hold.

Similarly, in a review entitled 'Abyssinian Aberrations', Frederick Hardman wrote in *Blackwood's Edinburgh Magazine*:

> We accept the book, and are grateful for it. With the author's tastes, depraved though we cannot but consider them, we purpose not to meddle.

[23]

Men of his stamp should be prized, like black diamonds, by reason of their rarity.[21]

Eccentrics and Noble Savages are rarely deemed useful; nor are such products as they may have to offer. Parkyns's narrative was (appropriately) taken to have leisure value but little practical worth.

The hostage crisis

In the 1860s the image of Abyssinia changed considerably from that presented by Parkyns. Differences between his perspective and that of his reviewers have been noted above, but the 1860s saw developments in the relationship of the two countries which may have been fed somewhat by the ideology of scientific racism but which had far more to do with the dynamics of foreign affairs and domestic social tensions. Parkyns's book was published before the Crimean War (1854–56), the Indian Mutiny (1857), the humiliation of Britain by Bismarck over Schleswig and Holstein (1864), the American Civil War (1861–65), and Governor Eyre's brutal suppression of the revolt in Jamaica (1865). These events contributed to a hardening of nationalist and racist sentiment, with the latter finding a new scientific outlet after the founding in 1863 of the Anthropological Society of London by James Hunt, who 'used its meetings and publications to proclaim the superiority of Anglo-Saxons over all others, and especially over nonwhite, peoples'.[22] At the same time there was renewed anxiety about class conflict at home. Arguments over Eyre's conduct were often linked explicitly to the rights or management of the working classes,[23] and similar issues had been prominent in the debates leading up to the 1867 Reform Act. Furthermore, in 1865 occurred the deaths of Lord Palmerston and Richard Cobden:

> two of the greatest political men of their time. Their deaths had a symbolic quality which contemporaries recognized. Palmerston had lived long . . . and had become identified with the established forces of society, the ruling class of the Regency still exercising its authority, still confident in its capacities. . . . Cobden, conversely, had died before his time, retired to Sussex as 'one of the great agricultural interest', aware that the great Radical hopes that had been pinned on him had not been fulfilled . . . The immediate future lay with what was to emerge in the dealings between the ruling-class heirs of Palmerston and the slowly gathering, rather disparate and not always mutually amenable popular forces which looked to John Bright for leadership.[24]

Barrister Bernard Cracroft had shown in his contribution to *Essays on Reform* (1867) that in the 1865 House of Commons there were at least

326 aristocratic members, with a 'good three quarters of the Commons all connected to each other, and to the Lords, by blood as well as by interest',[25] but the ruling class felt insecure none the less.

Within the terms of the debate over the 1867 Reform Act, the aristocracy sought to retain leadership and the middle class to gain it, while both groups agreed that the working classes should be kept subordinate. It was felt that the ruling classes needed to demonstrate their continued fitness to rule and to show themselves capable of national leadership. In this view:

> The wide and distinguished support for Eyre was symptomatic in some quarters of the growing conviction that in Britain itself a more authoritarian executive would remedy the ills in society and at the same time ensure the premier position of the existing elites.[26]

In 1866 Disraeli had seen the importance of enhancing Britain's imperial role as a means of pronouncing its position as a world power at a time when there were tremendous changes in the world, and in the following year he sensed that a successful show of imperial strength would 'serve as a focus for the energies of the whole nation' and offer a compelling 'foundation for national unity'.[27] Whilst, says Freda Harcourt, he may not have planned it in these explicit terms, the Abyssinian campaign launched this new phase of imperialism which, in its deliberateness and chauvinism, marked a clear break from the previous handling of imperial and foreign affairs.[28]

All these factors mean it is correct but insufficient for Douglas Lorimer to observe that 'In the mid-nineteenth century, a new vigorous racist ideology challenged the humanitarian traditions of the anti-slavery movement, and preached a new doctrine of racial supremacy'.[29] Lorimer's focus is, I think, too narrow and tends to elevate in a very mechanical way conscious ideologies above socio-economic pressures. If the interrelationship between the imperial sphere and domestic society is to be properly understood it has to be accepted that ideology is more complex and often more concealed than Lorimer's concept of athletic indoctrination would have it. To illustrate this I want to show how, in the second half of the 1860s, the British attitude towards Abyssinia took a turn that offered authors the sense of usefulness judged to be lacking in Parkyns. In part this was supplied by a policy decision, but the larger impetus came from the culture and was multi-layered. The full extent of the motives and of the ramifications was (and is) beyond the consciousness of any one individual or group.

In 1860 Plowden and Bell, two British residents (the former of whom had been British Consul at Massowa) who had guided Abyssinia's King Theodore were killed fighting a rebel chief (Garad, Theodore's brother-in-law) and it was commonly asserted that thereafter Theodore became a more autocratic and cruel ruler. Failing to obtain British and French help against hostile Moslems in neighbouring Eastern Sudan, Theodore's reaction against Britain intensified when Stern, an English missionary, brought to Abyssinia a copy of his own book containing derogatory remarks about the king, to whom they were translated. Stern and his companions were then held as captives. In 1862 Captain Cameron, British Consul at Massowa, received from Theodore a letter to Queen Victoria professing amity with her and common enmity against the Moslems, and asking for safe passage through Egypt for his ambassadors. But the letter got no further than the Foreign Office and met with no reply (a fact most British commentators, however bellicose, roundly condemned). Cameron was imprisoned and in 1864 Rassam, Resident at Aden, was also taken prisoner with his companions Dr Blanc and Lieutenant Prideaux after seeking to obtain the release of the others. All the captives came to be held at the rock fortress of Magdala (Fig. 1). Negotiations for their freedom came to nothing. After public debate as to whether and how to send out an expedition to force their release, a plan of action was decided upon. The plans utilised Britain's commercial and imperial influence:

> The right man to command the expedition sent from Bombay was fortunately found in Sir Robert Napier, a distinguished officer of engineers, who had done admirable service in the Second Sikh and the Indian Mutiny Wars. . . . Thousands of mules were purchased in Spain, Italy and Asia Minor; many hundreds of camels were brought from Arabia and Egypt. Elephants to carry mountain guns were taken with the expedition from the great port of western India, the force landing at Annesley Bay in the last month of 1867. About 12,000 troops were sent, with as many more men of the transport service and camp followers.[30]

The Indian connection is of course extremely important, but what I want to note here, in addition to the obvious material supplies and financial support obtained from India (as well as *matériel* bought or brought from other countries) is the idea of character-forming and empire-saving experience provided by service in that country. In a sense that concept is a corollary of the transformation of raw material obtained from colonies: India provides the requirements of individual and racial leadership.

The advance guard of four thousand men under Sir Charles Staveley arrived at Dalanta, within miles of Magdala, in April 1868. At Fahla Hill the advance party came under fire from the Abyssinians and had to be supported by the troops in the rear. Sanderson's account of the ensuing conflict reveals the importance to Britain of technology applied in a military context:

Figure 1 King Theodore's House at Magdala 1869.

The sailors unshipped their rocket-tubes from the mules' backs and in less than a minute sent one of the terrible missiles whizzing at the foe, followed by a regular discharge. The enemy had no experience of such engines of warfare, and paused in terror, while the horses plunged and broke away in flight. Then, rallying at the voice of the chiefs, the Abyssinians came rushing on, to be met by the fire of Snider rifles carried by the men of the 4th Regiment. This was the first engagement in which British troops ever used breechloaders, and the unceasing fire amazed and terrified the foe. Slowly at first, and then faster, they withdrew, pursued by the bullets and rockets.[31]

The first use of the Sniders and the fearful impact of the rockets is characteristic of the deployment of advanced military technology against enemies whose physical and cultural features are deemed inferior. It was said that this battle of Aroghee cost the Abyssinians at least five hundred men killed but the British only thirty wounded. Many of the chiefs subsequently surrendered, leaving the defiant Theodore under threat not only from the British but also from the Gallas, who were hostile to him. When the British stormed Magdala they found, in Sanderson's words, the following scene:

> Near the gate lay Theodore's body, bearing two wounds. His death was due to suicide by firing a pistol into his mouth. A few bodies of chiefs lay near the lower and the upper gates. A hundred prisoners were found in chains. The place was dismantled and destroyed by gunpowder and fire, and the expedition returned to the coast, leaving nothing of the fortress and town but blackened rock. The commander became Lord Napier of Magdala, G.C.B. In 1870 he was Commander-in-Chief in India. From 1876 to 1882 he was Governor of Gibralter; in 1890 he died Field-Marshal and Constable of the Tower.[32]

Several features of this account reflect changes in the British view of Abyssinia and illustrate the ways in which they are inscribed in literature and history. Such technological weaponry as Theodore possesses is used by him to destroy himself. His suicide is contrasted with the energy the British force has directed against him and his territory.

The social elevation of Napier, together with his military promotion, makes his reception quite different from that given to the agreeably eccentric Parkyns. I realise, of course, that the character of the military expedition made this difference inevitable, but that is partly my point. The response to travellers of any sort will vary with the nature of the journey, as, therefore, will the reaction to impressions of the foreign landscape and people. Clearly, then, there is a greater range of factors to be considered than many critics of travel writing and colonial discourse have traditionally allowed. With Napier's expedition, the preferment of white superiority is given institutional recognition, encouraging national support for Napier and signalling the collective function of his triumph. Writing in 1867, before the expedition's success, Dufton urged the use of force to free the captives whatever the British government's past errors and proclaimed: 'The national character must be maintained, the national honour vindicated, though it cost much treasure, and even blood'.[33] Dufton made no secret of the imperial rationale for this display of national strength. He was worried that:

> By the course we have hitherto adopted in the matter, we have in the eyes of the ignorant multitudes of Oriental nations lost a good deal of our prestige . . . And if this state of things were permitted to continue, the nations of India would soon learn to throw off their allegiances, and the Englishmen, who for the next twenty years will be seeking the sources of the Nile, would step into foot-chains wherever they went. This must not be.[34]

The issue of the captives becomes secondary to a demonstration of national and, by extension, imperial power *pour encourager les autres*.[35]

The narratives of the expedition marked a shift from personal adventure to national identification; from private pursuits to a public cause. Dufton urges the colonisation and exploitation of what he sees as one of the richest and most fertile countries in the world and which, he says, is at present occupied by people not far removed from savages. Dufton's prophecy was somewhat wide of the mark, and it didn't do him much good as he was killed by some Shohos in May the following year (1868) while in the service of the Intelligence Department. But the premise of his comments was certainly true: the trend was towards a perception of unified national interests. These were held to be embodied in the campaign and, as I shall contend, consequently in the narratives of the campaign also.

The official reward of Napier's leadership is very much linked with this developing sense of national identity. The title, Lord Napier of Magdala imposes his name on the Abyssinian scene as a tribute to his triumph and facilitates a kind of custodial entry of the African battle-scene into British culture and history. Magdala is appended to Napier: it has become part of his identity but is subordinate to his Britishness. It signifies his rise. Finally, it again distinguishes this discourse from that of Parkyns, whose Abyssinia Cottage must now seem an outdated quaintness.[36]

At the same time, England is at pains to broadcast its sense of justice and pity. The death of Theodore's widow in the British camp before the expedition left the country, and the death of their young son in England after some time spent in India under British care, supply a lesson in the destruction of innocence by a cruel party but also solicits applause for British compassion and charity. All these points were raised by Sir Samuel Baker on 5 June 1868:

> The rock of Magdala is the everlasting tombstone that covers the remains of Theodore, King of Ethiopia; at the same time it is an imperishable monument not only of British bravery and enterprise, but of British justice and moderation: unlike those savage wars that have reddened their paths with blood, and desolated the land by rapine, no single act of injustice has been reported throughout our long and difficult march, and England retires from Abyssinia respected by barbarians and honoured by the civilised world.[37]

The reporter

Someone later to be of great interest dined with Napier during the campaign. Henry Morton Stanley covered the expedition as a correspondent for the *New York Herald*, and wrote a book about the mission which he completed in 1869 but which was not published until 1874, when it appeared with another volume on the war against the Ashantee.[38] Stanley's presence further indicates the political and social changes occurring in the west as they were reflected in the Abyssinian crisis. These have a direct bearing upon the form and aims of the contemporary narratives.

Those who accompanied Napier were felt to be performing a useful role and one which contributed to British social cohesion as well as international influence. Observations on the country fed this impression of national purpose. Individual feats came to carry a representative status of a nature unavailable to Parkyns. This was inevitable given the sort of incident related by one concerned commentator, Beke, who reported Samuel, Theodore's steward, as pointing to the imprisoned British Consul and asking the latter's fellow captives '"Do you know who lies here? . . . This is Victoria!"'. Beke protested against the great indignity done to 'the name of Her Majesty and the honour of the British nation'.[39]

Even where successes were personal ones, such as Stanley's scoop through bribing the telegraph operator at Suez so that his dispatches were the first to be sent out (helped too by the subsequent fortuitous breakdown of the cable between Malta and Alexandria), making his report of the fall of Magdala the 'sole authoritative source for almost a week',[40] they assume a common value because they are felt to demonstrate salient or important emergent characteristics of the age. (The *Oxford English Dictionary*'s citations of 'scoop' in the journalistic sense both date from the 1880s, some time later.)

Stanley's journalistic coup, the magnitude of which impressed the *New York Herald*'s proprietor, James Gordon Bennett Junior, and helped decide him later that Stanley was the right man to seek out Livingstone, introduces a strident financial motivation to travel narratives of Africa. I shall look more closely at the idea of proprietary rights over such stories in a later chapter but I want here to assert that Stanley's oneupmanship over his rivals in the press (including G. A. Henty), which was criticised by some as fraudulent and by others as vulgar and brash, marks – heralds, I should say – a more transparently pecuniary and individual basis for the appearance of the narrative than, in the main, existed hitherto.[41] And I suggest that this fact, together with a much greater reticence about himself in this book than we have in his later works, may indicate a lack of precedent for a personal narrative of travel in Africa visibly having its *raison d'être* in individual financial gain. (Other travellers would, for example, cite the national

interest in advocating commercial expansion.) At a time when journalism, especially in America, was becoming a more individual affair,
with reporters gaining a higher profile, the parameters of the expression
of the self were not yet clearly defined.

I have argued elsewhere that Stanley's 1872 *How I Found Livingstone*
is a transitional text in this regard,[42] and that the consequences for the
descriptions of Africa and Africans are highly significant, but I think
that elements of this can be traced back to Stanley's narrative of the
Abyssinian campaign. In particular, the idea that the 1860s and 1870s
saw an increasing perception of self-identity according to one's relationship to the commercial nexus is well worth considering. Writing
near the beginning of the final decade of the nineteenth century, one of
Stanley's biographers made the following assessment of his subject's
time in Abyssinia:

> Stanley's career in Abyssinia was, from first to last, an unqualified
> success. Not only did he discharge his duties as correspondent with
> marked ability, but upon several occasions he made himself of great use to
> the officers of the English staff. He distanced the English correspondents
> by his graphic reports and the rapidity with which he forwarded his
> despatches to the coast. . . . In connection with this, however, and without
> in any way detracting from Stanley's personal ability, it must be remem-
> bered that he was being backed up by a millionaire, who spared no expense
> to obtain early news.[43]

This idea of individual achievement through a socially useful act, supported by a commercial network, speaks to the emergent values of the
period. It is tied closely to the rise of individual self-interest, which in
turn was linked to the construction of a more nationalistic umbrella
above it, maintaining the comforting sense of some kind of tie between
the individuals as the emphasis on individual self-help and social
mobility further eroded old class boundaries.[44]

The importance of spectacle in later Victorian years as part of this
process has been acknowledged by Cannadine and other historians and
the scale of the military expedition against Theodore could be said to
conform to that appetite. It is of course a spectacle which needs to be
described to those physically remote from it, and this would seem to
complicate the role of the narrator who must try to find within this
function some room for the accommodation of the more established
task of communicating one's own adventures.

It is true, of course, that although Stanley had spent his early years in
Wales he had gone to Abyssinia via America, where he lived for some
years and whence he took the name by which he is now known, but the
arguments over the American Civil War and republicanism would have

[31]

enhanced his awareness of the political positions of the time. Moreover, his experiences in Abyssinia gave him a direct impression of English class relationships, for the officers he met with behaved snobbishly towards him and, as a number of biographers have noted, he was humiliated by their bearing towards him.[45]

It may be this sense of humiliation which underlies Stanley's remarks on the Abyssinian peasantry:

> The poorest class of peasants, like the ancient Troglodytes, also find these cavernous recesses in the cliffs admirable habitations, and a protection against cruel chiefs and unjust masters. But, growing bold from impunity, and waxing stronger and insolent with numbers, the peasants generally select a chief from amongst themselves, and become the oppressors instead of the oppressed. (p. 40)

This may be a recognition of the oppression suffered by peasants, but the acknowledgement is tempered by the warning (and to Stanley's contemporaries it was still a very real fear) that the downtrodden will themselves exploit and maltreat others. He continues:

> This is the history of most of the towns in this neighbourhood, and, in fact, of those of the whole of Abyssinia. What the Abyssinians are today, not many centuries ago the warlike British barons were; or the Highlanders who used to make many a wild foray upon the more peaceful burghers of the Lowlands; or the robber counts of the Rhine. (p. 41)

Momentarily, then, Stanley brings the discussion threateningly close to home, apparently about to expose the historical limitations of British (and European) systems, and it may well be a sublimation of his treatment at the hands of the English officers which informs this near-justification of the Abyssinian peasants' behaviour. It is perhaps his consciousness of class discrimination and the peculiarities of its replication in race prejudice that permits the humour and relatively unassertive persona in his book on Magdala compared with his later writings.[46] In a sense Stanley's vision of a cyclical oppression is personally prophetic since he later came to aspire after some of the English values he reacted against in Abyssinia: his personally damaging greeting of Livingstone ('I presume') was influenced largely by his fear that the older man would turn out to share the coldness and reserve of the English officers Stanley had met in Napier's expedition; and he would later impose himself on blacks and subordinate white companions in similar fashion.

Against uncertain shifts, essential worth (by which I have in mind ideas of natural and material value) is also to be inferred from the ambivalent tone of Stanley's pronouncement on the power of money.

He writes of its influence in Abyssinia but what he says has relevance to the west too at this time of expanding commerce:

> the dollar in Abyssinia is an important genius; it causes water to flow from solid rocks; it brings forth food in abundance for 20,000 men and 60,000 animals; it makes the plains to overflow with goats and bleating kids; it causes the inhabitants to pull down their houses, and give their rafters to the Commissariat Department. (pp. 99–100)

I have mentioned the new military technology carried by the British force and the logistical support for the expedition. Stanley's paean to the dollar is in part a tribute to the strength of the finance behind such adventures. It also forms a literary re-enactment of that power, for the rhetorical structure of Stanley's clauses impresses upon the reader the sense of the country and its people and their property yielding to the dollar, and in that case it may be argued that it is the reader, in consuming this ideological image, who completes the act of purchase. Identification puts the readers in the position of those whose possession of the dollar has the country at their command, thereby offering them a vicarious empowerment which invites the private individual reader into the cohesive network of imperialist relationships at the expense of the blacks.[47] But at the same time the displacement on to Abyssinia of the growing power of money in America and Europe to transcend class barriers, to become in itself the means and principle of authority, suggests an uneasy reaction to the consequent overriding of individual worth. (The irony produced by the quasi-biblical structure of Stanley's rhetoric heightens this unease by invoking higher values only to locate them in the past.)

The discomfort is quite apparent from the terms of the debate in Britain over the Abyssinian question. The strategies devised for smoothing such conflicting feelings are well illustrated by the words of Sir Henry Rawlinson, who, speaking in the House of Commons in July 1867 in support of the dispatch of a military expedition, declaimed that those who opposed such an action 'disregard, or at any rate undervalue, the value of "prestige"'; a value with which Rawlinson pronounced himself well acquainted, having served for thirty years in the east. In a telling comparison he announced: 'I . . . look on "prestige" very much as I look on "credit" in finance. It is a power which enables us to achieve very great results with very small means at our immediate disposal'. It was therefore his position that 'I cannot subscribe to the doctrine now so prevalent of weighing the honour of England against gold and silver'.[48] Rawlinson's speech is framed so as to appeal to the very instincts from which he appears to distance himself. The reference to 'credit' ensures this. His stance also embraces, however, those survivors of the privi-

[33]

leged classes who find the facts of commerce vulgar. The appeal, then, is to a kind of aristocracy of motive. It is symptomatic of this attempted balance that some resolution should be sought by appealing to ever more prominent notions of national prestige. In narrative form, a similar process may be found in Stanley's account of the sacking of the imperial palace in Abyssinia, during which the generals, their staffs, and the members of the press 'were the only ones exempt from the picking and pocketing mania which had taken possession of all heroes' (p. 155). The description closes with a very measured conclusion which may be seen as an effort to re-establish the order of a social and economic hierarchy:

> The auction lasted two days. The total receipts amounted to £5,000. This sum was divided among the non-commissioned officers and men who were southward of the Bechilo, which gave each man a trifle over four dollars. (p. 169)

Although the awarding of such prize money was nothing new, the identity of the bidders and the competition between them hints at the challenges to power within British society. There is rivalry between the military's officer class, the scientific establishment (working out its position between professionalisation and popularism), and private wealth:

> Mr. Holmes, as the worthy representative of the British Museum, was in his glory. Armed with ample funds, he outdid all in most things; but Colonel Frazer ran him hard because he was buying for a wealthy regimental mass – 11th Hussars – and when anything belonging personally to Theodore was offered for sale, there were private gentlemen who outdid them both. (pp. 168–9)

These competing parties emblematise the forces connected with and feeding off African travel and exploration, which, in turn, influence the perpetuation or modification of African stereotypes accordingly.

Stanley encourages the possibility of geographical and social mobility, and we have here to note material changes too. A closer affinity with his audience is constructed than we find in Parkyns. This difference is made possible both by the newer imperialist ethos (fuelled by the nationalist impetus I have been discussing), and by the technological advances which went with it. Cables and newspapers, as well as professional journals, faster transport and improved communications, facilitated a more direct transmission of news and views than was possible just a few years before. Parkyns's voice is therefore heard as more remote – physically and culturally – than Stanley's. It is useful in this regard to be reminded that 'The word "telegraph" means "writing at a distance"'.[49] Even where the words that are read are published after the traveller's return, the fact of regular and undelayed contact whilst abroad means that they are received after some kind of contemporaneous bond has been established, though I hold this to be a trend rather than an absolute law. Several national and foreign newspapers sent correspondents to cover the Abyssinian campaign, and 'Each week the *London Illustrated News* depicted the progress of the army in its strange surroundings, giving an immediacy to the long and detailed reports in the daily and periodical press'.[50] Accordingly, Stanley solicits support, if not identification:

> Strains of music burst from the bands. The National Anthem, 'God save the Queen,' was never played or sung with greater effect or vigour than when the hoary crags of Magdala responded to its notes in an overwhelming chorus of echoes! (p. 149)

It is indeed a divinely approved anthem that has the once hostile, now conquered, landscape answering it. Little wonder that Stanley trumpets 'Though a little war, it was a great campaign' (p. 177).

There is also to be remarked upon a treatment of themes relating to the Abyssinians in 'universal' (or western aesthetic and religious) terms. This phenomenon, like the focus of the expedition itself, aims to divert class differences by appealing to the supposedly greater considerations of morality and the lessons of history. It is to be seen at its most salient in Stanley's description of the dead Theodore. The passage can in some ways be read as the end of the Noble Savage before the probing of the classifying sciences and the intrusive eye of the new journalism:

> The body of a native, seemingly half-famished; clad in coarse upper garments, dingy with wear, and ragged with tear, covering under garments of clean linen!
>
> The face of deep brown was the most remarkable one in Abyssinia; it bore the appearance of one who had passed through many anxious hours. His eyes, now fading, gave evidence yet of the piercing power for which they were celebrated. The mouth was well-defined and thin-lipped. The lower lip seemed adapted to express scorn, and a trace of it was still visible. As he gasped his last, two rows of white teeth were disclosed. Over his mouth two strong lines arched to a high aquiline nose. The face was broad, high-cheek-boned, with a lofty, prominent forehead, and overhanging eyebrows. The hair was divided into three large plaits extending from the forehead to the back of the neck, which latter appeared to be a very tower of strength. The body measured five feet and eight inches, and was very muscular and broad-chested. There was a character about the features, denoting great firmness or obstinacy mingled with ferocity; but perhaps the latter idea was suggested upon remembering the many cruelties ascribed to him. (p. 149)

[35]

The journalist's precise, carefully structured, words convey the contemporary fascination with specific, measured details of features, again signalling the popularisation of scientific discourse as it found its way into all kinds of prose descriptions of characters. They reveal too the importance to the imperial power of acquiring knowledge of its territory through mapping. The application of this process to the physical landscape is obvious, but Stanley's survey of Theodore's corpse is a corollary of this and exemplifies the type of possession that can be gained of subject people. One should not neglect to point out though that Theodore is looked upon as most definitely a unique leader of men, no matter how misguided his deeds. His face explains both his power (as conventional descriptions of members of the ruling classes did at home) and his abuse of it. Whatever his cruelties, he is admitted to be a man of some qualities. (This is common once the British have defeated an enemy whom they have formerly reviled lest the victory seem too hollow.) Even Frederick Myatt, whose 1970 book seems to share some of the attitudes that characterised the expedition, concedes that Theodore's retreat to Magdala was a great achievement.[51] The tension between these two positions is superficially resolved by the presentation of the dead king according to a recognisable intellectual motif:

> And this is how we saw the remains of him who had called himself THEODORUS, EMPEROR OF ABYSSINIA, THE DESCENDANT OF MENILEK; SON OF SOLOMON, KING OF KINGS, LORD OF EARTH, CONQUEROR OF ETHIOPIA, REGENERATOR OF AFRICA, AND SAVIOUR OF JERUSALEM, now dying – dead by his own hand! (p. 149)

The fall of Theodore recalls in part the old theme of the vanity of human ambitions, but it also borrows from the classical conception of the hero who has overreached himself and been struck down. In this case there is, for Britain, a self-aggrandising representation of the Fates, for not only did Theodore kill himself by firing his pistol into his mouth, but, from the evidence of Stanley and others, the weapon used was one given to him as a present from Queen Victoria. The gods are British.

Amongst the results of the expedition were that, in practical terms, the message to India had been sent, and the 'post-Crimean reforms in the army (a vital test, if not motive, of the expedition) had apparently been justified in the clearest possible way'.[52] In literary terms, the fact and circumstances of the action had a strong impact. The campaign and the crisis of which it was a part spawned several (complementary rather than conflicting) narratives and also produced a second edition of Parkyns's book. Interestingly, for it would underline Parkyns's individuality and the different attitudes to Abyssinia before and after 1860, Duncan Cumming claims that Parkyns 'declined to join the expedition on the grounds that many Abyssinians were his friends and that he had no intention of fighting them'.[53] And, in information which has more symbolic than intrinsic value, Cumming writes further that the name of Parkyns's son John (born of his Abyssinian wife Tures) was on the list of the prisoners freed at Magdala.

The capitalist

The impact of the Abyssinian question on political and literary positions was apparent even before the decision to send the expedition had been reached. Charles Beke had been highly critical of the British government for its negative reaction to his proposals for the commercial exploitation of Abyssinia and for what he saw as its political mishandling of the affair in endangering the missionary captives in order to cover up its mistakes. He brought out in 1867 a second edition of a work he had first published two years previously. Explaining his reasons for bringing out the book now and deferring his personal narrative until later because 'the public must be far more interested in the fate of the hapless British Captives in Abyssinia than in our [his and his wife's] personal adventures',[54] he nevertheless admits that:

> I have found it necessary, in order to render the present volume complete in itself, to refer to several matters connected with myself and my late journey, which would have appeared more suitably in connexion with that [personal] narrative, had it formed a portion of the single work originally contemplated. (p. iv)

Beke had been in Abyssinia from 1840 to 1843 and had, several times since then, appealed to the Foreign Office and to the Board of Trade for support for his enthusiastic espousal of commercial enterprise there.[55] Seizing on the growing interest in Abyssinia he was able to subordinate his personal experiences to perceived physical facts (introducing the former only to prove the latter) in pursuit of his larger concerns: the spread of civilisation and commerce. The result is a complicated text, containing overtly personal observations, scientific and economic musings, private and official correspondence, extensive references to official reports, and an appendix with letters from Beke to Russell and Palmerston, correspondence from the captives, and Beke's 1861 'Proposal for a Tram-road between the Cotton-fields of Ethiopia and the Coast of the Red Sea'. A sometimes desperate attempt to open up a campaign on all fronts, it reflects many of the strands which fed the crisis.

Beke argued that Africa had remained 'as it were a sealed book' because Europeans had approached it from the wrong direction. It was by following the road from the east that 'Africa will be regenerated by means of European commerce as the precursor of Christian civilization' (p. xi). As far as Abyssinia was concerned this would be done by cultivating the indigenous cotton, extracting the iron and coal found there, and by establishing 'a line of electric telegraph' across the country as 'an important portion of a chain connecting Europe with India, Australia, China, and the entire eastern hemisphere' (pp. 244–5). Peace and the release of the missionaries would be secured by an honest settlement of the political dispute and by attracting Theodore to the commercial opportunities for his nation. Profit and the divinity are on the side of peace:

> it is difficult to place a limit upon [Abyssinia's] capabilities under a more favourable state of things – the first grand step towards which is to induce the feelings of fresh wants in the minds of its inhabitants, who, to satisfy such feeling, would not be long in turning their lovely country to the uses for which it was assuredly intended by its Creator. (p. 250)

Beke calls for national and individual economic action to ensure that God's wishes are realised. He sees the roots of the current problem as lying in British policy in 1862 which sought to disengage from involvement with Abyssinia. The loss of commitment and interest, he claims, provoked Theodore to take his rash course, forcing Britain to take notice again of the country from which it had turned away, thus handing Theodore a kind of victory already and leaving British policy adrift and confused.

At one point in the book, generously declaring that he can bear personal losses for the greater good, he complains all the same that:

> For myself, I had fondly hoped that I might personally have had some share in the regeneration of a country to which I have devoted so many years of the prime of my life. But, according to all appearances, mine is likely to be the common fate of pioneers, projectors, and inventors, who, after sacrificing time, talents, fortune, health, nay even life ... in the furtherance of their views, find themselves, at the moment of fruition, superseded by others more fortunate, who reap the benefit and too often obtain likewise the credit of all their labours and sacrifices. (pp. 248–9)

There is something pathetic in his apologetic self-justification: 'I may seem to be constantly referring to myself; but mixed up as I am with so much that has occurred, it is impossible to avoid doing so' (p. 263). His apologies centre on the personal presence, not on his strident political pronouncements. What I am saying, in other words, is that Beke's devotion to commerce and 'civilisation' forces him to choose those aspects above his own record; that this priority has him highlighting the discourses which form the background to other travellers' narratives;

and that the imminent military expedition simply concentrated some of those cultural matters which facilitate the production of 'personal' testimonies. The capitalist ideology that in other travellers' accounts has given hidden support to their tales has, in Beke, come to the fore-ground, and he wants us to know the personal cost to him.

Beke's personal sacrifice makes him a kind of missionary to the expansion of western capitalism (as so many actual missionaries in fact were), granting others the chance to enjoy a direct involvement with the other country and to use a textual form more suited to the presentation of personal adventures. Both Beke and Napier, then, provide more 'useful', practical, and nationally beneficial roles than Parkyns. This must and does find its reflection in the shape as well as the content of narratives. And this is probably the place to note that Hotten claimed his book of extracts from travellers' tales to be in direct response to a call from *The Times* in October 1867 for a book that would do something to fill the general ignorance about Abyssinia.[56]

The emissary

I shall close this chapter by looking at a narrative of travel in Abyssinia from much later in the century in order to suggest how images and positions may shift subliminally as well as deliberately. The narrative is Gerald H. Portal's *My Mission to Abyssinia*, published in 1892,[57] and I proffer it as an illustration rather than an absolute summation of my argument. What this book reveals, I think, is how an individual voice, a personal narrative, may quickly once again be permitted after the sup-pression of a perceived threat. A significant feature of the product is its semblance of a return to an earlier pre-crisis mode. With the modesty affordable to a man representing a nation that has crushed its enemy a couple of decades earlier and seen a more sympathetic monarch enthroned, Portal, the Consul-General at Zanzibar, hopes that:

> As regards the simple story of our adventures . . . my readers may feel even the smallest fraction of the interest which was so thrilling at the time to ourselves. Few men, even among African travellers, have stood face to face with death so often in the course of a few months . . . and have lived, absolutely unhurt to tell the tale. (p. v)

It is thoroughly in keeping with the purportedly individual and inquisitive movement back into the country that the frontispiece of the book should bear a photograph of Portal 'in Abyssinian costume', stand-ing with spear, shield, and cloak (Fig. 2), and that Portal should declare his intention to write 'a personal narrative, and not a political treatise' (p. 1) as if the two spheres could be altogether separated. It is in keeping

[39]

Figure 2 G. H. Portal in Abyssinian Costume. From Gerald H. Portal, *My Mission to Abyssinia*

with the quite laboured effort to evoke past attitudes and perceptions that the photograph should offer such a manufactured representation. There is more than the simple fact of advances in photography that distinguishes Portal's depiction in Abyssinian dress from Parkyns's. Portal's adoption of a formal Victorian pose parallels his very deliberate entry into the country; Parkyns's ready abandonment of European garb, more humorously conveyed, belongs to an earlier discourse with a romantic survival.

Portal's introduction does more than contextualise his narrative: it reveals the events that have made possible the modified view of the Abyssinians and the reformulation of the individual British traveller's relationship to them. Briefly, Portal recalls how, in December 1883, news of the massacre at Melbeis in Kordofan of General Hicks Pasha, his English officers, and the ten thousand Egyptian soldiers with them, made it evident that Egypt would be unable to cope with the Mahdist rebellion in the Sudan. The decision to withdraw from the Sudan had left the garrisons along the Abyssinian frontier in a precarious position, finding 'themselves between the triumphant hordes of the Mahdi on the one side and the almost equally savage armies of the Negoos [the Negus, King Johannis] on the other' (p. 2). A treaty between Admiral Sir William Hewett and King Johannis had the latter giving safe conduct to Massowa in return for the cession of the fortresses on the Abyssinian frontier evacuated by Egypt and the equipment and goods collected from there. Trouble arose when Italian troops occupied Massowa and then Sahati. A body of Italian soldiers on their way to Sahati were attacked by a far larger force belonging to Ras Alula, the Abyssinian chief of the frontier province of Hamazen, in the battle of Dogali. Italian calls for vengeance gave way to reflection on the costs and possible losses of such an expedition. It is this consideration which provides the connection between the 1867–68 campaign and Portal's mission, the accomplishment of the former having allowed the latter the performance of the role which he now presents in a personal narrative. Portal explains that the English had greater influence than any other nation over Abyssinia because:

King Johannis owed not only his throne but life itself to the admirably-conducted expedition of Lord Napier of 1868 [which] had deeply impressed the king and the people of Abyssinia with the determination, honesty, and disinterestedness of a nation who sent a large army through the very heart of a distant and mountainous country, and who, having vanquished all opposition and effected its object . . . freed Abyssinia from the bloodthirsty tyranny of the mad King Theodore, placed Prince Kassa of Tigré on the throne, with the name of King Johannis, and then rapidly evacuated the country; paying fair prices for all provisions, for labour, and

[41]

for information, and finally leaving no trace of a hostile expedition except the existence of a badly-needed road . . . (pp. 111–12)

Regretting that Italy had waited nine months after its defeat at Dogali before asking for English mediation, Portal was entrusted on 17 October 1887 with the mission of making peace between Johannis and the Italians.

There is a clear difference posited between King Johannis, to whom rational appeals may be made (the purpose of Portal's travels) and the 'bloodthirsty tyranny of the mad King Theodore'. The replacement of Theodore has resulted in a more positive view of the Abyssinians. The people were judged by the character of their leader.

Portal was accompanied by Beech, who was serving in the Egyptian army, and by Hutchisson, Portal's reliable English servant. When they were all short of water: 'Poor Hutchisson was suffering dreadful pain, but he overcame his intense longing to lie down and quietly subside into oblivion, and struggled on with a pluck that is beyond all praise' (p. 52). Hutchisson's burden is valuable ideological baggage for Portal and his readers who will call for pluck from their subordinates.

The image of the faithful servant with its echoes of feudal order connects with the idea of an over-emphatic return to an earlier social mode. The year Portal's book was published was also the year in which Tennyson died. Alfred Austin, though not the first choice, became the new Poet Laureate. While not wanting to suggest any link between these two events, I do find significant the body of ideas about nation and community into which they circulate. Remarking that Austin's appointment must have owed more to his politics than to the quality of his poetry, John Lucas shows how Austin supplies:

> a kind of myth of an 'ideal' England of feudal relations, of a revived Young England. . . .
> . . . at the heart of the dream of Young England is a belief that the purity of the stock is bound up with the maintaining or, it may be, recovering of those feudalistic relations that had made 'old' England so fine a place. From which it will be seen that the myth-making proportions of this dream are as large as they are difficult to take seriously. Yet they affected many people.[58]

The kind of laboured revisioning of the past which I have touched upon, and will say more about shortly, has largely to do with the desire for the uncomplicated security of the feudal system.[59] The emphasis Portal places on the order and responsibility introduced after Napier's campaign and the enthronement of Johannis shows the advantages of this way of things and Britain's power to effect the move (even if things are a little more difficult at home). The scene is strengthened by the

[42]

presence of Hutchisson who in many ways is a sort of travelling version of the type of servant noticed by Lucas in much late-nineteenth-and early-twentieth-century literature and whose 'service implies that feudalistic structure which Alfred Austin and others offer as the ideal socio-political arrangement'.[60] Thus Hutchisson's loyal devotion shows his willingness to serve and his trust in his master:

> Hutchisson, who volunteered to accompany me in spite of the gloomy picture of the dangers and troubles before us which I drew for his edification ... behaved throughout with the greatest pluck, self-possession, and cheerfulness under difficulties. (p. 17)

'Self-possession' is of course a neat way of signalling the servant's unquestioning performance of his subordinate role.[61]

Two other features of the reconstruction of feudalism ought to be mentioned, and they are interconnected. They are the escape from the city and from technology, both of which are key elements in the creation of a mythical England. The presence of this myth from the 1890s to World War I in English poetry (especially) and novels has been well documented, but it has its manifestation in travel writing of the period also. The look away from the city was motivated in large part by theories of degeneracy derived from social Darwinism and having their literary expression in naturalism. As Lucas shrewdly observes, the survival of those who struggled for existence in the city and were deemed degenerate was a worrying indication that they were learning to adapt *down*.[62] With the growing movement of agricultural workers to the city, the search for a strong rural heart intensified, at the same time opening up an increasing division between myth and actuality, between the people and the message which was spoken for them.

Improvements in transport, weapons, communications, and so on are all associated with urban industrial production and may therefore become somewhat tainted with the dubious values and conditions of the city. To write of one's travels in a region where such advances do not exist is to present an arena in which pre-industrial life may be used either to support or to criticise contemporary Britain. A positive view would show the disadvantages of life without these developments or would acknowledge one's own technological material advantages while simultaneously demonstrating the retention of clean and honest pastoral values. A negative appraisal would complain of supposed qualities of rural life which have nearly been lost in England. In either case the depiction of rural life in the country visited feels heavily reconstructed because, for most of the travellers in these later years of the century, it is impossible to deny absolutely the felt or known-about urban situation.[63] (It is a fascinating juxtaposition that sees Parkyns and

Portal both cite Dickens, for example.)

Portal's praise of the road left by the British is a reminder of the power behind Napier's expedition, whilst his mention of the engineers having all departed removes from the scene the people whose conduct might have tarnished the image of such capabilities. (Much like the praise of the railways and detestation of the navvies who built them in Britain.) The process works conversely too. Which is to say that technology, or any kind of industrial product, can, in the 'wrong' hands, appear foolish or dangerous, thereby reconciling the British to their responsibility for such goods.

As Portal's party approaches a large village or town he becomes worried in case they are mistaken for Italians and then grows more alarmed to see women and children fleeing the site. Then:

> Luckily, however, our pacific gestures and mild demeanour attracted the attention of a stalwart young shepherd, armed with the universal spear and shield. With the help of the almighty dollar he was soon convinced of the honourable nature of our intentions, and then flew across the plain like a young gazelle, waving his spear to his fellow-townspeople and yelling the comforting word, 'Dahhân! dahhân!' (friends! friends!). (pp. 60–1)

Afterwards, as they are about to ride to the village outside which they had met the shepherd, there suddenly appeared from 'the bushes on our left ... about thirty or forty Abyssinian soldiers, all armed with Remington rifles' (p. 61). In their hands the rifles are an obvious threat. The worrying sight of the armed Abyssinians justifies the British exercise of force more generally and urges the introduction of the latest technology to accompany it. It also gives support to the Napier campaign even if the human traces of it have disappeared.

The almighty appeal of the dollar, to which Portal alluded, does function as a kind of bridge between pre- and post-industrial worlds (between city and country, Abyssinia and England) and significantly allows the market, in a literal and figurative sense, to be proffered as the site on which this meeting can take place. Thus Portal informs us that:

> markets are institutions of some importance in Abyssinia, and form part of a universal system which proves this country to be far ahead of the neighbouring tribes in the advance towards civilization. (p. 126)

He goes on to note that much of Abyssinia appears to be divided into commercial districts in which markets are held on certain fixed days of the week.

Descriptions of markets are commonplace in many of the travel narratives of East Africa and their purpose in justifying commercial entryism by the west is obvious, but there is more to it than this, and I see behind this attitude to the market a deep cultural need for this system of organised commerce to erase the differences between town and country at home. In doing so it establishes a certain view of commercial exchange as a stabilising essential of civilisation. With the focus on exchange in the marketplace (and often on the principle rather than the details) the people's characters need be described only so much as the narrator chooses. In other words, a town–country unity can be implied as well as a cultural difference predicated on 'race' posited, thereby manufacturing a national unity of the country from which the traveller has come.

For example, Portal, having proclaimed the existence of the markets as a sign of growth towards civilisation, then highlights what he sees as a deficiency in the means of exchange, rough bars of salt called 'tshô', complaining not just that 'It is difficult to imagine a more inconvenient and unsuitable form of currency than these bars of salt' (p. 127), but also, more revealingly, that 'they possess none of the qualities which are laid down by Adam Smith and Stuart Mill as necessary for a money-token or for a medium of exchange' (p. 128). The nod to the political economists here at once brands the Abyssinian system – and by dint of this its people – inferior and sets up a notion of an undivided Britain, the medium of exchange being taken as a yardstick against which other nations' currencies should be measured.

Against this, we have numerous instances of Portal attempting to reinforce, or restore, or decrying the loss of, a natural order. Just one example will suffice. Having described the making of 'tedge', a 'fermented drink greatly prized and drunk in large quantities by the Abyssinian aristocracy' (p. 66), he emphasises that the privilege of making the drink is confined to 'persons of rank and position' (p. 68) and that 'any common soldier or person of the lower orders convicted of encroaching on the privileges of the aristocracy in Abyssinia would have to pass through some very unpleasant moments before being considered to have purged his offence' (pp. 68–9). He then explains that:

> This excellent and sanitary law was made by the late King Theodore, who argued that the chiefs and upper classes could be trusted not to drink too much of the intoxicating liquor, whereas the lower orders, if allowed to make or drink tedge, would not know when to stop, and would seize every opportunity of getting drunk and of reducing themselves to the level of the beasts whom in many characteristics they already so nearly resemble. (p. 69)

The interest of this passage lies in Portal's reaction to the custom; not simply in his explicit statement about it but in his reasons for presenting it. There are points of comparison with Parkyns's use of

Abyssinian traits to criticise European practices and beliefs. Portal's conclusion from the circumstances of the preparation and consumption of 'tedge' is to wonder, in respect of this and similar rules:

> whether the 'Acts', 'Orders in Council', and 'Regulations' evolved from our beloved constitution and our beloved civilisation, were so very far superior in common sense to the edicts of this semi-savage potentate in his inaccessible ranges of African mountains. (p. 69)

It is a ruling-class desire to withhold certain things from the working classes and a dislike of government interference that seem to have motivated these remarks. Portal's writing on tedge lays bare his social sympathies but there is no real question of 'our' following the 'semi-savage potentate' (particularly after having driven him to suicide). The remote country, like the remote past, is invoked to isolate lost or threatened qualities.

For Portal, described by Lord Cromer (who had recommended him for the mission) as 'one of the best specimens of that class of Englishmen, pre-eminently healthy in mind and body, who, to the great benefit of their country, issue forth year by year from public schools',[64] the aspects of feudalism he portrays as attractive afford an opportunity to reflect on contemporary England, with the image of Abyssinians being managed accordingly. Watching the 'wildly picturesque and imposing spectacle' of 'Gooks' or 'Gûx' (p. 86), a kind of combat tournament, his conclusion is a much diluted version of the romantic construction of the Noble Savage:

> Has our higher education taught us to take light knocks and jostles, both moral and physical, with the smiling equanimity of Ras Alula's young men? In other words, has civilisation taught us to keep our temper much better than a semi-savage Abyssinian? (p. 91)

This is not so much a condemnation of British behaviour as a warning that the public-school ethos of fair play ought to be more widely held, and it is not irrelevant that Portal has been reminded by the turf which has been surrounded by a crowd of thousands of 'Lord's cricket-ground, of which, indeed, I thought somewhat wistfully on that day' (p. 87). These are unsurprising sentiments from one who was educated at Eton and played in the school cricket team.[65] The editor of his posthumously published travelogue of Uganda would later use Portal's life to exemplify 'the truth of the often-quoted opinion, that the qualities which often distinguish Englishmen in life are formed in large measure on the playing-fields'.[66] Even the women's contribution to the 'beauty of the scene' and the feeling that here were gathered 'all the best of Tigréan and North Abyssinian bravery, chivalry, and aristocracy' (p. 87) only reinforce the idea of a splendour that is as much in England's mythical past as it is geographically remote now.

The pathetic nostalgia of the evocation of chivalry (recalled some-times through temporal and here through spatial remoteness) is seen in the self-regarding view of Portal's class. Lord Cromer calls him 'chivalrous',[67] and Rodd describes his 'handsome face and knightly bearing' as typical of his 'family's origins in that southern school of chivalry, where French and English vied in feats of arms under the banners of King John and the Black Prince, in the days when lances were broken in the tilt-yards of Aquitaine'.[68]

The problems raised by the tilt towards the past are worked out more seriously by Portal, shortly after the episode discussed above, using a pastoral scene. Having 'halted for one hour only in a grassy meadow, through which flowed the Seisa, bright and clear as a Hampshire trout stream' (p. 109), Portal dwells on the attraction of permitting his party 'several hours of rest in the rich pasturage of this lovely valley' (p. 110), but decides, because of his anxiety over the twelve days already lost to his mission while at Ras Alula's, that they should not detain themselves further: 'No rest, therefore, could there be for us in the cool and pleasant valley of the Seisa' (p. 111). After crossing the Semayata mountains they encounter another range. The necessity of overcoming physical obstacles and proceeding on their way may also be read as a declaration that, having obtained what one requires from the pastoral and feudal environment, one should move on. This, after all, is true of the journey as a whole: once it has been accomplished one leaves the country and returns to one's familiar surroundings. And so:

> We might be weary, we might be sick, we might see the ribs of our mules daily defining themselves more and more prominently through the skin, and the men beginning to limp ominously as they toiled along the rocky path, but still, so long as we could move, so long even as we could be carried, our cry must ever be 'Push on, get forward.' (p. 111)

I am not arguing that the subtexts of feudalism and pastoralism that are to be found in Portal's book are characteristic of the dominant 'structures of feeling' of the time (in Raymond Williams's phrase), but I am suggesting that they are representative of a strong tendency and that, although there are different tropes for different countries, a focus on Abyssinia does reveal significant developments.

When Portal, travelling from Asmara to the capital Adowa, writes on the reason for the lack of hospitality (i.e. food supplies) to be found in the villages on the way, his explanation discloses the dark side of feudalism, thus offering another example of indirect commitment to the social system whose perceived deficiencies have led to the evocation of the pastoral and feudal in the first place. Portal tells of how every soldier of the king (and even their slaves) have the right to demand food and accommodation while travelling:

> The rations and lodgings are demanded 'in the name of Johannis, king of kings,' and woe betide any unfortunate villager who, emboldened by poverty and distress, shall dare to withhold his last handful of corn from the arrogant soldier. . . . It will readily be understood that this system . . . presses with great severity on villages like Gundet which have the misfortune to be placed on or close to a frequented road. (pp. 102–3)

These democratic sentiments rest uneasily on Portal's shoulders and probably owe more to a concern with the security of private property than with the condition of the villagers themselves. This alignment would therefore seem to be an apt illustration of the limitations of the recreated feudal scene: there may well be a turning away from the physical appearance and alleged degeneration of late-nineteenth-century Britain, but there will be no abandonment of fundamental economic and social principles where they conflict with the picturesque myth, thus giving rise to the unsatisfactory elements of the visited country. The three stages of this construction – the evocation of a pastoral setting, its placement in Abyssinia, and its restrictions when set against (or away from) the town or city – exemplify the processes I have outlined in my argument.

The outcome

Johannis rejects the peace terms conveyed by Portal not just because of Italian troop movements but for two other reasons also, which, as Portal reports them, bear more directly upon the images of a feudal society and pastoral country which he has evoked as a means of reconciling his readers to late-nineteenth-century Britain and Europe. The first is the fact of the Abyssinians' lack of 'practical experience of the power of Italy' (p. 164), suggesting, to European eyes, excessive confidence in their own numbers and force. The prospect of the crushing of an anachronistic world by a modern power is thus raised (anticipating the Italian aggression against that country between the two World Wars), though in fact the Abyssinians were to defeat the Italians at Adowa in 1896. Secondly, Portal argues that the acceptance of peace would leave the mobilised Abyssinian soldiers with nothing to do:

> these undisciplined and half-savage armies, some of them from the country of the Gallas, from Shoa, and from the extreme outskirts of Abyssinian dependencies, would refuse to return empty-handed to their own countries, and Abyssinia would soon be torn by a series of internecine struggles between the different Chiefs and Kings, the result of which it

would be impossible to foresee, but which would constitute a most
serious danger to the dynasty of King Johannis himself. (p. 166)

These words, taken from a Parliamentary paper, 'Mr. Portal's Mission to
Abyssinia' (1888), present even more starkly the threat to the feudal
nation which is endangered from without and within. The future of the
country when encroached upon by or juxtaposed with a modern
European power is limited in other ways. There is an impending disin-
tegration of the system, combined with an admission that many
changes would be for the better.

On re-entering the civilised world, Portal rejects in tone, if not in
actual words, the Abyssinia through which he has travelled. He offsets
against the hindrances with which his party met 'little acts of genuine
hospitality and kindness' and concludes that:

No one who has had any acquaintance with the Abyssinians can deny
their desperate bravery; thieves and liars, brutal, savage, and
untrustworthy they are by nature, but these evil national characteristics
are to a great extent redeemed by the possession of unbounded courage, by
a disregard of death, and by a national pride which leads them to look
down with genuine contempt on every human being who has not had the
good fortune to be born an Abyssinian. (p. 240)

In a postscript Portal reports the death, possibly by poisoning, of the
King's only son and the death of King Johannis himself in battle with the
Mahdists who for a while occupied some of the country. During the
ensuing civil war Menelek, king of Shoa, was supported by the Italians
and emerged as the strongest candidate for power. The Italians have
advanced to Asmara and have proclaimed a protectorate over the whole
country. Portal goes on to say that 'Outside Abyssinia proper a good deal
of progress has been made in the work of civilization and colonization'
(p. 249). The Colony of Erythrea (sic) has been declared. Massowa has
been cleaned up and improved and a railway run from there. A good road
to Asmara has been constructed. And 'From Asmara itself the shadow of
Ras Alula has disappeared' (p. 250). The hut from which the Ras passed
his cruel sentences 'is now perchance the residence of an Italian officer'
(p. 250).

If we accept the terms of Portal's evocation of the past then the way in
which Portal closes the postscript is of further interest for its absolute
consignment to the past of the country through which he has journeyed,
and for its simultaneous conferment upon Portal of the privileged position of the linking figure between the two worlds:

Thus has ended the independence of Abyssinia. With the death of King
Johannis died also that autonomy which had been the pride of this race for
many centuries. Although the benefits of a civilized Protectorate are very

evident, it is, I confess, with a feeling almost of sadness that I reflect that since I said farewell to Johannis at Afgol, on December 16, 1887, no other European can ever grasp the hand of an Independent Emperor of Ethiopia. (p. 251)

The restrained, qualifying, 'almost' keeps Portal safely in the civilized world. And thus he refrains from questioning the wisdom of Italy's policy towards Abyssinia and admits it may face obstacles from other nations, but concludes by remarking that 'we in England can only wish her every success in developing the immense natural resources of that beautiful, fascinating, but wild and unruly country' (p. 251). In fact, the Abyssinians were able to fight off the Italians and re-establish their independence until Mussolini's invasion, but Portal's words take us back to the justification of material exploitation, which is, as we have seen, never far away from political policy (Portal's book actually ends with an appendix that contains extracts from his reports on the forces of Abyssinia in a Parliamentary blue-book), and which, as we have also seen, colours the reaction to narratives like those of Parkyns which in their content and tone and form seem to evade the connection.

Notes

1 Malvern van Wyk Smith, '"Waters flowing from darkness": the two Ethiopias in the early European image of Africa', *Theoria* 68 (1986), 70. I am grateful to the author for supplying me with a copy of this article, from which much of the information on early images of Ethiopia is taken. My usage of 'Abyssinia' in this chapter is in keeping with nineteenth-century denotation, and not with any contemporary derogatory connotation.

2 Van Wyk Smith, 'The two Ethiopias', 71.

3 John Camden Hotten, ed., *Abyssinia and Its People; or, Life in the Land of Prester John* (London: John Camden Hotten, 1868; reprint ed., New York: Negro Universities Press, 1969), p. 13. Hotten's work is an interesting selection of extracts from previous travel narratives.

4 Geoffrey Best, *Mid-Victorian Britain 1851–75* (London: Fontana Press, 1979), pp. 21 and 71.

5 Best, *Mid-Victorian Britain*, p. 252.

6 For just one of many discussions of the Great Exhibition, see Asa Briggs, *Victorian Things* (Harmondsworth: Penguin, 1990), Chapter Two.

7 Mansfield Parkyns, *Life in Abyssinia: Being Notes Collected During Three Years' Residence in that Country*, 2 vols (London: John Murray, 1853). Page references to this work will be given parenthetically in the text.

8 See for example J. F. C. Harrison, *Early Victorian Britain, 1832–51* (London: Fontana Press, 1979), pp. 100–1.

9 Mansfield Parkyns to John Murray, 16 December [year not given], Archives of John Murray, London. All quoted letters from Parkyns are from this archive unless stated otherwise.

10 Mansfield Parkyns to John Murray, 24 July [year not given].

11 Burton's remarks are not inappropriate here: 'It would be preposterous to publish descriptions of any European country from information gathered ten years ago. But Africa moves slowly, and thus we see that the results of an Abyssinian journey (M. Antoine d'Abbadie's "Géodésie d'Ethiope") which took place about 1845, are not

considered obsolete in 1873'. Richard F. Burton, *Two Trips to Gorilla Land and the Cataracts of the Congo* 2 vols (London: Sampson Low, Marston, Low, & Searle, 1876), I, viii.

12 Quoted in Duncan Cumming, *The Gentleman Savage: The Life of Mansfield Parkyns 1823–1894* (London: Century Hutchinson Ltd, 1987), p. 79. On Tures and the son who apparently resulted from the union see pages 105 and 159–61 of Cumming's book, though the biography is best regarded with some caution.

13 For example, Clements Markham reports that Bell, an Englishman who helped organise Theodore's army, 'married an Abyssinian lady of good family in Bagemder', and that two Europeans each married a daughter from this union. There is no overt criticism, though the 'good family' is clearly important. Clements R. Markham, *A History of the Abyssinian Expedition* (London: MacMillan & Co., 1869), pp. 66 and 75.

Similarly, Henry Dufton, while more open about his own preferences, is nevertheless not as scornful as one might guess from Parkyns's secrecy. Dufton records declining with thanks a seventeen-year-old 'damsel', and meets with Europeans who 'have adopted the Abyssinian mode of living and dress, and some of them have married native ladies. Others have been more fortunate in securing for wives the half-caste daughters of Europeans, Mr. Waldmaier, our host, among the number, he being united to Miss Bell'. Henry Dufton, *Narrative of a Journey through Abyssinia in 1862–3* (London: Chapman & Hall, 1867), pp. 93–4. Parkyns, incidentally, met Bell in Egypt before entering Abyssinia, where he stayed with him in Adowa and travelled with him for some time.

14 Mansfield Parkyns to John Murray [n.d.], John Murray archives.

15 Vincent Crapanzano, 'On the writing of ethnography', *Dialectical Anthropology* 2, 1 (February 1977), 71.

16 Mansfield Parkyns to John Murray [n.d.], John Murray archives.

17 *The Athenæum*, no. 1364 (10 December 1853), 1507.

18 *The Athenæum*, no. 1364 (10 December 1853), 1507.

19 For a discussion of time in an industrialising society see E. P. Thompson, 'Time, work-discipline, and industrial capitalism', *Past and Present* 38 (1967), 56–97.

20 *The Athenæum*, no. 1364 (December 1853), 1508.

21 'Abyssinian aberrations', *Blackwood's Edinburgh Magazine* 75 (February 1854), 131. (The attribution to Hardman is by *The Wellesley Index*.)

22 Douglas Lorimer, 'Theoretical racism in late-Victorian anthropology, 1870–1900', *Victorian Studies* 31 (spring 1988), 406.

23 See for example Christine Bolt, *Victorian Attitudes to Race* (London: Routledge & Kegan Paul, 1971), pp. 83–5.

24 Richard Shannon, *The Crisis of Imperialism 1865–1915* (London: Paladin, 1976), p. 19.

25 Best, *Mid-Victorian Britain*, p. 263. See also Shannon, *The Crisis of Imperialism*, pp. 23–5.

26 Freda Harcourt, 'Disraeli's imperialism, 1866–68: a question of timing', *The Historical Journal* 23, 1 (1980), 93.

27 Harcourt, 'Disraeli's imperialism', 88.

28 Harcourt, 'Disraeli's imperialism', 89. I have drawn heavily on Harcourt's arguments here, but have done so necessarily since her perceptive essay has been overlooked by many commentators on the Abyssinian expedition.

29 Douglas Lorimer, *Colour, Class and the Victorians: English Attitudes to the Negro in the Mid-Nineteenth Century* (Leicester: Leicester University Press, 1978), p. 14.

30 Edgar Sanderson, *Africa in the Nineteenth Century* (London: Seeley & Co., 1898), p. 213.

31 Sanderson, *Africa in the Nineteenth Century*, pp. 214–15.

32 Sanderson, *Africa in the Nineteenth Century*, p. 217.

33 Henry Dufton, *Narrative of a Journey through Abyssinia*, p. 282.

34 Dufton, *Narrative of a Journey through Abyssinia*, pp. 281–2.

35 Soon after I began drafting the version of this chapter which appears in my Ph.D. thesis, the Gulf War broke out. Comparisons with the manipulation of British

hostages by both sides are irresistible, but how the Foreign Office must have hoped that, like Theodore with the pistol presented to him from Queen Victoria, Saddam Hussein would do the decent thing with his Supergun.

36 I see this type of naming as a general function of imperialism and of similar types of domination, and am certainly not making a special case for its manifestation in the late 1860s. After all, the *Dictionary of National Biography* informs us that Napier's middle name (Cornelis) commemorated the storming in 1810 of Fort Cornelis in Java, in which his father was engaged. I want rather to make the point that such incidents and their reception can tell us something about the direction in which the society of the time may feel itself moving; or, put another way, about the direction in which a society is pressured to move by those who are powerful within it.

37 Sir Samuel White Baker, 'On Abyssinia, or Ethiopia', *Proceedings of the Royal Institute* 5, 48 (1868), 418.

38 Henry M. Stanley, *Coomassie and Magdala: The Story of Two British Campaigns in Africa* (London: Sampson Low, Marston & Company, [1874]). All page references to this work will be given parenthetically in the text.

39 Charles T. Beke, *The British Captives in Abyssinia* (London: Longmans, Green, Reader, & Dyer, 2nd ed. 1867), p. 281. Beke, it has to be said, is highly critical of the British government, but this is largely because of its failure to promote trade with Abyssinia.

40 Frank McLynn, *Stanley: The Making of an African Explorer* (London: Constable, 1989), p. 69.

41 I allude here to Stanley's dispatches rather than to the narrative proper because of the delay in the latter's publication and because the immediate material and professional interest of the author was, in this case, in the former. But the publication of the book would itself have been a sign of the name he had made for himself with the 'finding' of Livingstone.

42 Tim Youngs, '"My footsteps on these pages": the inscription of self and "race" in H. M. Stanley's *How I Found Livingstone*', *Prose Studies* 13, 2 (1990), 230–49. On Stanley's journalism and expeditions in Africa see the relevant sections of Beau Riffenburgh, *The Myth of the Explorer: The Press, Sensationalism and Geographical Discovery* (London: Belhaven Press, 1993).

43 Arthur Montefiore, *Henry M. Stanley: The African Explorer*, 7th ed. (London: S. W. Partridge & Co., [n.d.]), p. 19.

44 On how industrial development, changes in social relationships, and the rise of the yellow press contributed to the enhancement of the ceremonial nature of the monarchy, see David Cannadine, 'The context, performance and meaning of ritual: the British monarchy and the 'invention of tradition', c. 1820–1977' in *The Invention of Tradition*, eds. Eric Hobsbawm and Terence Ranger (Cambridge: Cambridge University Press, 1983), pp. 101–64.

45 See for example Ian Anstruther, *I Presume: H. M. Stanley's Triumph and Disaster*, new edition (Gloucester: Alan Sutton, 1988), p. 37. Anstruther also notes that it was only a few years previously, in the Crimea, that William Howard Russell of *The Times*, who had been the first person ever to be sent by a newspaper to report on a campaign, had been treated 'with astonishing rudeness by the military command and had written that no more notice was taken of him than if he had been a crossing-sweeper' (p. 37). Anstruther remarks too that the military had been angered by Russell's strong criticism of the medical organisation.

46 This difference has been noted by Chamberlain, who writes of Stanley: 'His own character and judgment seem to have undergone a progressive degeneration as a result of years of loneliness, anxiety and malarial fever. There is a great difference between the tone of the first book he wrote describing the British Abyssinian expedition of 1868, in which he posed as a disinterested American observer . . . prepared to criticise both the Europeans and the Abyssinians, and his last book describing the Emin Pasha Relief expedition in which he almost exulted at atrocities'. M. E. Chamberlain, *The Scramble for Africa* (London: Longman, 1974), p. 29. My argument is that to personalise causes in this way is misguided and to look no deeper than tone is unsatis-

factory. In any case Chamberlain is misreading both books.

47 In writing of imperialism in this context I am referring to the idea of informal imperialism, about which there has been much debate. See for example, Ronald Robinson, John Gallagher, and Alice Denny, *Africa and the Victorians: The Official Mind of Imperialism*, 2nd ed. (Basingstoke: Macmillan, 1981), pp. ix–xxiii. My own focus however is on neither the 'official mind' of imperialism nor the purely economic factors involved in any continuity between informal and formal empire. Rather, I have in view the cultural and racial attitudes which contributed to and accompanied both forms of exploitation. I am in part considering the degrees of informality and formality in racial ideology.

48 *Hansard* 3rd Series, vol. 188, 24 July – 21 August 1867, cols 241–2.

49 Asa Briggs, *Victorian Things* (Harmondsworth: Penguin, 1990), p. 376.

50 Harcourt, 'Disraeli's imperialism', 102.

51 Frederick Myatt, *The March to Magdala: The Abyssinian War of 1868* (London: Leo Cooper, 1970), pp. 114–15.

52 Myatt, *The March to Magdala*, p. 177.

53 Cumming, *The Gentleman Savage*, p. 161.

54 Charles T. Beke, *The British Captives in Abyssinia*, p. iii. Further references will be given parenthetically in the text.

55 Beke's interventions are detailed by Percy Arnold, who calls him (among other things) 'enterprising and ever importuning'. Percy Arnold, *Prelude to Magdala* (London: Bellew Publishing, 1991), p. 15.

56 John Camden Hotten, ed. *Abyssinia*, p. 1.

57 Gerald H. Portal, *My Mission to Abyssinia* (London: Edward Arnold, 1892; reprint ed., New York: Negro Universities Press, 1969). Page references to this work will be given parenthetically in the text. Rennell Rodd, the editor of Portal's posthumously published book on Uganda, reports that *My Mission to Abyssinia* was first printed for private circulation among friends. See Sir Gerald Portal, *The British Mission to Uganda in 1893* ed. Rennell Rodd (London: Edward Arnold, 1894), p. xxviii.

58 John Lucas, *Modern English Poetry: From Hardy to Hughes* (London: B. T. Batsford, 1986), p. 1.

59 On this, and the idea of chivalry with which it closely connects, see Mark Girouard, *The Return to Camelot: Chivalry and the English Gentleman* (New Haven: Yale University Press, 1981). The vogue for chivalry can be traced back to the beginning of Victoria's reign, but in the late part of the century it has much to do with imperialism and a distaste for the city and for most of the people who lived in it. In other words, the Empire is seen as the arena for codes thought regretfully to be no longer tenable in much of Britain.

It is highly appropriate therefore that Rennell Rodd describes Portal's death from typhoid thus: 'It was a hard fate for a man who had encountered so many adventures, and passed so often through the fire, to fall victim to a sickness bred of city life'. Sir Gerald Portal, *The British Mission to Uganda*, p. xliv.

60 John Lucas, *Modern English Poetry*, p. 55.

61 Hutchisson would also accompany Portal to Uganda. Sir Gerald Portal, *The British Mission to Uganda*, p. 11.

62 John Lucas, *Modern English Poetry*, pp. 52–3.

63 In 1850 fifty per cent of the population in England and Wales lived in urban areas. By 1901 the figure was seventy-five per cent. Between 1841 and 1901 three million people migrated to cities. Shannon, *The Crisis of Imperialism*, pp. 14–15.

64 Introduction by Lord Cromer to Sir Gerald Portal, *The British Mission to Uganda*, p. xiii.

65 *Dictionary of National Biography*. The *D.N.B.* remembers Portal as 'a man of handsome presence and athletic mould, and possessed [of] tact, firmness, and daring'.

66 Portal, *The British Mission to Uganda*, p. xxvii.

67 Portal, *The British Mission to Uganda*, p. xiv.

68 Portal, *The British Mission to Uganda*, p. xxv.

CHAPTER TWO

Victorian writing; African eating: digesting Africa

Food and the town

Writing of the 1867 expedition to Abyssinia, Alan Moorehead claims that 'There has never been in modern times a colonial campaign quite like [it]', and, in a fascinating comparison, observes: 'It proceeds from first to last with the decorum and heavy inevitability of a Victorian state banquet, complete with ponderous speeches at the end'.[1] Moorehead's mind is, I presume, on the weight and show of planning, the number of ingredients, and the very public profile of the event. He is also thinking of Stanley's descriptions of the officers' dinners given by Napier.

In this chapter, however, I want to take Moorehead's simile much further. In nineteenth-century travel narratives descriptions of Africans eating are flavoured with a patronising amusement or tainted with disgust. And these responses are given to convey and confirm the cultural superiority of the British. The quote from Moorehead also links the ritual of eating with a heavy articulacy. But I want to look closely at *how* this lofty position is maintained, and shall argue that underlying the European attitude is an implicit condemnation of 'primitive' society for lacking the rituals of preparation and consumption which are a feature of technological, capitalist societies.

Increasing distance between food and its consumers had been given moral and social status during developments since the Middle Ages, with a movement away from communal dishes and vessels, and from direct physical contact with the food:

> Once the spontaneous, direct, and informal manners of the Middle Ages had been repressed, people began to feel shame. ... new inhibitions became the essence of 'civilized' behaviour, distinguishing adults from children, the upper classes from the lower, and Europeans from the 'savages' then being discovered around the world.[2]

By around the beginning of the sixteenth century, table manners began to be modified, moving towards the behaviour with which we are now familiar. The threat of the knife as a weapon was removed, and the fork allowed one to avoid manual contact with food.[3] The cultural value of these changes was given the support of technological capitalism in the second half of the nineteenth century at the expense of pre-capitalist societies. In the latter, the absence of mediating layers was important, given, as Jack Goody has noted,[4] nineteenth-century developments in the preservation, mechanisation, retail and transportation of food and in the increasing intervention of a whole series of agents between the producer and consumer of food (particularly in distribution).

In nineteenth-century Britain the adaptation to life in towns had important effects on food and eating habits, as John Burnett has remarked. The separation between producer and consumer increased. By 1850 fewer bakers were their own millers and fewer publicans their own brewers. Instead, by mid-century:

> both dealt with remote, highly capitalized and mechanized producers, to whom they were frequently bound by ties of indebtedness. In other trades, such as grocery, the wholesaler or agent had become interposed between retailer and purchaser and had often acquired a dominating position.[5]

Features of urban life that contributed to consumer dependence on professional services included the unsuitability of living conditions, through overcrowding and lack of equipment, for culinary preparations; and the number of women who worked in factories or at other domestic trades and who therefore had little time for cooking.[6] In one way we can see this distance as receiving a kind of displaced justification through the ever more contemptuous portrayal of immediate, spontaneous gratification practised by Africans. And not only Africans. The industrial poor in Britain were described in similar terms. The 1842 *Report on the Sanitary Condition of the Labouring Population of Great Britain* contained the following account:

> The bone-pickers are the dirtiest of all the inmates of our workhouse; I have seen them take a bone from a dung-heap, and gnaw it while reeking hot with the fermentation of decay. Bones, from which the meat had been cut raw, and which still had thin strips of flesh adhering to them, they scraped carefully with their knives, and put the bits, no matter how befouled with dirt, into a wallet or pocket appropriated to the purpose. They have told me, that whether in broth or grilled, they were the most savoury dish that could be imagined. I have not observed that these creatures were savage, but they were thoroughly debased. Often hardly human in appearance, they had neither human tastes nor sympathies, nor even human sensations, for they revelled in the filth which is grateful to dogs, and other lower animals, and which to our apprehensions is redolent only of nausea and abomination.[7]

It is an interesting passage. On my first few readings of it I focused on the strips of flesh still attached to the reeking bones and was reminded of James Bruce's tale of Abyssinians cutting and eating raw a steak from a living cow (to which I refer below). Yet I was unsure what it was that made these 'creatures' just debased, not savage. Then I saw that the crucial difference between these scavengers and the Africans is that the former employ implements to scrape the meat *carefully* and that its storage in a wallet or pocket gives to them the benefit of forethought and future provision that raises them above the Africans who allegedly have no thought for the morrow.

The scorn of African eating habits is a distraction too from a serious and widespread consequence of the growing distance between producer and consumer in urban Britain: food adulteration. As Burnett has said: 'Food adulteration is essentially a phenomenon of urban life. . . . As soon as there emerged a consuming public, distinct and separated from the producers of food, opportunities for commercial fraud arose'.[8] Burnett very firmly locates the root causes of food adulteration in the changes associated with industrialisation and urbanisation, with the widening division between producer and consumer coinciding with the abandonment of the medieval regulation of food standards:

> partly because of administrative difficulties but, more fundamentally, because of a changed conception of the role of the State and a doctrinaire belief in the efficacy of free competition to ensure the best interests of the consumer.[9]

From 1815 when the Assize of Bread was repealed 'there was no general attempt by government to intervene between producer, retailer and consumer in order to regulate the price or quality of food'.[10] There was little significant improvement in the quality of food until effective legislation was passed in the 1870s. The year 1850 had in fact marked 'a decisive turning-point in public attitudes'[11] about food adulteration, for in that year Thomas Wakley, editor of the *Lancet*, and Dr Arthur Hassall planned a rigorous inquiry into the matter. Their reports were published weekly in the *Lancet* between 1851 and 1854 and in 1855 were compiled for separate publication. More accessible versions were reprinted in the newspapers and in periodicals. Hassall's examination of thirty common foods, drinks, and condiments proved, in the words of Burnett, that:

> Serious, and often dangerous, adulteration existed of practically every food which it would pay to adulterate. . . . By now it had become quite impossible to obtain several basic foods in a pure state.[12]

The first Adulteration of Foods Act was passed in 1860. Under its terms various local authorities could appoint public analysts who would, for a fee of 10s 6d, examine samples of food and drink complained of by private citizens. Although judged to be largely ineffectual, it did, in intervening between purchaser and seller, go against the principle of *laissez-faire*, and thus set a precedent which helped the eventual appearance in 1872 of the Adulteration of Food, Drink and Drugs Act, which made it an offence to sell a mixture containing ingredients intended to add weight or bulk unless the composition was declared to the buyer. Administrative inconsistencies contributed to the Sale of Food and Drugs Act, 1875. This Act provided only for a heavy fine and then imprisonment for a second offence for those who practised adulteration injurious to health, and even then guilty knowledge had to be proved against the seller, but:

> Within a decade of the passing of the new Act, a remarkable improvement had already been effected in the quality of basic foods – so much so that a good case may be made out for regarding the 1880s as the crucial period in the suppression of adulteration and the establishment of food purity.[13]

Although it seems that for some time prior to 1875 the quality of food and drink had begun to show 'noticeable improvement',[14] most of the travel narratives I refer to in the present chapter were produced by and reported to the society which was becoming more and more aware of its substandard food and of the roots of this in the very processes (urban industrial capitalism) which were the moving pride of the age.

In some cases such advances were directly linked with the activities of those who wrote the kinds of narratives with which I am concerned. For example: 'As with the early canning industry, much of the production of biscuits had first of all been directed to the needs of travellers, explorers and the armed forces'.[15]

In addition to the fact of exploration and imperialism stimulating industrial productivity in the constitution and packaging of foodstuffs, there is the matter of complex layers; of users feeling themselves to be part of a sophisticated and well-functioning network. The network places one socially and culturally. In the first half of the nineteenth century, 'the choice of foods, their manner of preparation, order of service and even the times of eating, all became matters of high social importance and class demarcation',[16] an idea which is quite apparent in the literature of the time. In a tantalising essay Barbara Hardy has noticed how, for instance, in *Great Expectations* 'Almost all characters and groups are given moral and social definition by their attitudes to food and hospitality'.[17] Ceremony and appreciation are very much to the fore here, as they will be seen to be in the travel writing. More generally, the network mirrors the specialisation of occupation and the definition of social role in other spheres, and connects members of different classes and regions through their relationship to the product, making them feel they are performing usefully within a harmonious and hierarchical system. It also convinces one that one's products and manners of usage and one's system of organisation are all of a higher quality than those of other societies. I am happy to let T. S. Eliot make this point clear:

> If we take culture seriously, we see that a people does not need merely enough to eat (though even that is more than we seem able to ensure) but a proper and particular *cuisine:* one symptom of the decline of culture in Britain is indifference to the art of preparing food.[18]

The notion of a 'proper' cuisine has quite evidently to do with a scale of values, and this is why Eliot could talk of a decline in culture indicated in part by carelessness in preparation. Standards and elaboration in culinary practice are a concern of many of the travellers to East and Central Africa and it is my argument that in this preoccupation we see a sort of synecdochic justification of the behaviour of the west. This is not surprising, for as Claude Fischler has stated:

> Food is central to our sense of identity. The way any given human group eats helps it assert its diversity, hierarchy and organization, and at the same time, both its oneness and the otherness of whoever eats differently. Food is also central to individual identity, in that any given human individual is constructed, biologically, psychologically and socially by the food he/she choses [*sic*] to incorporate.[19]

Raw states

Keeping our gaze on Abyssinia for the moment, examination of a trope common to many of the narratives of travel in that country, that of the Africans eating raw flesh, supports Fischler's contention, though I wish to complicate it. The image, attributed in the main to James Bruce's account, in the late eighteenth century, was of his witnessing Abyssinians cutting two steaks from the buttock of a living cow, whose skin they then repaired with skewers or pins and a plaster of clay. The episode recounted by Bruce rebounded as much on himself as on the Abyssinians: many people in Britain refused to believe it and he was teased about it on his return home. The point I wish to draw from this is the distance created between the white observer and narrator and the black Africans who are watched. Later travellers would often refer to Bruce's claim, sometimes jokingly, sometimes negatively; yet the fact is that it helped advance the white writer within a literary tradition whilst fixing the Abyssinians in apposition to Bruce's narrative: did they or did they not eat raw flesh from a living beast? As one nineteenth-century commentator remarked: 'several subsequent travellers seem to have visited that country more with a view to criticise Bruce's statements than to add to our knowledge of the country'.[20] In part, then, Bruce's incident serves as an example of how travellers would journey with a predetermined model,[21] but it also reveals how they may shape their own identity, and therefore sense of belonging, in relation to the home or host country. Mansfield Parkyns, for instance, uses Bruce as a means of becoming apparently more self-reflexive:

> In some few cases I may have fallen into a common error, that of putting down as customs incidents which I may have seen, but which, in reality, may happen scarcely once in a hundred years. I make this remark on account of the reputation poor Bruce got.[22]

I have shown in my first chapter how Parkyns fashions himself as something of an outsider, looking in on both cultures, and how this posture attracted charges of eccentricity. Here, looking specifically at images of eating, one can begin to see how this position is reached. Although announcing his firm belief that Bruce saw what he said he had seen, Parkyns combines his own subsequent carefulness with a criticism of his home culture in a way that helps lend his voice the perceptibly personal quality I have described above. Bruce's account and the British public's fascination with it allow him to do this. So that, commenting on the debate over the steak cut from the live cow, Parkyns opines:

> I have heard it remarked that it was scarcely possible to believe human beings capable of such cruelty. In answer to this I would merely observe that no one should venture on such a remark in a country where salmon are crimped, and eels skinned, alive; nor should they talk of cruelty of any sort till the state trials, and other books, showing the horrible death which many of our ancestors suffered for their adherence to the Stuart family, be out of print, and the old sentence for high treason forgotten.[23]

Parkyns here employs his perception of the manners of eating as a particular means of criticising features of British society through a certain image of Africa. I have already shown how, in a more general way, Parkyns constructs an individual role for himself and establishes a space between or overlapping the two cultures (bringing into use his 'nigger' eye and his European one). But his presentation of culinary matters has that position signified in a textual as well as a figurative way. Again picking up Bruce, Parkyns denies that in defending the earlier traveller he has any 'extraordinary story' of his own to tell, though wishes that he had. Rather, 'All that I profess to do is to enter more particularly into the customs of the people I have visited than has hitherto been done'.[24]

Figure 3 'An Abyssinian Devouring Raw Beef' From John Camden Hotten, ed.,
Abyssinia and its People; or, Life in the Land of Prester John

The self-deprecation is thus followed by the expression of a more precise entryism than has been practised before. This seems to work in two principal ways. One involves the amount of detail contained in the narrative; the other concerns Parkyns's own situation *vis-à-vis* the Abyssinians. The first discloses a vertical structure; the second a horizontal movement. In the former case, Parkyns's account of table customs stresses the hierarchical aspects of consumption:

> When the master of an Abyssinian house takes his meals, all his servants stand round the doorway and look on; which custom, though it has at first a disagreeable effect to a stranger, is in reality a mark of respect to their superior, showing that they are in attendance on him, and not merely eating his bread and idling their time away. The master's feeding-time, in fact, is a sort of muster for the servants.[25]

Parkyns goes on to describe how, when bread is passed round, the finest sort is placed at the top, with increasingly inferior varieties beneath it. The arrangement is made because the nobler guests are seated first and get the best bread, are followed by the more humble guests, who then take their places and receive the second class of bread, and so on, so that the coarsest is taken by the servants and poor friends.

This socially stratified system of distribution, characteristic of feudalism, may be seen as upholding class differentiation in British society, with its correlation between social and culinary quality. Reay Tannahill, for instance, has noted how the choice of the middle classes in the first half of the nineteenth century when entertaining was 'usually a reflection of an adaptation of what was eaten on the next higher level of the social scale'.[26] And it is probably not surprising that Parkyns, born – on the side of one of his parents – into the landed gentry, should see things this way. But juxtaposed with this recognition of a vertical social scale is the representation of Parkyns's movement into the Abyssinian mode. For, as a footnote to his remarks on the servants' tearing meat with their fingers, Parkyns informs the reader that he himself ate with his fingers for six years and even continued to do so by preference when in Egypt up to the day he boarded the steamer homewards. With some glee, one suspects, Parkyns relays the horror of the friends to whom he told this, with the effect of clearly signalling his individuality. He uses food, one might say, to try to 'other' himself, joyfully impressing upon the reader his ability to depart from the ways of one culture and gain an entry into another. Through the position he adopts on eating he realises his self-elected function as a cultural traveller, acting a vicarious (and therefore safely distanced) role for his home society. Thus, writing of a meal of turtles on his journey prior to reaching Abyssinia, he reports how:

In the evening their flesh was made into a sort of soup, or rather stew, of which I was invited to partake. It was in one large wooden bowl, round which sat about twenty connives. My own black servant sat next to me, and every one dipped his hand, armed with a piece of bread, into the same dish. At the time of my voyage to Jedda this sort of communism in feeding was rather extraordinary to me; but since that time I have for years been in the constant habit of 'dipping my finger in the dish' with niggers, and think even now that that mode of eating is far more convenient, and, as it is practised in the East, quite as cleanly as the use of knives and forks; and, after all, 'fingers were made first'.[27]

This illustrates what I have called the horizontal movement of Parkyns's entryism. It has him crossing over from one side to the other, blurring the normally clear standards. One may adapt here Fischler's description of the 'omnivore's paradox'; that is, the tension between:

neophobia (prudence, fear of the unknown, resistance to change) and neophilia (the tendency to explore, the need for change, novelty, variety). Every omnivore, and man in particular, is subject to a kind of Batesonian double bind between the familiar and the unknown, monotony and change, security and variety.[28]

The salient figures of this process in the above quoted passage from Parkyns are blackness (the 'black servant'); the sharing in the group activity ('communism') in contrast both to bourgeois privacy and aristocratic distancing; and the directness of the manner of eating: that is, the absence of a sophisticated social ritual and of a mediating technology. The lack of the latter two qualities, thereby soliciting our disapproval (which Parkyns is, of course, playing against in order to highlight his distinctive persona), works to effect an identification of technological capitalism with morality. For the conventional white traveller, politeness in eating consists of social and cultural intervention through the use of implements and ceremony.

Generally, the lack of social ritual or mediating utensils is taken to signify a strong connotation of immorality or, where the image is of the Noble Savage rather than the degraded savage, of an amoral state. As has been shown, the latter condition may be evoked in the late romantic or early Victorian age as a means of freeing oneself – even if only imaginatively – from the constraints of British culture so that the figurative escape makes possible an actual acceptance of the familiar and the routine. Attitudes to food suggest this quite clearly, as we see in James Bruce's account of a banquet of raw flesh at which:

The company are so ranged that one man sits between two women; the man with his long knife cuts a thin piece, which would be thought a good beef-steak in England, while you see the motion of the fibres yet perfectly

Figure 4 African celebratory feast in Boma, Zaire. Dr Falkenstein 1876.

distinct, and alive in the flesh. No man in Abyssinia, of any fashion whatever, feeds himself, or touches his own meat [the women cut up the meat and wrap it in seasoned bread]. In the mean time, the man having put up his knife, with each hand resting upon his neighbour's knee, his body stooping, his head low and forward, and mouth open very like an idiot, turns to the one whose [bread] cartridge is first ready, which is so full, that he is in constant danger of being choked. This is a mark of grandeur. The greater the man would seem to be, the larger piece he takes in his mouth; and the more noise he makes in chewing it, the more polite he is thought to be.[29]

Here the greater differentiation in eating seemingly robs the male of action. He is reduced to idiocy. The ritual of eating is mocked for its apparent dependence upon women and upon the men's helpless gluttony. (It is true that afterwards each man does drop a small portion into the mouth of each of his female neighbours, but it is a habitual act of gratitude.) The passage reads almost as a parody of culinary consumption, and has the result of normalising British customs. The men's

[63]

implements are redundant and their particular brand of conspicuous consumption is rendered grotesque. There is an unattractive lack of productiveness in the scene.

But there is another point to be made. The eating of the meat whose fibres are still distinct and alive in the flesh is an image of a natural act performed without the meliorating processes of civilisation. In this regard, and to support my view of the growing moral force of technology, it is worth remarking, when recalling the continued fascination of Bruce's account, on the effect of railways upon the movement and image of food in Britain. Tannahill reminds us that in London meat had customarily been brought in on the hoof for slaughter in the city, but by the 1850s ready-dressed carcasses were being transported to London from places as distant as Aberdeen. Tannahill quotes one contemporary as commenting that Aberdeen had become 'a London abattoir'.[30] Bruce's writing goes on to make a connection between the lack of restraint in this sphere and the absence of constraint in sexual activity. The uninhibited pleasure derived from the latter provides the reader with a kind of voyeuristic enjoyment purified by his or her consciousness of the interceding barriers erected in 'civilised' society. So, having told of how the cow which has supplied the feast remains outside bleeding to death, Bruce writes:

> In the mean time, those within are very much elevated; love lights all its fires, and everything is permitted with absolute freedom. There is no coyness, no delays, no need of appointments or retirements to gratify their wishes; there are no rooms but one, in which they sacrifice both to Bacchus and Venus. The two men nearest the vacuum a pair have made on the bench by leaving their seats, hold their upper garments like a screen before the two that have left the bench; and, if we may judge by sound, they seem to think it as great a shame to make love in silence as to eat. Replaced in their seats again, the company drink the happy couple's health; and their example is followed at different ends of the table, as each couple is disposed. All this passes without remark or scandal; not a licentious word is uttered, nor the most distant joke upon the transaction. These ladies are, for the most part, women of family and character.[31]

As Jack Goody, for one, has noted, food and sex are often linked in perceptions of cultures (the eating of the fruit of knowledge in the Garden of Eden is, of course, at the heart of the Christian tradition) and may present a picture of hierarchy within a culture. What Bruce gives us is a scene in which, both in food and sex, there is an absence of the physical and moral codes of restraint to be found in western society. The screen formed by the diners' garments to hide the couple who have left the bench serves, in the scene as it is written, to preserve whites' morals and to excite the imagination. Goody has observed that in polygamous African cultures the wife with whom the husband is sleeping is normally the one who provides him with food and that the cooking of food by the woman is often seen as reciprocating the sex function of the male.[32] There is a connection here with Bruce's narrative, to which the white male audience responds by vicariously enjoying the immodest sexual favours of the women who have fed the men, whilst perhaps seeking to obscure the relationship of culinary preparation to sexual union in their own European culture.

In the main, at the time Bruce was writing and even up to Parkyns's time (and, with rare exceptions, after Parkyns), aspects of the romantic view of the savage (the absence of labour, the providential supply of food, freedom from restraint) were accepted, even if satirised. Later in the nineteenth century, in the late 1860s and the 1870s, the more aggressive view of blacks became predominant and often emphasised their supposed technological deficiency and mental incapacity. This is reflected in the descriptions of food preparation and consumption. Stanley may, as in other matters, be seen as signalling this transformation. With this shift of vision the very freedom from restraint which was seen as positive or ambivalent is now undesirable. Sometimes this is conveyed directly; at others obliquely. In Stanley's 1872 *How I Found Livingstone* the explorer's emblazoned rhetoric complements the immersion in ritual and the shunning of simplicity:

> The Doctor said he had thought me a most luxurious and rich man, when he saw my great bath-tub carried on the shoulders of one of my men; but he thought me still more luxurious this morning, when my knives and forks, and plates, and cups, saucers, silver spoons, and silver teapots were brought forth shining and bright, spread on a rich Persian carpet, and observed that I was well attended to by my yellow and ebon Mercuries.[33]

The hierarchy paraded here is a racial one, shown in Stanley's possession of coloured attendants and, of course, by the rich paraphernalia of civilisation: its culinary utensils mark not just a functional difference between cultures but one of material wealth. The classical allusion elevates Stanley's cultural position, and the setting of his cutlery and vessels on a rich Persian carpet suggests the appropriation of wealth from a subordinate culture. The distancing involved is obvious and is indicated too by the great bath-tub, the monument to hygiene supported by a black porter. The former workhouse orphan Stanley is also raising his status within western society, showing himself to belong spectacularly to the culture on whose margins he originally existed. We are a long way here from Parkyns's fingers!

[65]

The representation of Africans' reactions to this type of scene – or to this type of scene on a much less grand scale – is frequently used to aid the constitution of the white person's identity. Thus James Mounteney-Jephson, who accompanied Stanley on the Emin Pasha Relief Expedition in the late 1880s, notes in his diary the following about a village chief:

> He brought me some fish & he & a great many of his people came & sat round as I ate my dinner, and stared at every mouthful I took, they were evidently very much astonished at my plates, knife, fork, spoon, etc. & could not understand how it was I did not touch any food with my fingers.[34]

Complaints about the rudeness of the staring Africans were commonplace in the travel literature by this time, but Jephson utilises the image not just to validate the cultural superiority of travellers who possess the means to consume the product without soiling their hands through touching it, but also to demonstrate that this superiority extends to intellectual advantage. He is able without difficulty to read the Africans' incomprehension of his performance: 'they were *evidently* very much astonished ... & could *not understand*'. It is not the rightness of Jephson's mode of eating that is challenged; rather, it is the nature of his power to eat in this way that is quizzed, as an almost supernatural awe is communicated.

The absence of western implements indicates, then, the absence of civilised processes, including intellectual ones, and at the same time may be cited to justify on the one hand the importation – by force if necessary – of western technology, or on the other the treatment of Africans as savages incapable of improvement. Morality (the lack of it) and eating thus become closely linked. And so an updated version of Parkyns's communism of eating is a reluctant one, forced by hunger. Parke, also on the same expedition as Jephson and Stanley, describes sharing with his companion and a group of 'Arab-Africans' a meal of curried chicken and rice:

> It was very good; but as eight or ten savages were eating out of the same dish with their hands, the display was rather calculated to blunt the appetite a little. All the same, however, we both ate freely; for hunger is not over-nice, and serves to dissipate silly prejudices.[35]

But the prejudices are *not* completely removed, for the continued distaste is evident. Furthermore, even when the food is cooked and hygiene is observed, the moral condition is a raw one, for Parke immediately afterwards asserts: 'Like all good Mohammedans, these people always wash their feet, hands, and mouths before eating a meal; I wish the friction would remove some of their peculiar morality'.[36]

The same freedom from control that had been envied is now an anarchic, dangerous state requiring condemnation and, if judged desirable, the imposition of order, thereby reinforcing the traveller's sense of belonging to his society to the exclusion of others. Eating serves as a paradigm of culture. Farb and Armelagos, summarising Lévi-Strauss's idea of the culinary triangle, have written that 'Eating is important . . . because, although food is a part of Nature, humans impose their own cultural categories upon it'.[37] It is not without significance that the proliferation of descriptions of an unrestrained appetite for raw flesh should have occurred with and after the circulation of new anthropological and political theories of 'primitive man'. In his book *Victorian Anthropology*, George Stocking sums up the attitude of Herbert Spencer and some of his contemporaries thus:

> Just as the moral character of primitive man was premised on a direct, unmediated expression of internal passional nature, so was the intellectual character of primitive man premised on a direct, unmediated apprehension of external nature.[38]

And E. B. Tylor, who has been described as the 'first major anthropologist in the world', classed as the first of three stages of cultural evolution a 'savage' stage characterised by subsistence on wild plants and animals and the use of Stone Age tools.[39] Marx, writing in 1857 on production and consumption, illustrates a point by saying that 'Hunger is hunger; but the hunger that is satisfied with cooked meat eaten with fork and knife is a different kind of hunger from the one that devours raw meat with the aid of hands, nails and teeth'.[40] Such classifications encouraged the ranking of societies, with European nations at the head (that is, at the top of the scale and being the thinking part of the world).

So, when we have at different times in the narratives of Sir Samuel White Baker references to his men eating the raw liver of a victim, and Arabs eating raw organs of animals and the raw flesh of a camel, and the greed shown in cutting up a hippo,[41] then we know that immediate gratification and an inability to reflect in other matters are also implied. An unstructured, unsophisticated political economy may also be under attack here as Britons came to terms with the complexity of their own.[42] The implication is that Europeans are necessary for the propagation of correct ideas concerning the distribution of food, and that control in distribution may improve the manner of consumption. Burton, in 1860, makes this quite clear. Writing of himself and Speke, he declares:

> When a bullock is killed one of us must be present. The porters receive about a quarter of the meat, over which they sit wrangling and screaming like hyænas, till a fair division according to messes is arrived at. Then,

unless watched, some strong and daring hand will suddenly break through the ring, snatch up half a dozen portions and disappear at a speed defying pursuit; others will follow his example, with the clatter and gesture of a troop of baboons, and the remainder will retire as might be expected, grumbling and discontented.[43]

The denotation of bestiality and the need for surveillance are important, especially coming as they do from Burton the military officer and anthropologist. Disorder in eating signifies social disorder and a lack of an effective social differentiation. The presence of whites is necessary to introduce an efficiency predicated on distinction. Behaviour which ignored the proprietorship of food merited strong condemnation. As Burnett has noted, for instance, until 1857 transportation remained the penalty for poaching, which thereafter was punishable by imprisonment or a heavy fine.[44]

Burton is outspoken in his denunciation of the Africans' lack of distinctions, and the sweep of his hostile gaze is proof of the purpose to which accounts of food are put by travellers whose systems they nourish. 'The East African is greedy and voracious', declaims Burton. This is not to say that the East African's appetite should be indulged; quite the opposite, for, 'Like most barbarians, the East African can exist and work with a small quantity of food'. This kind of opinion becomes a classic justification for the rations one gives one's porters (and it is based on similar beliefs about the working classes at home: they don't need the same quantity and quality of things as enjoyed by their betters). Burton is an accomplished writer as well as an agile thinker and it is characteristic that he is able neatly to attach to this view another dearly held stereotype: that of the Africans as incapable of thinking of and saving for the future. So, the porters may eke out their daily allowance of one and a half pounds of grain by finding herbs and roots so that it will last several days, but, 'generally, upon the barbarian's impulsive principle of mortgaging the future for the present, he recklessly consumes his stores'.

I have maintained in this chapter that food is a convenient focus for divergent or antagonistic cultural behaviour and ideologies, and it certainly does nothing to weaken my case that Burton also observes: 'In morality, according to the extended sense of that word, the East African is markedly deficient',[45] and goes on to assert that:

> The want of veneration produces a savage rudeness in the East African. The body politic consists of two great members, masters and slaves. Ignoring distinctions of society, he treats all men, except his chief, as his equals.[46]

The shameful and socially harmful consequence is shown in the fact that the African 'has no rules for visiting', will drop in uninvited, 'barking' loudly, and will, choosing the best place in the room, contaminate the rug or bedding with his 'unwashed person'. The disregard of social rank and the transgression of courtesies that would exist in civilised societies are manifestations of the inferior condition of the savage, of which culinary manners are but a visible symptom.

The raw state of African society, of which the quality and consumption of food are emblematic, fails to recognise superiority. Burton and many of his compatriots are personally and politically troubled by the non-observance of gradations because it threatens Britain's 'prestige' and power abroad and the ruling classes' dominance at home. Burton's complaint – 'The curiosity of these people, and the little ceremony with which they gratify it, are at times most troublesome'[47] – is a common one, especially when provoked by the staring of the blacks (often while eating). And Burton also complains about the nuisance of Africans who peer into one's tent and who, 'uncouth figures . . . half-clothed except with grease', run after the caravan uttering 'cries that resemble the howls of beasts more than any effort of human articulation'.

There is, on the face of it, a paradox in all this. Why should natural behaviour disgust the senses and yet the mechanics of power in 'civilised' societies be justified as natural? Taken separately, each part of the paradox is easily explicable, but the paradox is only apparent, for it finds its resolution, I think, in Darwinian (and quasi-Darwinian) conceptions of evolution. Thus those who were familiar with the terms of the debate (as Burton was) could deride 'unimproved' nature as exhibited by 'primitives' whilst having no difficulty in arguing for the naturalness of the appurtenances of complex industrial societies on the basis of their being the result of natural progress. Emphasising the normality of development or transformation could become a powerful vindication of one's own place in the status quo. Burton again exemplifies such thought:

> In intellect the East African is sterile and incult, apparently unprogressive and unfit for change. Like the uncivilised generally, he observes well, but he can deduce nothing profitable from his perceptions. His intelligence is surprising when compared with that of an uneducated English peasant; but it has a narrow bound, beyond which apparently no man may pass.[48]

This short passage epitomises the stand. The mentality of the East Africans is unproductive (with resonances of sexual and agricultural failure) and seemingly incapable of fructifying. They are deemed to be locked into their present state, with no chance of progression to a higher condition. They can see but not think. They are not equipped to transform the raw material of perception into a worthwhile product. The comparison with the English peasant indicates the domestic implications of the comments. In short, the tenor of the remarks is that the Africans and the English peasants need someone to think for them and to make them productive, or to show them how to be so. A key word is 'profitable'. The British ruling class is required to manage and govern the Africans if the existence of the latter is to be a useful one, financially, morally, or culturally. The question of value, itself highly culture- and class-bound, is assumed to be an objective fact, so that potential and actual British exploitation of Africans could be justified by religious or scientific authority, in either case reflecting the domestic political situation. This is so even when political shifts see the blurring or crossing of class boundaries. Terence Ranger has shown how, in the early colonial days in Rhodesia and Kenya, it was more profitable for whites to run a farm store and to trade with the Africans for the surplus food they produced than to grow crops themselves:

> By so doing they performed a vital function since the labour forces of the early colonial economies depended entirely on African produced food. Hence, for a time, it was gentlemanly to run a store or to buy grain and cattle from Africans.[49]

The Africans, as in Burton's view, are used as if they were themselves in some kind of raw state. The fruits of their labour are consumed in order to feed the colonial work force which will, in turn, apply itself to the raw materials that will be appropriated and, often, exported by the whites, who might then return them in a finished state. And in the process white traders have their own status enhanced, as do white labourers who impress their superiority upon the blacks. The Africans are simply lowly agents of transformation whilst the whites enjoy the profit of the process. This process stands in metaphorical relation to the very fact of cuisine which, as Fischler reminds us, 'can . . . first be taken to mean the process whereby man transforms raw materials before and, with a view to, eating them'.[50]

The whites' use of food in securing their dominance was nothing new. Peter Hulme, examining the colonial encounter between Europe and the New World, has pointed out how, in *The Tempest*:

> Caliban makes it plain . . . that Prospero's most powerful weapon over him is the withholding of food – the food that Caliban is himself responsible for collecting and preparing. . . . Prospero is dependent upon Caliban's labour for his food supply and general material requirements; Caliban is forced by Prospero's magic to labour in order to be able to eat even a small portion of the food he prepares.[51]

This type of relationship, particularly, as Hulme remarks, with its conclusion of slavery being replaced by feudalism as Caliban grants the wishes of the European colonist and 'voluntarily' recognises his natural superiority, is not at all dissimilar to the situation in Africa (and one could draw parallels between Prospero's magic and the nineteenth-century traveller's literacy, which was reportedly seen by many Africans as a supernatural power). Furthermore, as Fischler again has pointed out, in transforming the nutritional raw materials from the state of nature to the state of culture, a cuisine can be seen as playing with and taming the forces of nature and of the supernatural: 'It is an act so magical that one remembers the strange kinship between cookery and witchcraft'.[52] It is my contention that the effect of the writing I examine is to draw on this sense of power. I shall enlarge in a moment on the idea of food and eating as synecdochic of the relationship between the two continents.

Before I do so, however, it should be acknowledged that the condemnation of the Africans' selection and distribution of food was not total, even where meat was concerned.[53] A rare identification with the eating of an animal's intestines (in this case those of a giraffe) is made by William Baldwin, who recommends their flavour and remarks that 'The Kaffirs know well the best of parts of every animal, and laugh at our throwing them away'.[54] Even though some caveats need to be introduced – Baldwin was travelling mainly in South Africa and was writing early in the 1860s – important points can be made from his statements. First, he was a hunter, and this was a pursuit which involved a displacement of sexual frustration or aggression.[55] It ought not to come as a surprise that Baldwin should distinguish himself from other travellers by aligning himself with the native diet. Nor should it shock us that Baldwin's admiration of 'Kaffir' food is accompanied by a favourable outlook on their women and politics. After all, we have seen that detestation of the former is usually conjoined with loathing of the latter. And so we find the hunter praising the figures of the women ('Finer-made girls than some of the well-fed Kaffirs, I suppose, are not to be found. . . . they are lithe and supple as a willow wand'), and cherishing the idea of the absolute power of the chief (whom other travellers might have despised as capricious and despotic):

> They say perfect happiness does not exist in this world, but I should say a Kaffir chief comes nearer to it than any other mortal; his slightest wish is law; he knows no contradiction; he has the power of life and death in his hands at any moment, and can take any quantity of wives and put them away at pleasure; he is waited upon like an infant, and every wish, whim, and caprice is indulged to the fullest extent.[56]

I am not trying to make a case for Baldwin as an enlightened lover or sympathiser of Africans (his disparaging remarks on the 'Hottentots', for example, will not support this), but I do want to use him to show that, far from there being any objective view of African food and eating habits, whites' reactions to the African diet are intimately linked with the responses to the general culture, and that these responses are rooted in the culture of the observer rather than in that of the observed. This is given literal illustration in a picture of Baldwin enjoying the hospitality of the 'Kaffir' chief as he is served, and fanned while eating, by pretty, semi-naked women. There is no question but that the authority which enjoys service in the one sphere may command service in the other. The stripping away of elaborate ritual, the simple presentation of dishes by the semi-clad females, gives the scene an uncomplicated sensual enjoyment that is an escape from frustration. Some hunters, of course, were as aggressive in their denunciation of the Africans as they were in the engagement of their professional or sporting activities; but, given their immersion in the blood of the indigenous animals, it seems unsurprising that others, like Baldwin, were ready to 'always do in Rome as Rome does – eat (if I can) whatever is set before me, and shut my eyes if I feel qualmish' and found that 'Nothing approaches the parts most relished by the natives in richness of flavor, and racy, gamy taste'.[57]

The raciness and gaminess tell us that we are dealing in part here with the call of the wild. Just as many of the hunters were seeking to flee the complications of western society, so it follows that several voices from that society spoke out against the bloodlust they abhorred. Those adventurers and explorers (more frequent from the 1860s onwards) who embraced sophistication and complexity reveal just as clearly the perception of food and eating as an index of cultural progression. They may spurn what Baldwin happily digests, but their distaste is, as an indirect endorsement of the standards of their home culture, no less grounded in their own society than is Baldwin's flight from delicacy and politeness.

Eating and writing

A point I now need to make, but which has been implicit in much of what I have already said in this chapter, is that the accounts of eating which work towards the establishment of a hierarchical differential between European and African habits are expressed in *writing*. For writing is itself regarded as the sign of a superior society. Literacy is taken to be the mark of culture that has attained a degree of intellectual and technical sophistication incomprehensible to pre-literate worlds. Hence the great number of anecdotes telling of the Africans' superstitious reverence or fear of paper that has been or is being written upon. African boys, soon to become pupils, are shown thinking writing to be 'witchcraft'.[58] An Italian traveller, Casati, complains of how:

> Troublesome events were the cause, later on, of my losing some of my notes (a lot of fables), obtained from the lips of some Negroes belonging to the principal races that I met; the foolish and cruel suspicion of a king thought them worthy of the funeral pile.[59]

This was held to be a not uncommon threat, and it finds its most famous expression in another of Stanley's narratives in which the explorer is accosted by a group of Africans who are worried after he had been seen by their people writing notes the previous day. The ensuing scene, one of Stanley's most memorable set-pieces, exhibits the west's cultural codes on the matter with even greater flourish than one would have expected from the audacious reporter. Stanley quotes one of the Africans as relaying their fear thus:

> This is very bad. Our country will waste, our goats will die, our bananas will rot, and our women will dry up. What have we done to you, that you should wish to kill us? We have sold you food, and we have brought you wine, each day. Your people are allowed to wander where they please, without trouble. Why is the Mundelé so wicked? We have gathered together to fight you, if you do not burn that tara-tara [paper] now before our eyes. If you burn it we go away and shall be friends as heretofore.[60]

If writing is taken (as intended) as a sign of culture, then Stanley's potential antagonists see it as harmful to nature, a view transmitted by the images of death, decay and infertility. Their ignorance prevents their conceiving that culture can be acquired or admitted without destruction. Therefore culture must be destroyed. The Africans may be capable of entering satisfactorily into a relationship of exchange, selling food, but their recognition of civilisation goes no further. Stanley's response to this ultimatum is to go to his tent, while:

> my brain was busy in devising some plan to foil this superstitious madness. My note-book contained a vast number of valuable notes; plans of falls, creeks, villages, sketches of localities, ethnological and philological details, sufficient to fill two octavo volumes – everything was of general interest to the public. I could not sacrifice it to the childish caprice of savages.[61]

Stanley's brain (his powers of reflection and reason are contrasted with the superstition of the Africans) has collected knowledge which is at the service of Europe and America whose publics it will also entertain. The fact that the knowledge is also of those Africans who are now ready to immolate it suggests that the latter have no self-knowledge and underscores the importance of power in relation to knowledge. Like children, the Africans must be protected from themselves; the destruction of the

[73]

notes would postpone or ruin altogether any chance of their improvement. Stanley's brain finds a dramatic solution. He burns a substitute tome, a well-thumbed volume (Chandos edition) of Shakespeare, which he passes off as the offending note-book. The information Stanley has collated may have been saved by this ruse but the 'episode of the Burning of Shakespeare' inscribes in flame the image of the African as anti-culture.

Stanley elsewhere would play around with, modify, even argue against this image. But it was and remains a potent symbol. Stanley knew this because he manufactured it. Norman Bennett records that in his diary Stanley wrote that the sacrifice he had offered was not the Shakespeare volume but a worthless piece of paper scribbled over carelessly.[62]

Stanley presents the book-burning episode as dramatic evidence of the Africans' distance from culture which, unless guided, they would sooner conflagrate than assimilate. This and less spectacular scenes were used by anthropologists and racial theorists to support 'scientific' ideas about 'primitives'. Sir John Lubbock, in *The Origin of Civilisation and the Primitive Condition of Man*, quotes or summarises several travellers including Denham, Park, Caillié, and Burton on the Africans' fear of writing and drawing.[63] As with observations on other matters, these reports thus found popular and scientific circulation.

The Africans' lack of writing, like their lack of table manners, can disturb as well as amuse. The point of view and the medium in which it is communicated always insist on the Africans' role as object. Mrs Pringle, travelling through East Africa to aid a Christian mission, writes:

> In the first place, you must picture me sitting cross-legged, *à la Turque*, under our thatched-roof bower, my knees forming my writing-table, and before me a perfect crowd of natives on the river-bank – every woman, child, and baby the small village possesses having turned out to inspect and watch the movements of the Inglese. The noise and jabbering they are making are most distracting; at the same time, they are very respectful, and anxious, poor things, to help us.[64]

The Africans' unfamiliarity with writing hinders the white's performance of it, in terms both of their stares and the absence of the proper instruments. Here Mrs Pringle has to make a natural writing-table from her knees. There are obvious parallels here with eating, which activity the blacks are supposed not to practise properly. The sentimental notice that the 'poor things' want to assist but do not know how to is designed to appeal to the nineteenth-century sense of duty that one should show them. The society that can show them how to help has as two of its salient accomplishments the arts of writing and of eating with good manners.

When the European traveller writes or eats, his or her personality is reflected in the preference to do so at a distance or 'in private' – even when someone like Parkyns dips his finger in the dish with blacks it is manifestly an act in opposition to the norm since there would otherwise be no need to draw attention to it – and the prominence given to the actual or potential disruption of either task by African inquisitiveness or hostility is a profound symbol of cultural disturbance. Eating and writing are directly linked in this function: in both cases the European body is sustained through the consumption of Africa. Even when travellers eat their own food in their own way the descriptions of them doing so still use African culture to validate their own behaviour; and, more often than not, African labour is used for support.

The accounts of Africans eating are thus framed in a form not just inaccessible to them but which is itself a mark of a culture from which their lowly position in the hierarchy of cultures or 'races' excludes them. Jack Goody has recognised the 'link between literacy and the elaboration of the repertoire' and has, quite correctly, seen this link in terms of the way in which the development of literacy helped societies formalise hierarchical distinctions in the distribution and consumption of food (what we could call the pecking order) and offer increased sophistication or specialisation:

> And so writing has been instrumental in preserving and often . . . in creating, those inequalities in the rights of people to the means of production that in the past have led to social differentiation of a radical kind.[65]

Goody acknowledges that increased literacy may aid social mobility by allowing education in the ways (the menus and table manners) of the higher classes or castes, but, as the above quotation indicates, he knows the dangers not only of restricted literacy but of the hegemonic power of the proffered ladder of mobility.

Food, commodity, and identity

There is another side too to the image of food. For if the adventurers and explorers and the readers of their narratives find their sense of themselves in the distance they maintain from African ways, then just as surely do they discover confirmation of their identity in the western food they take with them. Thomas Richards (although speaking of products generally rather than food specifically) gets this right when, in his otherwise disappointing chapter on 'Selling darkest Africa', he argues that:

> In the hands of 1890's advertisers the commodity was represented as the bulwark of Empire ... As an inert object the commodity did not change wherever it was taken, and whenever commodities were taken into the colonial world they asserted their 'Englishness' as against everything irremediably foreign.[66]

(This is what the travellers in my next chapter wished for: the comfort and surety of identity from the objects they took with them.)

With food and drink there is an organic Englishness whose virtues are ready to be taken internally. This is so even with items not indigenous to Britain, in which cases the attachment to them of English properties (that is, worthy national characteristics) is a pronouncement of the country's long-standing mercantile prowess and of its newer imperial influence.

We shall take tea as an example. And we do so in the company of Stanley, whose image is used in an advertisement of 1890 for the United Kingdom Tea Company, which depicts him drinking tea with Emin Pasha, to whom he remarks 'Well, Emin, old fellow, this cup of the United Kingdom Tea Company's Delicious Tea makes us forget all our troubles' and from whom he receives the reassuring reply 'So it does, my boy'.[67] There is, of course, a mutual reinforcement here: tea is a calming drink, and Britons are calm, phlegmatic people. Trouble may be stirring but the more important brewing is that of the tea, which allows us to collect ourselves. I use the first person plural because that is how the advertisement and the ideology to which it belongs works. Outside the whites' tent a group of Africans, whose features cannot be distinguished, struggle to bring in further crates of the tea. They are in our service, labouring to bring us the sweet comfort (as are the unseen pickers in India and Ceylon, who nowadays are graceful women working for us). Less obvious (because perhaps subliminal) messages of assurance for the British consumer are found in the text of the advert which informs us that the tea is 'Supplied to the Members' Refreshment Rooms of the Houses of Parliament' and that it will be 'Delivered to any Address Carriage Paid'. The parliamentary endorsement is an authoritative attestation to the strengths of Englishness and tea (and to the English taking tea), while the delivery offer incorporates every Briton into this network of national refreshment. Finally, we are told that the stores are held in London at 'Imperial Warehouse'. I will have more to say about the cultural reception of the Emin Pasha Relief Expedition in a later chapter, and shall look more closely then at the promotion and appropriation of images derived from it, but I hope I have done enough for now to show some of the ways in which the substance and manner of consumption are used to provide an important index to individual and social character. It's true there may be a certain jokey quality to the tea advert, but when we compare all its references and codes to passages like the following one from *The Sunday Reading for the Young* (1877) then we do have a further, clear illustration of what I have been saying. The passage comments on a group of Africans shown in a drawing and, simply making explicit what is implied in any number of texts, states: 'They are but one degree removed from the level of brute creation – the sole trace of civilization about them is that they cook their food, and that, it may be assumed, in the crudest manner'.[68]

I want to sum up, then, by saying that the white travellers' descriptions of eating are written and distributed in a form suggestive of nineteenth-century western technology and capital; that the act of writing is used to give the narrators a spatial, social and intellectual distance from the diners who are described; that this distance empowers whites with a level of reflection denied to the Africans who are engaged in either a spontaneous, uncontrolled display of gluttony or a base parody of European rituals; that the observation by Britons of Africans feeding themselves fixes the latter in the whites' cultural gaze as anthropological curiosities whose apartness from them confirms the Europeans' cultural superiority; and that the particular constructions of this relationship may shift according to the political and intellectual forces of the nation from which the writers are journeying. Power and knowledge are wholly bound up with these perceptions and descriptions. Just eleven years ago the authors of *Consuming Passions* were writing: 'once the anthropologist finds out where, when, and with whom the food is eaten, just about everything else can be inferred about the relations among the society's members'.[69]

It should not come as a great surprise then that in those enduring texts of the troubled years of the *fin de siècle*, when Britain was engaged in a morbid introspection over its apparently fracturing identity, the perceived splits and tensions should be fearfully signalled by eating habits. In Wells's 'The Time Machine' (1895), the Morlocks, descendants of the proletariat, are almost certainly cannibals, feeding off the decadent Eloi, and the Time Traveller returns from his encounter with them casually revealing a hunger for meat; Dracula's dietary habits in Bram Stoker's 1897 novel are well known; and Kurtz in Conrad's *Heart of Darkness*, as Tony Tanner has shown,[70] can be seen as cannibalistic, as he opens 'his mouth wide', giving him 'a weirdly voracious aspect, as though he had wanted to swallow all the air, all the earth, all the men before him'.[71] I have deliberately held back from cannibalism. It is a subject in itself and would lead me away from the main arguments in this chapter, but the presence of white cannibalism, whether actual or metaphorical, in the disturbing narratives of the 1890s underlines the importance of representations of eating in image-formation and projections of cultural identity.

So it should certainly come as no great shock that Karega, one of the principal characters in Ngũgĩ's novel *Petals of Blood*, reported seeing his hope 'in the new children, who have nothing to prove to the white man [and] who do not find it necessary to prove that they can eat with knife and fork'.[72]

Notes

1 Alan Moorehead, *The Blue Nile* (London: Hamish Hamilton, 1962), p. 230.
2 Peter Farb and George Armelagos, *Consuming Passions: The Anthropology of Eating* (Boston: Houghton Mifflin Company, 1980), p. 205.
3 On these developments see especially Norbert Elias, *The Civilizing Process: The History of Manners*, trans. Edmund Jephcott (Oxford: Basil Blackwell, 1978).
4 Jack Goody, *Cooking, Cuisine and Class: A Study in Comparative Sociology* (Cambridge: Cambridge University Press, 1982).
5 John Burnett, *Plenty and Want: A Social History of Diet in England from 1815 to the Present Day* (London: Nelson, 1966), p. 81.
6 Burnett, *Plenty and Want*, p. 33.
7 Quoted in Gertrude Himmelfarb, *The Idea of Poverty: England in the Early Industrial Age* (London: Faber & Faber, 1984), p. 358.
8 Burnett, *Plenty and Want*, p. 72.
9 Burnett, *Plenty and Want*, p. 81.
10 Burnett, *Plenty and Want*, p. 82.
11 Burnett, *Plenty and Want*, p. 190.
12 Burnett, *Plenty and Want*, p. 191. The information about the *Lancet*'s probe is taken from pp. 190–1.
13 Burnett, *Plenty and Want*, p. 207. The information on the Food Acts is from pp. 204–7.
14 Burnett, *Plenty and Want*, p. 197.
15 Goody, *Cooking, Cuisine and Class*, p. 157.
16 John Burnett, *Plenty and Want*, p. 54.
17 Barbara Hardy, *The Moral Art of Dickens* (London: Athlone, 1970), p. 153.
18 T. S. Eliot, *Notes towards the Definition of Culture* (London: Faber & Faber, [1948] 1962), p. 27.
19 Claude Fischler, 'Food, self and identity', *Social Science Information* 27, 2 (1988), 275.
20 John Camden Hotten, ed., *Abyssinia and Its People; or, Life in the Land of Prester John* (London: John Camden Hotten, 1868; reprint ed., New York: Negro Universities Press, 1969), p. 23.
21 Descriptions of banquets of raw flesh in Abyssinia date back to at least the sixteenth century (see Hotten, *Abyssinia and Its People*, pp. 21–2), but this really reinforces my point. These accounts belong to the times at which Europe was constructing its hierarchy of good manners. It was Bruce who popularised the image, and the nineteenth century – with its own emphasis on manners to counteract the threatened collapse of class distinction – which became fascinated by it.
22 Mansfield Parkyns, *Life in Abyssinia: Being Notes Collected During Three Years' Residence and Travels in that Country*, 2 vols (London: John Murray, 1853), I, 2.
23 Mansfield Parkyns, *Life in Abyssinia*, I, 2–3.
24 Mansfield Parkyns, *Life in Abyssinia*, I, 3.
25 Mansfield Parkyns, *Life in Abyssinia*, I, 384–5.
26 Reay Tannahill, *Food in History* (London: Eyre Methuen, 1973), p. 333.
27 Mansfield Parkyns, *Life in Abyssinia*, I, 62.
28 Claude Fischler, 'Food, self and identity', p. 278. Fischler has in turn taken the idea of the 'omnivore's paradox' from Paul Rozin, 'The selection of foods by rats, humans and

other animals', in *Advances in the Study of Behavior*, vol. 6, eds J. S. Rosenblatt, R. A. Hinde, E. Shaw, C. Beer (London: Academic Press, 1976).

29 Summarised in John Camden Hotten, ed., *Abyssinia and Its People*, pp. 39–40.
30 Reay Tannahill, *Food in History*, p. 348.
31 Summarised in John Camden Hotten, ed., *Abyssinia and Its People*, pp. 40–1.
32 Jack Goody, *Cooking, Cuisine and Class*, p. 114.
33 Henry M. Stanley, *How I Found Livingstone: Travels, Adventures, and Discoveries in Central Africa; Including Four Months' Residence with Dr. Livingstone*, new edition (London: Sampson Low, Marston, Searle, & Rivington, [1872] 1887), p. 344.
34 Dorothy Middleton, ed., *The Diary of A. J. Mounteney-Jephson: Emin Pasha Relief Expedition 1887–1889* (Cambridge: for the Hakluyt Society at the University Press, 1969), p. 243.
35 Thomas Heazle Parke, *My Personal Experiences in Equatorial Africa as Medical Officer of the Emin Pasha Relief Expedition* (London: Sampson Low, Marston & Company Limited, 1891), p. 138.
36 Thomas Heazle Parke, *My Personal Experiences*, p. 138.
37 Peter Farb and George Armelagos, *Consuming Passions*, p. 105.
38 George Stocking, *Victorian Anthropology* (New York: The Free Press, 1987), p. 225.
39 See Francis L. K. Hsu, 'Rethinking the concept "primitive"', *Current Anthropology* 5 (1964), 169. The reference is to Tylor's book *Anthropology* (1881). Tylor's third, 'civilised' stage begins with the acquisition of writing.
40 David McLellan, *Marx's Grundrisse* (London: Granada Publishing, 1971), p. 35.
41 The references are to Sir Samuel White Baker, *Ismailia: A Narrative of the Expedition to Central Africa for the Suppression of the Slave Trade Organized by Ismail, Khedive of Egypt*, 2 vols (London: Macmillan & Co., 1874), II, 354–5; and to the same author's *The Nile Tributaries of Abyssinia and the Sword Hunters of the Hamran Arabs* (London: Macmillan & Co., Limited, [1867] 1907), pp. 40, 314, and 172.
42 This complexity was manifest in Napier's Abyssinian campaign in which, as Moorehead observes, at least twelve non-combatants were required for the support of each fighting man, so that the army 'was now planned and managed like some great industrial organization'. Alan Moorehead, *The Blue Nile*, p. 233.
43 Richard F. Burton, *The Lake Regions of Central Africa: A Picture of Exploration*, 2 vols (London: Longman, Green, Longman, & Roberts, 1860), I, 358.
44 Burnett, *Plenty and Want*, p. 120.
45 Richard F. Burton, *The Lake Regions of Central Africa* II, 334–5. Unless stated otherwise, all quotations used in the present discussion of Burton are taken from these two pages.
46 Richard F. Burton, *The Lake Regions of Central Africa*, II, 336.
47 Richard F. Burton, *The Lake Regions of Central Africa*, II, 336.
48 Richard F. Burton, *The Lake Regions of Central Africa*, II, 337.
49 Terence Ranger, 'The invention of tradition in colonial Africa', in *The Invention of Tradition*, eds Eric Hobsbawm and Terence Ranger (Cambridge: Cambridge University Press, 1984), p. 218.
50 Fischler, 'Food, self and identity', p. 284.
51 Peter Hulme, *Colonial Encounters: Europe and the Native Caribbean, 1492–1797* (London: Methuen, 1986), pp. 131–2. Hulme later makes another pertinent point: that in the early seventeenth century Amerindians' agricultural practices were misconstrued, leading to the charge that they were nomadic and failed to settle or cultivate the land; leading in turn to the charge that they had no right or claim to the land (see pp. 157–9).
52 Fischler, 'Food, self and identity', p. 284.
53 To be fair to Burton (though I see no compelling reason why we should be), he does himself recommend 'Congo chop' in one of his books, but even there he has nothing positive to say about African eating habits, and the native food is seen as desirable principally because it is suited to the environment: 'foreigners will certainly fare better and . . . outlive their brother whites, when they can substitute African stews for the roast and boiled goat and cow, likest to donkey-meat, for the waxy and insipid

potato and for heavy pudding and tart, with which their jaded stomach is laden, as if it had the digestion of north latitude 50°'. Richard F. Burton, *Two Trips to Gorilla Land and the Cataracts of the Congo*, 2 vols (London: Sampson Low, Marston, Low, & Searle, 1876; reprint ed., New York: Johnson Reprint Corporation, 1967), II, 251.

I don't believe this recommendation affects my argument in any way; rather, it prescribes a menu for the efficient absorption or utilisation of the land.

54 William Charles Baldwin, *African Hunting: From Natal to the Zambesi, including Lake Ngami, the Kalahari Desert, etc., from 1852 to 1860* (New York: Harper & Brothers, 1863), p. 243. There may be an ironic dig here at those recipe books and domestic manuals which decried wastage.

On Baldwin see John M. MacKenzie, *The Empire of Nature: Hunting, Conservation and British Imperialism* (Manchester: Manchester University Press, 1988), pp. 105–9.

55 On the connection between hunting and sexuality see for example MacKenzie, *The Empire of Nature*, pp. 42–3. MacKenzie's book has some useful observations on the relationship between hunting, masculinity, and imperialism.

56 William Baldwin, *African Hunting*, p. 243.

57 William Baldwin, *African Hunting*, p. 243.

58 J. Cooke Yarborough, ed., *The Diary of a Working Man (William Bellingham) in Central Africa, December 1884, to October, 1887* (London: Society for Promoting Christian Knowledge, [n.d.]), p. 95.

59 Major Gaetano Casati, *Ten Years in Equatoria and the Return with Emin Pasha*, trans. Mrs J. Randolph Clay and Walter Savage Landor, 2 vols (London: Frederick Warne & Co., 1891) I, 48–9.

60 Henry M. Stanley, *Through the Dark Continent: Or the Sources of the Nile around the Great Lakes of Equatorial Africa and down the Livingstone River to the Atlantic Ocean*, new edition (London: Sampson Low, Marston, Searle, & Rivington, [1878] 1890), p. 571.

61 Henry M. Stanley, *Through the Dark Continent*, p. 571.

62 Norman R. Bennett, ed., *Stanley's Despatches to the New York Herald 1871–1872, 1874–1877* (Boston: Boston University Press, 1970), p. 387.

63 Sir John Lubbock, *The Origin of Civilisation and the Primitive Condition of Man: Mental and Social Condition of Savages*, 3rd ed. (London: Longmans, Green, and Co., 1875), pp. 21–5. Lubbock cites similar reports on Amerindians.

64 M. A. Pringle, *A Journey in East Africa Towards the Mountains of the Moon*, new edition (Edinburgh and London: William Blackwood and Sons, 1886), p. 172.

65 Jack Goody, *Cooking, Cuisine and Class*, p. 192.

66 Thomas Richards, *The Commodity Culture of Victorian England: Advertising and Spectacle, 1851–1914* (Stanford, California: Stanford University Press, 1990), pp. 142–3.

67 The advert is reproduced and briefly discussed in Richards, *The Commodity Culture*, p. 139, and is also reproduced in Leonard de Vries, *Victorian Advertisements* (London: John Murray, 1968), p. 120. Richards's source is *The Graphic Stanley Number*, 30 April 1890, and de Vries's is the *Illustrated London News*, 1 March 1890.

68 Quoted in Jan Nederveen Pieterse, *White on Black: Images of Africa and Blacks in Western Popular Culture* (New Haven: Yale University Press, 1992), p. 35.

69 Farb and Armelagos, *Consuming Passions*, p. 4.

70 Tony Tanner, '"Gnawed bones and artless tales" – eating and narrative in Conrad', in *Joseph Conrad: A Commemoration. Papers from the 1974 International Conference on Conrad*, ed. Norman Sherry (London: Macmillan, 1976), pp. 31–2.

71 Joseph Conrad, *Heart of Darkness*, ed. Robert Kimbrough, 3rd ed. (W. W. Norton & Company, 1988), p. 59.

72 Ngũgĩ wa Thiong'o, *Petals of Blood* (Oxford: Heinemann, [1977] 1986), p. 167.

CHAPTER THREE

Beads and cords of love

The context

In this chapter I shall look at the ambivalent space occupied by some travellers and explorers in East and Central Africa. Any idea that ambivalence is due to the nature of a racial fetish runs the risk of effacing important differences within the colonising country by perceiving contradictions and illogicalities as symptoms of a collective, national subconscious. This perspective entails precisely the same phenomenon of the construction of a national identity through the elision or transcendence of political difference that we see in the rallying round Victoria in the second half of the nineteenth century. I therefore want to trace various signs of ambivalence, which I shall attempt by considering the social identity of some travellers, their attitudes to writing and journeying, and their relationship to Africans and to goods. I shall be making particular mention of beads, which occupy the dual role of currency and commodity. All these factors are connected. Some are applicable to certain travellers more than others. My aim is not to claim a particular type of ambivalence for any one traveller but to show how texts deal with material causes of ambivalence and ambiguity in ways that psychoanalytic theories of race fetish have difficulty acknowledging.

It seems to me that when Bhabha writes of race fetish and the supposedly obsessive repetition of the 'mythical moment of disjunction'[1] between cultures and races, he is in danger of escalating psychic tendency into material inevitability. This will not do, and in examining manifestations of the subject's ambivalence I hope to suggest something of their origins. Once these are understood and seen in their material settings they should be demystified.

James Casada is just one historian who has already called for a consideration of the explorers' family backgrounds, social status, education, and pre-African careers.[2] His study of ten explorers yielded the interesting observation that only two of them were eldest sons, that none completed a university degree, and that although fathers' occupations varied considerably their social status was similar, often involving a military or religious role. Outside from, and at opposite ends of, this bourgeois pattern were Stanley and Baker. Eight of the ten men were bachelors at the beginning of their explorations.[3] However, while Casada's advice is important, his conclusions are unhelpfully evasive.

Having made the effort to look outwards at society, Casada reduces his focus again to the individual, so that Africa is viewed merely as an outlet for personal tensions,[4] and the explorers' attitudes towards Africa are seen as affected by the 'motivational factors of allurement and escapism' because, for example, the 'alluring enticement of Africa attracted them in the same way their colorful beads and gaudy cloths attracted the natives'.[5] This is indeed blaming Africa for wearing a short skirt.

I shall not consider every traveller to East and Central Africa, and I have already said in my Introduction why I am not writing on Livingstone (though his influence is strongly felt throughout this chapter). Nor is my focus on the geography or the history of the region. My attention in this chapter is on literary tropes, and on how their apparent role in the service of the west in fact can be made to reveal troubling divisions. I thus consider the social role both of the traveller and of commodities. My working definition of a commodity is taken from Appadurai, who suggests that 'the commodity situation in the life of any "thing" be defined as the situation in which its exchangeability (past, present, or future) for some other thing is its socially relevant feature'.[6] The notion of exchangeability takes on immense significance in the present context.

To give some consistency of conditions I have selected for this chapter mostly narratives whose authors went to the same areas around Lake Tanganyika and through Uganda. Their journeys span the period covered by my study, so that the importance of physical signs of ambivalence can be gauged against historical changes.[7] Some of the narratives I look at are generated by the search for the sources of the Nile, but my interest is in neither the geographical 'discoveries' nor the personal disputes associated with those expeditions, the stories of which have been told often before. Casada has opined that the search for the Nile sources shows how Afromania was a disease defying rational explanation.[8] Casada's misdiagnosis itself seems to defy rational explanation.

Briefly to set the scene against which the tensions were played out, however, Burton and Speke undertook an expedition to East Africa from 1856 to 1859, sponsored by the Royal Geographical Society. (They had previously travelled together in 1855 on an ill-fated trip to Somaliland, on which both men were wounded in an attack by Somalis.) On this journey they 'discovered' Lake Tanganyika, but Burton prevented Speke from exploring the lake as thoroughly as he would have wished. On the return journey, however, Speke surveyed a lake, which he named Victoria and was convinced was the source of the Nile. Burton vehemently and publicly disagreed, and from 1860 to 1862, with James Augustus Grant, Speke travelled on a second expedition (again dispatched by the Royal Geographical Society) to prove that Lake Victoria was the source of the Nile. Speke made further finds. In the words of Stanley:

> He christened the falling effluent, where it drops from the level of the lake and escapes northerly into the Victoria Nile, 'Ripon Falls,' in honour of the Earl of Ripon, who was President of the Royal Geographical Society . . . and the arm of the lake from which the Victoria Nile issued, Napoleon Channel, as a token of respect to the Paris Geographical Society, who had honoured him with a gold medal for the discovery of Lake Victoria.[9]

But on his last expedition Livingstone heard information from the Arabs that Victoria was really five lakes, and speculation by armchair geographers left the facts uncertain. Livingstone, on 2 April 1867, had been the next European to see Lake Tanganyika. On 14 March 1869 he arrived in Ujiji on the eastern side (where he was 'found' by Stanley in November 1871) after having travelled along nearly all the western shore from the south end to Kasengé, an island which Speke had visited in 1858. The lake was then explored for a few weeks by Stanley and Livingstone and then, from August 1872, by the latter alone on his last journey. In February 1874, on his trip across Africa from east to west, Cameron arrived at Ujiji and proceeded to Lake Tanganyika, where he discovered the Lukuga creek, which he decided was the lake's outlet; and then journeyed up the west coast as far as Kasengé Island before returning to Ujiji. Stanley's *Through the Dark Continent* expedition sought to solve some of the questions left unanswered by the previous journeys.

By the mid nineteenth century, East Central Africa, previously left to the Portuguese and Arabs, became the focus of British concern. As Hammond and Jablow observe:

> Britain's colonies in Asia, primarily India, were her major concern. . . . The Suez Canal – the new, short route to India completed in 1869 – placed East Africa in a position of strategic importance. Increasing pressures of international rivalry, especially with France and Germany, made it imperative for Great Britain to maintain dominance in East Africa to further safeguard the 'jewel in the imperial crown'.[10]

Speke's cords of love

Speke's *Journal of the Discovery of the Source of the Nile* was published in 1863. James Grant, who would later serve as Head of the Intelligence Department in the Abyssinian Campaign,[11] acted as an important go-between for Speke and his publisher, Blackwoods. Grant's comments on Speke's manuscript throw interesting light on responses to travel narratives at this time. Grant expressed to Blackwood his feeling that the manuscript should be revised because: 'many parts are *slightly indecent* + too slangy in expression for the general public . . . & I should like to see it cut down to half its dimensions – the scenes have so much repetition in them'.[12] Yet he was at the same time hopeful that 'care will be taken that Speke's peculiar style of expression be not altered in his book'.[13]

Just a few days after Grant's expressed wish to Blackwood, the publisher reassured him that 'The book is being kept strictly in Speke's own particular dialect and it will be as genuine a book of travels as ever was published'.[14] Assuming (as I think we must) that this last claim is free from irony, we may note the correlation between distinctive accent and authenticity. It has to do with the moment of intersection between well-to-do amateurism and the new professionalism. The attraction is that the latter is invested with the supposed uncomplicated and disinterested honesty of the former. Four years earlier Blackwood had told Speke on accepting his papers on the discovery of the source of the Nile for *Blackwood's Edinburgh Magazine*:

> I am sure we adopted the wisest course in simply correcting your plain honest narrative & not attempting any literary adornment. The narrative is plain sensible English now & very graphic. As you happily expressed a confounded fellow making you talk about 'Azure skies' would have been intolerable.[15]

It is a wonderfully British sleight of hand that has the writing at once a 'plain honest narrative' and corrected. The intervention is quite characteristic of the mediation between product and consumer in the second half of the nineteenth century. Thus: 'You would see that I altered slightly your rather specific description of the extreme nudity of your African family'.[16] It might be said that Blackwood is clothing Speke for public viewing. Another example is furnished a year later, with Blackwood's comments on Speke's account of his Somali adventures taken by *Blackwood's Edinburgh Magazine*, the proofs of which Blackwood sent to Speke with an apology for proof-reading that was not as careful as it should have been because:

> constantly where I get interested I forget to note whether you are writing

good or bad English. It is a most quaint & interesting narrative. There is a reality about your description of the escape from the Somali which is better than the finest writing. It grieved me to the heart to alter the part where the dread horror came upon you but it was necessary.

The publisher and readers enjoy consuming what they take to be the 'reality' of Speke's adventures but require that it conform to their perspective. The narrative should appear to be that of an actual person so that the lack of literary worth is held up as proof of the material contained in it. Blackwood is explicit in his praise of the 'reality' of Speke's description over the 'finest writing'. The opposition of these terms tells us much and we find precisely the same separation and values in the *Quarterly Review*'s article on Speke's *Journal*:

> If it does not possess literary merit, to which its author probably never aspired, it abounds with very extraordinary incidents; and this graphic narrative affords probably a clearer insight into savage life than any more artistic production could have given.[17]

The reviewer shares Blackwood's assumptions about the distinctiveness of voice assuring the validity of the experience, but extends this point along a logical progression: the greater reliability of its observations on its environment. It is felt that a finer artistry would detract from such a record, in both material and purpose.

Speke himself thought along similar lines. On sending the manuscript to Blackwood he explained 'I could not cut any of it down, or it would spoil it [sic] truthful effect'.[18] Scale and comprehensiveness would also seem to be considerations here, and it is interesting that as a writer his view of authenticity pulls against the economy urged by Grant.

Speke was as enamoured of his new-found literary profile and of its financial rewards as any fledgeling author. In respect of payment for the narrative of his Somali adventures used in *Blackwood's Magazine* he thanked the publisher for having: 'made me quite a literary character – I feel as proud as Punch ... Sixty pounds!! its [sic] wonderful to contemplate on'.[19] A few months previously Blackwood had sent Speke £80 as payment for his papers on the discovery of the Nile sources published in the *Magazine*, with the words 'They are most interesting & valuable papers & will I trust cause the name of J. H. Speke to be long remembered in the world'.[20] The designation 'valuable', though signifying empirical worth, is nevertheless a further indication of how financial value has become attached to scientifically important information. In 1860 Speke received £60 for his narrative of his Somali adventures used in the *Magazine*. There is, then, a pecuniary interest for the author, one

Figure 5 Speke with copy of *Blackwood's Magazine* 1864

which may make him more attuned to the tastes and requirements of the audience, but which certainly has him enter the literary marketplace. In 1863 Blackwood guaranteed Speke 'the five thousand pounds [John] Murray offered & some similar arrangement as he proposed for the contingent profits'.[21]

As an additional influence on Speke's writing there was the question, already alluded to, of his standing with Richard Burton, a matter which contributed to the very existence of Speke's book. Writing to Blackwood from Africa, Speke expressed his wish that:

> the whole of my writings . . . appear in the form of a book either in the Winter or next spring season; as by that time Burton's writings will have had a good fair start of me. But a book I must have to do justice to myself and those who accompanied me on that expedition.[22]

The urge to self-justification, which was much in evidence in the quarrel with Burton, might be placed in a social context. Speke's father was a descendant of a Frenchman who came to England with William the Conqueror and, while the father lived during his retirement a quiet life on his estates, Speke's mother 'came of a more ambitious background. Her father's family were merchants, among the richest in England, whose huge stone-built manor, Didlington, stood as the symbol of their material success'.[23] The parallels with Parkyns's parentage are hard to ignore, though whereas Parkyns was able to manufacture or play to the image of an eccentric, Speke's situation is much more ambiguous and often fraught. He served in India and fought in the second Sikh War in 1849, as did James Grant.[24] He viewed Africa through eyes that had seen India, and this contributed another kind of filter to his vision.

Maitland has noted that after both the 1856–59 expedition to Central Africa and the 1860–63 expedition Speke failed to hand over his journals to the Royal Geographical Society for first publication, a neglect which ran counter to the Society's official policy. Speke gave lectures to the Society but, claims Maitland, with the publication of his articles in *Blackwood's Magazine* towards the end of 1859, the Council of the Society began to feel that Speke had, after all, 'behaved ungenerously by withholding his material from the *Journal* and seeking instead the wider, more profitable recognition of the public'.[25] This, according to Maitland, was a factor in the Society's reticence over Burton's criticism of Speke in *The Lake Regions of Central Africa*.

The Royal Geographical Society showed disdain towards one who had circumvented social rules by ignoring a gentleman's agreement and decided to pursue his own interests instead. Roy Bridges gives as a reason for the Society's first-publication policy the hope that 'prestige and, perhaps, financial advantage could be gained from first revealing to the world the details of a new discovery'[26] – but the friction between the two parties is indicative of the movement towards individualism and of the pressures on scientific bodies to grow closer to the 'public', a direction perhaps taken later in the 1860s by anthropology, but one the Royal Geographical Society was slow to follow.

Bridges has shown that between 1848 and 1877 the number of the Society's subscribers increased from around six hundred to three and a half thousand, coinciding with the 'classic period of East African exploration', and concludes that 'There seems little doubt that interest in the exploits of the East African explorers was a potent factor' in this growth. Bridges admits that the Society's 'very existence was made possible by the subscriptions of an increasingly prosperous Victorian bourgeoisie and its outgrowth in India', but believes it difficult to prove a 'connection with expansive capitalism convincingly except at the very general level'.[27] His survey of membership leads him to suggest that 'the "scientific interest" arose . . . not so much from a commercial middle class but from a bureaucratic and functional bourgeoisie'.[28] So, although the Society may in one sense have had 'genuine scientific' aims, these have to be contextualised. As Bridges puts it in another essay:

> The image which Speke and others built up of Africans as backward people needing European rule undoubtedly influenced the assumptions which imperial rulers made when they took control some twenty years later; European overrule in East Africa was almost a duty. A corollary of this attitude was that East Africa's economic resources could not be tapped until order was established. When it was, Speke implied, European rule would pay dividends.[29]

Speke's *Journal of the Discovery of the Source of the Nile*, which was the first of his published books but which covered the second expedition, opens with a concise illustration of the employment of a strikingly individual voice to validate its impressions. Thus:

> If my account should not entirely harmonise with preconceived notions as to primitive races, I cannot help it. I profess accurately to describe naked Africa – Africa in those places where it has not received the slightest impulse, whether for good or for evil, from European civilisation.[30]

The crucial word is 'entirely': there is sufficient space for a divergence that will uphold Speke's personality, but that space is used to confirm many general ideas *because* of its supposed location outside the ruling elite with the respected voice. The concept of virgin land – in the sense of its being unvisited by Europeans – helps create this position. Speke dresses it in prose for others to inspect. He has penetrated it and now passes it into circulation.

Speke asks us to reflect 'on ourselves, who have been so much better favoured, *yet have neglected to teach them*, than on those who, whilst they are sinning, know not what they are doing' (p. 1; my emphasis). The statement is an undeniable exhortation to active influence. We are still on the first page of his introduction, and this appeal to take up an educative mission must therefore frame whatever follows in the narrative. For instance:

> experience *will* not teach the negro, who thinks only for the moment . . . the curse of Noah sticks to these grandchildren by Ham, and no remedy that has yet been found will relieve them. They require a government like ours in India; and without it, the slave trade will wipe them off the face of the earth. (p. 45)

When Speke's party approaches Karagué,[31] the tone of his narrative changes somewhat from the emphasis on Africans' alleged laziness and imbecility. They reach this promising territory by marching through the deep valley of Lohugati:

> which was so beautiful we instinctively pulled up to admire it. Deep down its well-wooded side below us was a stream, of most inviting aspect for a trout-fisher, flowing towards the Nyanza. Just beyond it the valley was clothed with fine trees and luxuriant vegetation of all descriptions . . . in the far background were the rich grassy hills of Karagué and Kishakka. (p. 161)

The paradisiacal scene is completed when the party rest after crossing the stream and are visited by:

> all the inhabitants, who were more naked than any people we had yet seen. All the maidens, even at the age of puberty, did not hesitate to stand boldly in front of us – for evil thoughts were not in their minds. (p. 161)

Nakedness is attractive here. Of course the narrative voice is projecting on to the 'maidens' an absence of 'evil thoughts' just as much as if it had read evil thoughts into them. It is a sly manipulation of pronominal reference since the evil thoughts pertaining to the maidens, if they were to be found anywhere, would be the possession of Speke and his companions. But Speke wants to paint a picture of innocence so that he can clothe the valley and perhaps its people with the equipage of civilisation. Biblical authority, the Protestant work ethic, and the demise of the romantic Noble Savage all tell us that such a state of easeful innocence is not to be preserved. As George Stocking has shown, in the nineteenth century 'Political economy posed much more sharply [than in the eighteenth century] the implicit antagonism of civilization to nature, whether external or internal to man'.[32] After 1830 it had more specific reference to contemporary British experience, widening the opposition between savagery and civilisation. Stocking emphasises the increasing association of human productivity and labour with civilisation, arguing that it was this which led to the demise of the Noble Savage idea, which he terms the 'fantasy of a precapitalist mentality that saw labor as the curse of fallen man exiled from the

[89]

Garden'.[33] Stocking is perhaps too rigid in his placing of the line between capitalism and pre-capitalism, but his words do contextualise Speke's construction of the valley most usefully. Speke tells King Rumanika:

> To observe and admire the beauties of creation are worth much more than beads to us. But what led us this way we have told you before; it was to see your majesty in particular, and the great kings of Africa – and at the same time to open another road to the north, whereby the best manufactures of Europe would find their way to Karagué, and you would get so many more guests. (pp. 171–2)

Or he may have told the king this; we do not know exactly. The point, though, is that he says so to his readers and therefore the role he hopes commerce will play in the opening up of the country is highlighted. At the same time Speke seems anxious that he should not be taken for a trader himself: a desire born partly of the wish to have the king treat him in a certain way and partly of the view of traders held in Britain. He uses the image of beads, which are both ornament and currency, to communicate to us his anxiety. There is still something vulgar about money-making activities whilst idle leisure is even more unacceptable. Immediately before the passage quoted above are the lines:

> we have had our fill of the luxuries of life; eating, drinking, or sleeping have no charms for us now; we are above trade, therefore require no profits, and seek for enjoyment the run of the world. (p. 171)

Furthermore, when he gives Rumanika his revolving pistol it is 'in return for his great generosity as well as to show I placed no value on property, not being a merchant' (p. 170).[34] Speke and his companions may see themselves as above trade but here they appear to be in the service of it, at least in the sense of paving the way for it; a posture that lends credence to Roy Bridges's description of the explorers as constituting, 'by origin or adoption', a service class.[35] The irony is that Speke so signally employs commodities in his efforts to emphasise his superiority to those who trade in them. And, as my comments on his status as author suggest, this procedure applies particularly to his book itself. This should not be a complete surprise for, as Bridges rightly says, explorers – especially those searching for the Nile sources – could inspire feelings of nationhood which cut across class lines.[36] In part this depends on the fostering of a common attitude towards black people, but it is inevitable that the explorer's text, as the document which is supposed to help manage this unity, should itself contain the tensions that make the effort necessary in the first place.

Before departing, and leaving the sick Grant, Speke hands Rumanika some gifts, including a hammer, knife, gilt pens, letter paper, and gold and mother-of-pearl shirt studs, to show his appreciation of the king's kindness and of his restraint from mendicity. The goods are a mixture of the useful and the ornamental; things one would give to an artisan and to a gentleman, reflecting both the difficulty of knowing what to give to an African 'king' and the pressures for social compromise between classes at home. Apart from the worth this hand-out places on British goods, with the hope of creating further wants, it carries a conservative message for domestic society: reward will be made to those who do not clamour for it.

When the king's mother offers him two girls for wives he does not refuse them (though does not admit that he took them as wives), but is confident of the rewards of a kind of emotional *laissez-faire*: 'I did not follow her advice to chain either of them with iron, for I found cords of love, the only instrument white men know the use of, quite strong enough' (p. 299). It is not facetious to remark that Speke's cords of love are a personalised version of the sort of relationship envisaged by many for the colonies.

Speke tells Kamrasi, king of Unyoro, that he has come to find if he would be willing to trade by exchanging ivory for European goods and that he should make friends with Mtésa because 'unless the influence of trade was brought in to check the Waganda from pillaging the country, nothing would do so' (p. 403). Although Kamrasi is reported by Speke to be of a milder disposition than Mtésa, the traveller nevertheless complains that 'he wanted to fleece us of everything', which is an obstacle to free trade, as is the widespread custom of 'hongo', the paying of tribute, about which Speke constantly grumbles throughout his book. The commercial unattractiveness is given physical reflection: 'Nothing could be more filthy than the state of the palace and all the lanes leading up to it' (p. 413). The uncleanliness hints at a degraded moral state, which inevitably has its political dimension too:

> Kidgwiga told us today that king Kamrasi's sisters are not allowed to wed; they live and die virgins in his palace. Their only occupation in life consisted in drinking milk, of which each one consumes the produce daily of from ten to twenty cows, and hence they become so inordinately fat that they cannot walk . . . The brothers, too, are not allowed to go out of his reach. This confinement of the palace family is considered a state necessity, as a preventive to civil wars. (p. 420)

This idea of unproductive consumption is anathema to Speke. Nothing is given back to the people and the uselessness of the way of life is represented by the immobility of the sisters and brothers. Their restriction of movement is, of course, to be contrasted with Queen Victoria's visits around the British Isles, an important factor in the rise in popularity of the monarchy.

When Kamrasi asks, through a messenger, 'What medicine will attach all subjects to their king?' and Speke replies 'Knowledge of good government, attended with wisdom and justice, is all the medicine we know of' (p. 437), the British circumvention of superstition replaces it with rationality and objective qualities of fairness and propriety: invisible bonds of love again.

Speke has a passage on the land and people around Lake Victoria which is a remarkable model of the concise ordering of stereotypes in the support of western economic and political activity. I quote it at length:

> To look upon its resources, one is struck with amazement at the waste of the world: if instead of this district being in the hands of its present owners, it were ruled by a few scores of Europeans, what an entire revolution a few years would bring forth! An extensive market would be opened to the world, the present nakedness of the land would have a covering, and industry and commerce would clear the way for civilisation and enlightenment.
>
> At present the natural inert laziness and ignorance of the people is their own and their country's bane. They are all totally unaware of the treasures at their feet. This dreadful sloth is in part engendered by the excessive bounty of the land in its natural state; by the little want of clothes or other luxuries, in consequence of the congenial temperature; and from the people having no higher object in view than the first-coming meal, and no other stimulus to exertion by example or anything else. The great cause, however, is their want of a strong protecting government to preserve peace, without which nothing can prosper. Thus they are, both morally and physically, little better than brutes, and as yet there is no better prospect in store for them.[37]

Speke and his *Journal* were roundly criticised by Burton, whose attacks challenge the construction of the African landscape and people in Speke's narrative. A forum for Burton's views was provided by his publication in 1864 of *The Nile Basin*, which combined a lecture given by Burton to the Royal Geographical Society in November 1864 (accompanied by a preface) with James Macqueen's hostile reviews of Speke's *Journal* from the *Morning Advertiser*. At one point Burton accuses Speke of not knowing 'the use of words':

> 'A village built on the most luxurious principles' is a mass of dirty huts; a 'king of kings' is a petty chief; a 'splendid court' is a display of savagery; and the 'French of those parts' are barbarians somewhat superior to their neighbours.[38]

There are numerous examples in *The Nile Basin* of such disparaging

remarks which, however distasteful or simply plain racist, do nevertheless expose the constructedness of Speke's discourse. Their criticism is
of the kind of dressing and elaboration which Blackwood seems to have
favoured. These examples are to be found mostly in Macqueen's part of
the book, whilst Burton seizes upon Speke's inaccuracies and vagueness
to discredit his conclusions, enabling him to reiterate that 'I cannot but
believe the Tanganyika to be the Western lake-reservoir of Father Nile'
and that the question of the real sources of the Nile is 'thrown further
from discovery than before' (p. 64).

Macqueen, a so-called armchair geographer born in 1778 and formerly
manager of a sugar plantation in the West Indies, begins his reviews by
writing against Speke's placing of information in the hands of the
Blackwood publishers before putting it in the public sphere, a proceeding he will not let us forget:

> *Blackwood* having spoken out as strongly as its author dictated, we beings
> of the lower sphere, considering that the interdict has been removed, may
> now reverently and humbly approach the subject proclaimed by the same
> authority to be of the highest importance, and equally the property of all
> kindreds and tongues, to examine calmly and minutely the narrative. (p.
> 69)

In most part his case relies upon a racist distaste for Speke's close
proximity to the Africans and for the suggestiveness of some of the
writing. Macqueen wishes to preserve the physical distance associated
with moral distance and general superiority. Allied to his outrage at
Speke's implicit flirtations with African women is his shock that some
of the people 'are represented to us as more polished than ourselves, and
as equal to our gay neighbours on the other side of the Channel' (p. 97).

Grant's modesty and the cooking pot

If we see in Speke's letters to his publisher and in his entry into the
literary marketplace at the expense of the Royal Geographical Society's
gentlemanly codes a pecuniary interest, Grant's narrative has the
appearance of a higher-class disdain of trade. Grant's first words are 'It is
not without considerable anxiety and reluctance that this volume is
submitted to the public',[39] and he represents himself as persuaded by
Speke that he should publish his experiences and observations of Africa.
Moorehead has called Grant 'the most modest and self-effacing man
who ever entered the turmoil of African exploration',[40] which is not
only wrong, but worryingly so. Grant writes in his Preface:

> The scenes and descriptions here recorded are from life – transcripts from
> my Journal made on the spot, without any reference to books, or any

attempt at embellishment. Some of the details may appear trifling – all of them are very imperfectly related; but they are at least *true*. (p. ix)

This is not modesty. It is the arrogant self-deprecation, the unctious false humility, of one who knows himself to be in a position of power. In the ignoring of other books anti-intellectualism consorts with a desire to assert the author's individuality through a blindness to the mediating layers of capitalist production. He refers to his 'friendly publishers' (p. x) as if there were no commercial transaction at all. Grant is informing us that he is a gentleman. He walks; he doesn't explore. The modest, self-effacing explorer even tells us that the title of his narrative came from a remark made to him by the Prime Minister, Palmerston, who said to him 'You have had a long walk, Captain Grant!' (p. x).

If Grant were comfortable and secure in his status then I do not think he would use Palmerston in this way or be so self-conscious about his self-consciousness. And if he were happy with the state of Britain I do not think he would make comparisons of the following kind: 'At Mineenga, we met several parties or gangs of slaves in chains, and my thoughts reverted to the happy village-life in our own country, a pleasing contrast to such painful and revolting scenes' (p. 72). Grant may not be seeing British village life accurately, and he does not seem to see city life here at all. Or, rather, he does not wish to see it. His writing is deceptive. He lulls the reader, by several remarks complimentary to Africans, into accepting him as a fair judge of the people he describes.

For Grant commodities provide an index to character. Morality and beauty may be identified in relation to goods, or judged according to one's attitude towards them. Mtésa is portrayed turning over the pages of books 'as a monkey would' (p. 224), an image which promotes every comprehending reader of Grant's story above the African king. More striking, because more unusual, is a scene in which Grant is introduced by two strangers to a Watusi woman, 'a beautiful ladylike creature' (p. 131), whose 'small breasts were those of a crouching Venus – a perfect beauty, although darker than a brunette!' (p. 132). In the following account exchange is disguised and eroticised:

> After the fair one had examined my skin and my clothes, I expressed great regret that I had no beads to present to her. 'They are not wanted,' she said: 'sit down, drink this buttermilk, and here is also some butter for you.' . . . I shook hands, patted her cheek, and took my leave, but some beads were sent her, and she paid me a visit, bringing butter and buttermilk, and asking for more presents, which she of course got, and I had the gratification to see her eyes sparkle at the sight of them. This was one of the few women I met during our whole journey that I admired. (p. 132)

The unnamed woman's goodness is proved by her gift without hope of reciprocity. Her goodness is then rewarded by the very objects whose previous absence proved her a generous person. Her delight at the subsequent presents brings her into the familiar pattern of exchange, bringing with her her good character. Her attractive generosity is of course suggestive of much else besides. There is in this romantic episode a construction of a feudal, pre-capitalist endorsement of capitalism, and it is thus significant that the man is succoured by the beautiful lady at a small settlement within a 'wild jungle' (p. 131).

Another instance of the inculcation of western values through one's relationship to commodities is furnished by the actions of his 'cookboy', M'Kate, who voluntarily undertook alone one day a 36-mile round trip to recover a cooking pot he had left behind and 'which was certainly not worth the journey. It only proves what men will do with kind treatment' (p. 360). It is absolutely crucial, of course, that the object is not in itself worth the labour expended on its retrieval, for what impresses Grant is that M'Kate has learned so thoroughly the importance of property that he will subordinate himself to it as a matter of principle, irrespective of its value. This gives a lesson about service which is applied to the working classes at home and, when this rule is under threat, to subject peoples abroad. M'Kate is bound to the cooking pot by cords of duty, if not love. So it is in this light that we should see Grant's attitude towards his narrative's dedication (of it and himself) to Speke, and his substitution of duty and affection for the material factors of its production. It is significant also that Grant includes an appendix listing the 'personal kit' he and Speke took with them (pp. 449–52), with comments on the reliability of various items. By such means he hopes to keep himself above them. This is Grant's modesty and self-effacement: he will not fetch the cooking pot.

Burton's baubles

One traveller who unashamedly drew attention to his own role was Burton, of whose prodigious output I shall, because of space and topic, consider only one or two narratives. His preface to *The Lake Regions of Central Africa*, which has been hailed as possibly 'one of the best explorer's journals ever written',[41] contains a bold announcement of his plans and method. The purpose of the expedition it records (which took place from 1856 to 1859) was to ascertain the limits of the 'Sea of Ujiji', and to determine the exportable produce of the interior and the ethnography of its tribes. The Foreign Office donated £1000 and Burton was given two years' leave of absence from regimental duty by the Court of Directors of the late East India Company.

In *The Lake Regions of Central Africa*,[42] Burton confidently asserts, like most of his contemporaries, that East and Central Africa lack historical interest and contain no useful works. What is especially interesting about Burton's stance though is his criticism of western features and codes, particularly where he perceives morality to be hindering truth, but, unlike proponents of the Noble Savage view, Burton does not adopt the refuge of the society of the savage. He remains, in many senses, outside both societies.

Burton deploys an articulated consciousness of language and codes in a way that, with his marked sense of self, plays around with the relationship between writer and reader. At times utilising a mocking tone, he foregrounds writerly and readerly expectations, sometimes to subvert them; at others to confirm them through a heightened awareness of them. That is to say, he occasionally purports to make visible or audible the structures or rules affecting the normal agreements between author and audience.

The freedom of movement within and between certain discourses highlights the writer's occupancy of a special place. This latter site may appear variously as one of transcendence or exile, but the overall scope of movement signifies privilege, as well, of course, as the donning of masks and disguises for which Burton would become so noted.

African people and their culture are frowned upon in both popular and scientific learned discourse which encapsulates the Africans even more completely than would otherwise have been the case. They are knowable both in popular and in academic parlance. Their knowability fixes them and conjoins the popular and educated discourses of Britain, so that British social differences are elided by their common knowledge of Africans. In this sense Burton, traditionally seen by critics and biographers as himself a marginal figure, actually becomes the Briton *par excellence*, flitting between two realms and bringing about an apparent reconciliation.

Objects and wealth are again a means of using the image of Africans to achieve this. As with other travellers I discuss in this chapter, Burton deploys attitudes to value as an indicator of physical and cultural maturity:

> The African preserves the instincts of infancy in the higher races. He astonished the enlightened De Gama some centuries ago by rejecting with disdain jewels, gold, and silver, whilst he caught greedily at beads and other baubles, as a child snatches at a new plaything. To the present day he is the same. There is something painfully ludicrous in the expression of countenance, the intense and all-absorbing admiration, and the greedy wistfulness with which he contemplates the rubbish. (I, 147–8)

Classic ethnographic techniques may be observed here: the generalised reference to the whole race by the singular noun; the idea of an eternal infancy; both these ideas in contrast to the differentiated European traveller from centuries ago, thus giving Europe a history denied to the unchanging Africans; the ignorance of commodity value in western economic systems used to signify a child's lack of knowledge of what is universally known to adult man; and the projection of this last ideological point on to individual Africans whose features and gestures are framed against it, so that these cannot but be seen as proof of their perpetual immaturity. Nor should we overlook the way in which all western children, and by implication, all western people, are made homogeneous. We are to assume that all western children are excusably ignorant of value and that all western adults are properly aware of it. To compare Africans' attitudes with those of a western child is not just to belittle Africans but to deny the existence of different stances within Britain. Complaints against grabbing were levelled against the working poor.

I have said throughout this chapter that travellers promote commerce and at the same time reveal unease about the signs and effects of the meeting of cultures; that this discomfort is often focused on the role of commodities as they are freed from the realm of one culture and enter another. There is no doubt that Burton shares the views of other of his countrymen in desiring the promotion of civilised commerce. Burton the anthropologist offers a secular condemnation of the results of the lack of commerce where missionaries would be concerned more with religious aspects. He writes:

> Nor can even lucre prevail against the ingrained indolence of the race – an indolence the more hopeless as it is the growth of the climate. In these temperate and abundant lands Nature has cursed mankind with the abundance of her gifts; his wants still await creation, and he is contented with such necessaries as roots and herbs, game, and a few handfuls of grain – consequently improvement has no hold upon him. (II, 328)

In saying that not even money can buy the East African out of indolence, Burton is suggesting that the Africans cannot be commoditised in European systems. On one level the gifts of nature condemn the Africans to a lack of labour and an absence of wants – a sure way of happily reconciling the west to the post-lapsarian state – and on another the people are unworthy and incapable of admission to the west's capitalist economy: commerce and capitalism may in time stop slavery (II, 366) but there is another connotation too. Racial characteristics are thought to have so deeply affected the Africans that even a money economy would do little to alleviate their basic condition. Thus

[97]

their character is witnessed in such commercial dealings as they do have:

> If they cannot obtain the very article of barter upon which they have set their mind, they will carry home things useless to them; any attempt at bargaining is settled by the seller turning his back, and they ask according to their wants and wishes, without regard to the value of goods. Grumbling and dissatisfied, they never do business without a grievance. (II, 329)

Quite how people whose wants have yet to be created can ask for things according to wants is not vouchsafed us, unless it be that, as children who are subject to 'sudden fits of fury' (II, 329), they act irrationally. It is apparent that the Africans are to be blamed for having no sense of value according to western notions of worth.

The 'Wajiji', lacking in the art of commerce, are deficient also in the niceties of polite society. Amongst them there 'appears to be little family affection' (II, 69). They are 'rude, insolent, and extortionate; they demand beads even for pointing out the road; they will deride and imitate a stranger's speech and manner before his face' (II, 68–9). Manners, the markers of class in Britain, acquire racial judgement here. Their asking for beads for showing the road would, one thinks, demonstrate quite an understanding of value and commerce, but Burton is railing against their commodification of information, which he believes the west should be free to appropriate. Macqueen credited Africans with common sense for knowing 'that as labour and property come more and more into demand they ought to obtain more for both',[43] but Macqueen is an iconoclastic figure.

It might be said too that the sort of mirroring about which so many travellers complain (seeing the Africans, like apes, as imitators) is in large part precisely the anxiety of objectification which I have suggested applies to commodities. It applies too to the self. Hence the complaints of rudeness and of staring. Burton is just one of many travellers who are disconcerted by being stared at. He categorises the types of stare to which he is subjected. Both the categorisation and the humour are ways of dealing with the deep discomfort at the shifting of the subject object relationship. Burton's categories include: 'the stare furtive', 'the stare open', 'the stare curious or intelligent', 'the stare stupid', 'the stare discreet or indiscreet', 'the stare flattering and the stare contemptuous', 'the stare greedy', 'the stare drunken', and 'the stare cannibal' (II, 128–9). More than some travellers Burton employs humour to turn this disquieting attention to his advantage by turning to his readership for a reconstitution of his subjectivity. His audience is reminded that he is explorer and ethnographer.

[98]

Cameron: the umbrella and the loin cloth

Verney Lovett Cameron, the first Briton to cross Africa from east to west, journeyed from Bagamoyo on the east coast to Benguella in Angola, a trip which took him two years and nine months. In his writings he clearly put himself in the service of capitalism, which he presented as the great civilising influence. Cameron's travels had a great influence on expansion into Central Africa and he was one of the first to suggest the probable course of the Congo River.

Born in 1844, the son of a clergyman, Cameron had joined the Royal Navy at thirteen and had spent eight months in the Red Sea during the Abyssinian campaign. In 1872 the Royal Geographical Society had belatedly accepted his offer to find Livingstone. He was accompanied by his friend W. E. Dillon, who was a naval surgeon, and by Lieutenant Cecil Murphy of the Royal Artillery. In 1873 news reached them of Livingstone's death. Murphy decided to accompany Livingstone's body to the coast while Cameron and Dillon would go to Ujiji and thence follow up his explorations. But on 18 November Dillon, ill from fever, committed suicide, leaving Cameron to go on alone. Cameron found ninety-six rivers flowing into the Tanganyika and the large river the Lukanga flowing out of it. He proved that the Lualaba was the headwater of the Congo, and 'by tracing the watersheds of the Nile, Zambezi and Congo rivers, he was able to define broadly the limits and areas of the principal hydrographic basins of Central Africa'.[44] He was given a Royal Geographical Society Gold Medal and an honorary doctorate from Oxford University. At the time of the expedition he held the rank of lieutenant. After it, he was promoted to commander.

Unlike Speke, Cameron seems to have been a reluctant author; at least at first. Apologising, as did many of the travellers, for the shortcomings of his narrative, he confessed: 'As a fact, I never contemplated writing a book of travel',[45] and his diary was put into narrative form by Sir Clements Markham for publication in the *Proceedings of the Royal Geographical Society* while he was still in Africa.[46] Cameron writes that it has been his object to make his book 'a guide by which my footsteps may be traced by those interested in the exploration of Africa, rather than a personal narrative of adventure and travel' (I, vii). Cameron's reduction of his individuality to his footsteps is a fascinating one. It places him in a subordinate position to his nation – emphasised by the dedication of the narrative to 'Her Majesty Queen Victoria by her humble and obedient servant the author' (I, v), which reads like State patronage through the monarch – and focuses attention on the country rather than the traveller, but they are after all *his* footsteps, and we can look only where he has trodden. What interests me about Cameron are the literary means by which his identity is constructed through the championing of capitalism and the representation of the Africans who stand on the other side of the relationship. His discomfort with his service bothered him for years afterwards. In the early 1890s, when contributing to a history of African exploration, he declared:

> To write about my own journey in a work like the present is obviously a somewhat difficult task; for the balance has to be held between what necessarily bulks large in one's own memory – viz., the personal part of the work, and what were the results obtained from a scientific and geographical point of view.[47]

The self is preserved by this false dichotomy which duplicitously objectifies the scientific basis of capitalist expansion. My reading of this is confirmed by the fact that in the same essay Cameron stands by his earlier conclusions and wishes that his calls for commercial activity in Africa had been taken up on a larger scale.[48]

In Cameron's eyes a vital factor in civilisation is an appreciation of the value of goods. A dramatic scene – which has its parallel in other narratives, including Stanley's – involves the rescue from fire of Cameron's books, journals and instruments by his servant Jumah and one or two others. Cameron reports: 'Whilst we were clearing out of the tent I asked Jumah if his kit was safe. He replied, 'Potelea mbali, ponya mabooku' (Let it be d—d, save the books)' (II, 113). One of Jumah's rewards for this selfless recognition of value, which is contrasted with Bombay's selfishness and with the ignorance of those blacks who have yet to learn the worth of European culture, is to have his portrait included in the text immediately after the account. Jumah's knowledge of the books' importance is transmitted in his language. The status of the books has crossed linguistic and cultural boundaries. Before this movement has been made Africans are ridiculed for their inappropriate handling of goods, of the function and value of which they may have no conception. On the case of one man who insisted on being given a pair of worthless goggles which the traveller's party pretended were of great value, Cameron muses:

> it is generally so with uncivilised men when something new catches their eye; they must have it, coûte qui coûte. Yet a few days later, just like children tired of a new toy, they are ready to throw or give it away. (I, 110)

The man's desire for the goggles is portrayed as representative of the primitive culture, whose members are attracted to objects by superficial looks instead of a real understanding of practical or aesthetic worth. They have not been educated into the proper creation or expression of wants and their cultural immaturity is communicated to us through the image of physical inexperience; they have not grown up because they do not appreciate value. Their quickness to tire of new things is a dangerous resistance to being defined by their relationship to particular goods, as was happening in Britain.

The ideology of Cameron's writing is insidious. It gulls the reader into readily granting it a liberal premise. Yet it relies upon a humour which dehumanises those who do not share the author's system or values. A further example is furnished by the misuse of another object:

I was greatly amused by one of the guides who displayed much pride at possessing an umbrella. He kept it open the whole day, continually spinning it round and round in a most ludicrous fashion; and when we came to some jungle he added to the absurdity of his appearance by taking off his only article of clothing – his loin cloth – and placing it on his head after having carefully folded it. The sight of a perfectly naked negro walking under an umbrella was too much for my gravity, and I fairly exploded with laughter. (I, 206–7)

Here the humour depends upon the juxtaposition of objects: the entry and inappropriate usage of one destabilises the other. One can see in this an implicit warning about the cultural confusion which can arise from an unthinking imposition or admission of European goods. The feeling of unease generated by Africans in European dress or with western goods was widespread and there were frequent attempts to laugh it off nervously.

Cameron's role in promoting commerce means that his identity is, more visibly than with many other travellers, defined in relation to goods. Indeed, it could be said that he draws it from them. They determine in some ways his mission, his self-perception, and his reception. He is visited by Kasongo, a chief, who:

made many enquiries as to my nationality and business, and I informed him that it was from my country that cloth and other articles used in trading in Africa were sent; and my object was to visit the people who purchased these things and to see their countries, so that I might be enabled to tell my Sultan what they wanted, and increase the trade for the benefit of both sides. (II, 23)

Not only Cameron but the nation is constructed in terms of its products, the importance of which must grow as the explorer aims to increase wants, which will be done by getting the Africans to think of themselves in relation to articles.

For the individual such a degree of identification with, or subordination to, commodities can mean in some situations a loss of selfhood as well as a bestowal of belonging. In *Across Africa* one can detect a tension between the two urges. Overwhelmingly, the conscious and tangible feeling is for a shelter under the umbrella of national and cultural affiliation, but there are several moments in the narratives that remind us of the character of the man whose footsteps we are tracing. As with Parkyns, a way of asserting one's personality is to portray the Africans and one's relations with them in a manner that cuts against the conventional stereotypes. In doing this, Cameron, in at least one episode, employs, like Speke, eroticism. The wives of Russuna (who is a chief and friend of slave-trader Tippu-Tib) are 'the handsomest women I had seen in Africa', and:

> On the second day all fear of me and bashfulness had vanished, and they came in a body to see me. I soon had them all sitting around me looking at pictures and other curiosities; and after a long time they began to wax so much more familiar that they turned up the legs and sleeves of my sleeping suit, which I always wore in camp, to discover whether it was my face alone that was white. (II, 16)

Cameron enjoys constructing his identity through the eyes of the exotic women, thereby making himself the object of voyeurism. For the heterosexual male reader this scene may work on two levels: the visual consumption of the image and the imagined occupancy of Cameron's position. The degree of sensuality and the lack of stated physical repulsion make Cameron's individuality come across clearly. But in the end closure must occur. After all, Cameron can neither go any further himself nor (in print at any rate) permit the women to do so:

> Indeed, they ultimately became so inquisitive that I began to fear they would undress me altogether; to avoid which I sent for some beads and cowries and gave them a scramble, and thus withdrew their attention from my personal peculiarities. (II, 16)

After the titillation normality is restored by the intervention of commodities. But the humour masks deep complication. We are meant to smile at the women's priorities in valuing the beads and cowries more than the human (in contrast to Speke's lack of care for beads) yet this is exactly the view to which Cameron would have us believe he subscribes: he is professedly in the service of commerce (though he would of course attach greater worth to goods according to the western reader's own scale). The passage is both a recognition of human value and a rejection of it. Nor should one miss the tone of 'personal peculiarities', for what is meant by this is his colour, which is an additional way of subordinating his personal identity to a larger collectivity.

Bound up with the need to create wants is the self-persuasion that the British would be acting in the Africans' interests:

> Many people may say that the rights of native chiefs to govern their countries must not be interfered with. I doubt whether there is a country

in Central Africa where the people would not soon welcome and rally round a settled form of government. The rule of the chiefs over their subjects is capricious and barbarous, and death or mutilation is ordered and carried out at the nod of a drunken despot. (II, 335)

The horrors of the slave trade provide a convincing reason to act, and a determination to do so can thus bring upon the actors a moral justification while enjoying economic rewards too:

> Africa is bleeding out her life-blood at every pore. A rich country, requiring labour only to render it one of the greatest producers in the world, is having its population – already far too scanty for its needs – daily depleted by the slave-trade and internecine war.
> ... And should England, with her mills working half-time and with distress in the manufacturing districts, neglect the opportunity of opening a market which would give employment to thousands of the working classes, it will ever remain an inexplicable enigma.
> Let us hope that the Anglo-Saxon race will allow no other nation to outstrip it in the efforts to rescue thousands, nay, millions of fellow-creatures from the misery and degradation which must otherwise infallibly fall to their lot. (I, 209–10)

It must be recorded that Cameron's objections to slavery are often made explicitly on commercial grounds:

> The loss of labour entailed by working gangs of slaves tied together is monstrous; for if one pot of water is wanted twenty people are obliged to fetch it from the stream, and for one bundle of grass to thatch a hut the whole string must be employed. On the road, too, if one of a gang requires to halt the whole must follow motions, and when one falls five or six are dragged down. (II, 147–8)

The tone of Cameron's narrative should not blind us to his call for the deployment of the technology and communication systems of the west in the furtherance of trade. There is a distinctly practical side to his book. He recommends the acquisition of a port, such as Mombasa, from the Sultan of Zanzibar and the construction of a light railway from there to Lake Tanganyika which would soon earn money because of the ivory trade to Zanzibar; he urges the placing of steamers on the Zambesi, Congo, and Kwanza and the establishing of depots; he calls for the utilisation of money, missionaries, and for those 'interested in scientific research [to] come forward and support the King of the Belgians in his noble scheme for united and systematic exploration' (II, 337). It is these profitable aspects of civilisation which Cameron is keen to pursue; as for the imposition of other manifestations of culture, he is more reluctant, reflecting, I think, the tension or ambivalence to which I have already referred. We must not, he says, attempt:

to force our European customs and manners upon a people who are at present unfitted for them. . . . The forcing system, so often essayed with so-called savages, merely puts on a veneer of spurious civilisation; in the majority of cases the subject having, in addition to the vices of his native state, acquired those belonging to the lowest dregs of civilisation. (II, 338)

Cameron wants to provoke more than a passive, vicarious response to his narrative, for it is 'not by talking and writing that Africa is to be regenerated, but by action' (II, 337). We should note his class prejudice against the 'lowest dregs', to whom the vices belong.

It is hard to ignore the extent of cultural force attached to depictions of goods and objects in *Across Africa*. Cameron asks:

Why are not steamers flying the British colours carrying the overglut of our manufactured goods to the naked African, and receiving from him in exchange those choicest gifts of nature by which he is surrounded, and of the value of which he is at present ignorant? (II, 334)

In an old ideological manoeuvre, the Africans are said not to have any real claim of ownership over their environment because the objects the Europeans cherish may not have needed cultivation or exist in such plenitude that they are 'gifts of nature', and the Africans, having no knowledge of how much the west covets them, are belittled for possessing no sense of their worth. So significant cultural and economic force applies to the description of the Africans and their environment. Nor should we forget the more direct and physical power that can be used when thought necessary. A reminder comes when, after the end of his journey, Cameron meets in Sierra Leone Captain Bradshaw of the 'Encounter', formerly 'my old captain in the *Star* during the Abyssinian campaign' (II, 279–80).

Nevertheless in 1937 Cameron's biographer praised his subject's modesty and his restraint, in both his travels and his record of them:

Few travellers or explorers have so deliberately eschewed all exaggeration in their narratives, or made so light of a really hazardous undertaking. He avoided all striving after effects or the semblance of sensationalism.[49]

Foran sees this as having ironically contributed to Cameron's fall from public consciousness, an assessment with which Hooker, writing more than three decades later, concurs: 'It is in some ways to his credit that he has not achieved more fame; at least his memory lacks notoriety'.[50] There are dangers in extrapolating too much from what is seen to be an admirable, gentlemanly reserve. Foran moves from hailing Cameron's 'cool courage, constant tact, resourcefulness, unswerving determination, innate modesty and utter truthfulness',[51] to claiming that: 'He was actuated by higher motives than personal renown. He served a cause, not empty notoriety. . . . Cameron inevitably subordinated self to actual scientific and geographical discoveries'.[52] This indeed evinces seduction by Cameron's narrative persona. The subordination of self to ventures other than scientific and geographical discovery is ignored; a strange omission since Foran does refer elsewhere in the book to his subject's involvement with the Central African and Zoutpansberg Company, his chairmanship of the London Committee of the Companhia da Zambesia, an Anglo-Portuguese concern for the exploitation of the Zambesi Valley; and his role in founding the Anglo-Belgian Katanga Company, of which he was a director.

The white man with the open hand

Evidence of the changing situation of the author and of a corresponding change in the nature of expeditions is seen in Stanley's dedication of *Through the Dark Continent* to the proprietors of the *Daily Telegraph* and the *New York Herald*, the backers of the expedition. In this narrative Stanley employs a number of different discourses as he moves from the position of marginality I described in my first chapter to that of popular hero. His manoeuvres manipulate images of Africa and Africans. As does Conrad in *Heart of Darkness*, Stanley questions certain stereotypes of Africans, only to be bound by and perpetuate others. He criticises, for example, those explorers who have derided the Wangwana, the Zanzibari porters. Departing from those such as Burton who have claimed that the blacks are devoid of love and affection, are the link between the simian and the European, and are perverse and disobedient, Stanley pronounces:

> I find them capable of great love and affection, and possessed of gratitude and other noble traits of human nature: I know too, that they can be made good, obedient servants, that many are clever, honest, industrious, docile, enterprising, brave and moral; that they are, in short, equal to any other race or colour on the face of the globe, in all the attributes of manhood. But to be able to perceive their worth, the traveller must bring an unprejudiced judgment, a clear, fresh, and patient observation, and must forget that lofty standard of excellence upon which he and his race pride themselves, before he can fairly appreciate the capabilities of the Zanzibar negro. The traveller should not forget the origin of his own race, the condition of the Briton before St. Augustine visited his country, but should rather recall to mind the first state of the 'wild Caledonian,' and the original circum-stances and surroundings of Primitive Man.[53]

Stanley may be thumbing his nose here at the vanities of the English ruling class, so we should not overlook the influence of personal feelings on racial representation. Neither should we be duped into accepting too anti-racist a reading of the latter reminiscence. It anticipates Marlow's 'And this also has been one of the dark places of the earth' in Conrad's *Heart of Darkness*,[54] and, like that reminder, depends upon the 'has been'.

Although Stanley declares his hope that he is 'free from prejudices of cast, colour, race, or nationality' (p. 31), he nevertheless describes the Zanzibaris as having just entered the Iron Age and now subject to the attention of nations which have improved above them over four thousand years. The consequence of this disparity of progress is a self-issued invitation for western intervention, under the guise of a higher authority:

> They possess beyond doubt all the vices of a people still fixed deeply in barbarism, but they understand to the full what and how low such a state is; it is, therefore, a duty imposed upon us by the religion we profess, and by the sacred command of the Son of God, to help them out of the deplorable state they are now in. (p. 31)

Thus, despite (or rather through) Stanley's emphasis on the virtues of the blacks, the impetus is towards a movement of cultural imperialism. Whatever the humanitarian postures assumed by Stanley in *Through the Dark Continent*, the fact is that the text reinforces western superiority at the same time that it presents Stanley's own qualities. He pays tribute to the Wangwana for their contribution to the explorations of Livingstone, Speke, Grant, and Burton, but then concludes: 'It will depend altogether upon the leader of a body of such men whether their worst or best qualities shall prevail' (p. 33).

Stanley's comments on power and virtues draw attention to individual qualities, doing away with notions of class as a determinant of virtue. This can be seen when Stanley relates an incident involving Uledi, 'the coxswain of the *Lady Alice*, the best soldier, sailor, and artisan, and the most faithful servant, of the Expedition' (pp. 566–7). Uledi has saved thirteen people from drowning and, although reported as not handsome (his face is marked by remnants of smallpox), Stanley says of him: 'handsome is that handsome does' (p. 567). He goes on:

> I never sought in him for the fine sentiments which elevate men into heroes; but the rude man, with his untutored, half-savage nature, was always at my service. He was a devotee to his duty, and as such he was ennobled; he was affectionately obedient, as such he was beloved; he had risked his life many times for creatures who would never have risked their own for his, as such he was honoured. Yet – this ennobled, beloved and honoured servant – ah! I regret to speak of him in such terms – *robbed me.* (p. 567)

Stanley's judgement of the man by his deeds is in accord with the increasing attention, from the mid nineteenth century onward, to achievements rather than birth as the measure of the individual. One finds the same discourse employed in discussions of the working classes in England, though of course this had to compete with the still insistent pronouncements on birth as a determinant of value. The tensions and contradictions produced by this clash of discourses are often and interestingly apparent in the writings of Stanley, whose own position, as I have indicated in my first chapter, was notoriously complex. Here, however, Stanley does not disguise the idea of the nobility of servitude for it attests to his own power. If the qualities traditionally found in a particular class can now be found in any, then the stable indicator of character is to be proved by one's attitude towards property. Uledi had made a favourable impression by being a good servant and by saving the lives of other servants of Stanley; his fall from grace occurs with his theft of beads, articles which have helped Stanley confirm his own rectitude:

> Beads abstracted! at such a time, when every bead is of more value to me than its bulk in gold or gems, when the lives of so many people depend upon the strictest economy, when I have punished myself by the most rigid abstinence from meat in order to feed the people! (p. 567)

There is more. Stanley's affinity with nature justifies the future exploitation of its resources. Capitalism is naturalised. At a time of expanding technology and urbanisation Stanley enters primitive nature so that his recommendations receive cultural and natural sanction. Here is surveillance with a purpose:

> It is a spot from which, undisturbed, the eye may rove over one of the strangest yet fairest portions of Africa – hundreds of square miles of beautiful lake scenes . . . hundreds of square miles of pastoral upland dotted thickly with villages and groves of banana. From my lofty eyrie I can see herds upon herds of cattle, and many minute specks, white and black, which can be nothing but flocks of sheep and goats. I can also see pale blue columns of ascending smoke from the fires, and upright thin figures moving about. Secure on my lofty throne, I can view their move- ments, and laugh at the ferocity of the savage hearts which beat in those thin dark figures; for I am a part of Nature now, and for the present as invulnerable as itself. As little do they know that human eyes survey their forms from the summit of this lake-girt isle as that the eyes of the Supreme in heaven are upon them. How long, I wonder, shall the people of these lands remain thus ignorant of Him who created the gorgeous sunlit world they look upon each day from their lofty upland! How long shall their untamed ferocity be a barrier to the Gospel, and how long shall they remain unvisited by the Teacher!
> What a land they possess! and what an inland sea! How steamers afloat

on the lake might cause Uriri to shake hands with Uzongora, and Uganda with Usukuma, make the wild Wavuma friends with the Wazinza, and unite the Wakerewé with the Wagana! A great trading port might then spring up on the Shimeeyu, whence the coffee of Uzongora, the ivory, sheep, and goats of Ugeyeya, Usoga, Uvuma, and Uganda, the cattle of Uwya, Karagwé, Usagara, Ihangiro, and Usukuma, the myrrh, cassia, and furs and hides of Uganda and Uddu, the rice of Ukerewé, and the grain of Uzinza, might be exchanged for the fabrics brought from the coast; all the land be redeemed from wildness, the industry and energy of the natives stimulated, the havoc of the slave-trade stopped, and all the countries round about permeated with the nobler ethics of a higher humanity. But at present the hands of the people are lifted – murder in their hearts – one against the other . . .

Oh for the hour when a band of philanthropic capitalists shall vow to rescue these beautiful lands, and supply the means to enable the Gospel messengers to come and quench the murderous hate with which man beholds man in the beautiful lands around Lake Victoria! (p. 143)

Stanley is secure in his elevated position. He likens himself to God in his unobserved watchfulness.[55] He enters into nature, the better then to subdue and tame it. Under the cloak of bringing knowledge of God he serves capitalism. Technology is a force for pacification, which will lead to trade and thus to civilisation. Capitalism saves the beauty of nature from the cultural ugliness of the Africans whose destruction of one another is matched by their unproductive use of the environment.

A little later in the text we have explicit confirmation of the calming powers of trade:

The wide wild land which, by means of the greatest river of Africa, we have pierced, is now about to be presented in a milder aspect than that which has filled the preceding pages with records of desperate conflicts and furious onslaughts of savage men. The people no longer resist our advance. Trade has tamed their natural ferocity, until they no longer resent our approach with the fury of beasts of prey. (p. 539)

This general principle is given more specific illustration when Stanley entertains the 'great magic doctor of Vinyata' with 'exceedingly sweet coffee and some of Huntley and Palmer's best and sweetest biscuits' (p. 79) and presents him with empty sardine boxes, soup pots and empty jam tins. The result is the making of blood-brotherhood. The next day the 'magic doctor' is given another present as well as some beads for his wife and his children. But armed conflict with the 'savages' of Wanyatara soon breaks out. The lesson learned from this is of the uselessness of forebearance with people too savage to understand its principles. The mark of the 'savages' is that they do not reciprocate material gifts with the gratitude that will produce benefits for the west.

[108]

Stanley justifies an armed response thus:

> Our position, as strangers in a hostile country, is such that we cannot exist as a corporate expedition, unless we resist with all our might and skill, in order to terminate hostilities and secure access to the western country. (p. 82)

Conversely, those who show a positive response to western generosity are granted the status of civilised beings, with objects and commodities again the means by which the favourable position is recognised. It is in this context that one of Stanley's African nicknames is especially significant. Much has been made by biographers of Stanley as 'Bula Matari', or stone-breaker, a name given to him while he was blasting a path through rock for a railway, and which his widow had carved on his tombstone. Stanley and his biographers deliberately promoted the sobriquet as a symbol of his hard qualities (and I have more to say about this in my final chapter). Less often quoted is the title Stanley mentions in *Through the Dark Continent*. At the 'hospitable village of Mombiti' in the 'rich country of Usukuma' (p. 86) Stanley is able to purchase plenty of food for his porters, to whom:

> Long arrears of rewards were due ... for the many signal examples of worth they had shown; and here I earned anew the flattering appellation bestowed upon me three years previously in Africa – 'The white man with the open hand' – 'Huyu Msungu n'u fungua mikono.' (p. 86)

There is a powerful elision here. The image of the white man with the open hand obscures the fact that Stanley is purchasing the provisions, which are actually supplied by the Africans. The white man receives credit for facilitating the exchange which produces a beneficial movement of goods. He is seen as holding the power to sustain and reward his employees. The cultural act of purchase has precedence over – because it controls – the natural means of sustenance. It is therefore possession of the means of exchange that endows Stanley with the superior position. The point is reinforced in the Nyamwezis' song of triumph:

> Kaduma's land is just below;
> He is rich in cattle, sheep, and goats.
> The Msungu [white man] is rich in cloth and beads;
> His hand is open, and his heart is free.
>
> To-morrow the Msungu must make us strong
> With meat and beer, wine and grain.
> We shall dance and play the livelong day,
> And eat and drink, and sing and play. (p. 92)

In so far as he can fortify the people and be their apparent provider

Stanley plays a mercantile God, keeping all the time a beady eye on their land.

Notes

1 Homi K. Bhabha, 'The other question: difference, discrimination and the discourse of colonialism', in *Literature, Politics and Theory: Papers from the Essex Conference*, eds. Francis Barker, Peter Hulme, Margaret Iversen, Diana Loxley (London: Methuen, 1986), p. 170.
2 James Allen Casada, 'The imperialism of exploration: British explorers and East Africa, 1856–1890' (Ph.D. thesis, Vanderbilt University, 1972), p. 18.
3 Casada, 'The imperialism of exploration', pp. 26–8.
4 Casada, 'The imperialism of exploration', p. 100.
5 James A. Casada, 'The motivational underpinnings of the British exploration of East Africa', *Proceedings of the South Carolina Historical Association* (1973), pp. 64; 62.
6 Arjun Appadurai, 'Introduction: Commodities and the Politics of Value', in *The Social Life of Things: Commodities in Cultural Perspective*, ed. Arjun Appadurai (Cambridge: Cambridge University Press, 1986), p. 13.
7 The original version of this chapter in my Ph.D. thesis also looked at women writers to the same region. To allow for a more focused discussion of their narratives, however, I have revised and extended that section, which is to be found as 'Buttons and souls: some thoughts on nineteenth-century women travellers to Africa', paper given at the 1992 Sociology of Literature Symposium, 'Writing Travels', University of Essex.
8 Casada, 'The imperialism of exploration', p. 96.
9 Henry M. Stanley, *Through the Dark Continent: or The Sources of the Nile around the Great Lakes of Equatorial Africa and down the Livingstone River to the Atlantic Ocean*, new edition (London: Sampson Low, Marston, Searle, & Rivington, Limited, [1878] 1890), p. 12.
10 Dorothy Hammond and Alta Jablow, *The Africa that Never Was: Four Centuries of British Writing about Africa* (New York: Twayne Publishers, 1970), p. 49.
11 James Allen Casada, 'The imperialism of exploration'. Casada also notes (p. 55) that another explorer, Verney Lovett Cameron, whom I discuss below, also served in Napier's expedition.
12 J. A. Grant to Blackwoods 1863. Blackwood Papers 4181, National Library of Scotland, Edinburgh. (Hereafter NLS.)
13 J. A. Grant to Blackwoods, 18 September, 1863. Blackwood Papers 4181, NLS.
14 Blackwood to Grant, 23 September 1863. MS 30360, NLS.
15 John Blackwood to Speke, 3 November 1859. MS 30359, NLS.
16 John Blackwood to Speke, 3 November 1859, NLS.
17 [J. H. Tremenheere], review of Speke's *Journal of the Discovery of the Source of the Nile*, *Quarterly Review* 115, 229 (1864), 105.
18 Speke to Blackwood, 3 March 1860. Blackwood Papers 4143, NLS.
19 Speke to Blackwood, 28 March 1860. Blackwood Papers 4154, NLS.
20 Blackwood to Speke, 3 November 1859. MS 30359, NLS.
21 Blackwood to Speke, 23 June 1863. MS 30360, NLS.
22 Speke to Blackwood, 21 July 1860. Blackwood Papers 4143, NLS.
23 Alexander Maitland, *Speke* (Newton Abbot: Victorian (& Modern History) Book Club, 1973), p. 13.
24 Speke and Grant had met in India in 1847. See James Augustus Grant, *A Walk across Africa or Domestic Scenes from my Nile Journal* (Edinburgh: William Blackwood & Sons, 1864), p. ix.
25 Maitland, *Speke*, p. 107.
26 R. C. Bridges, 'Sir John Speke and the Royal Geographical Society', *Uganda Journal* 26 (1962), 39.
27 R. C. Bridges, 'Europeans and East Africans in the age of exploration', in *The Exploration of Africa in the Eighteenth and Nineteenth Centuries* (University of

Edinburgh Seminar Proceedings, 1971), p. 126. This essay may also be found in the *Geographical Journal* 139, 2 (June, 1973), 220–32.

28 Bridges, 'Europeans and East Africans', p. 130.

29 Roy C. Bridges, 'John Hanning Speke: negotiating a way to the Nile', in *Africa and Its Explorers: Motives, Methods, and Impact,* ed. Robert I. Rotberg (Cambridge, Mass.: Harvard University Press, 1970), p. 135.

30 John Hanning Speke, *Journal of the Discovery of the Source of the Nile* (London: J. M. Dent & Co., [1863] 1906), p. 1. Further references to this work will be given parenthetically in the text.

31 In 1860, in what is now Uganda, on the northern and western borders of Lake Victoria, there were three separate kingdoms: Bunyoro in the north, Buganda in the centre, and Karagué to the south, on the western shore of the lake. Kamrasi, who ruled Bunyoro, was in enmity with Buganda. Rumanika, ruler of Karagué, was the weakest of the three rulers, and so tried to remain on good terms with the other two. Mtésa, at this time, had only recently gained power. This information is to be found in, among other places, Alan Moorehead, *The White Nile* (Harmondsworth: Penguin Books, 1963), pp. 55–8.

32 George W. Stocking, Jr, *Victorian Anthropology* (New York: Free Press, 1987), p. 35.

33 Stocking, *Victorian Anthropology*, p. 36.

34 Stanley later writes that this gun 'had an honoured place, and Rumanika loves to look at it, for it recalls to his memory the figures of his genial white friends Speke and Grant'. Henry M. Stanley, *Through the Dark Continent*, p. 302. Thus do gifts become enshrined in ideology and text.

35 Roy Bridges, 'The historical role of British explorers in East Africa', *Terræ Incognitæ* 14 (1982), 10.

36 Bridges, 'Historical role', 11.

37 John Hanning Speke, *What Led to the Discovery of the Source of the Nile* (Edinburgh: William Blackwood & Sons, 1864), pp. 344–5.

38 Richard F. Burton, 'The Nile Basin' and 'Captain Speke's Discovery of the Source of the Nile' by James Macqueen. New introduction by Robert O. Collins (London: Tinsley Brothers, 1864; London: Frank Cass & Co., 1967), p. 28. Further references to this book will be given parenthetically in the text.

39 Grant, *A Walk across Africa*, p. vii. Further references will be given parenthetically in the text.

40 Moorehead, *The White Nile*, p. 62.

41 Moorehead, *The White Nile*, p. 33.

42 Richard F. Burton, *The Lake Regions of Central Africa: A Picture of Exploration,* 2 vols (London: Longman, Green, Longman, & Roberts, 1860). References to this work will be given parenthetically in the text.

43 In Burton, *The Nile Basin*, p. 92.

44 W. Robert Foran, *African Odyssey: The Life of Verney Lovett Cameron* (London: Hutchinson & Co., 1937), p. 13.

45 Verney Lovett Cameron, *Across Africa*, 2 vols (London: Daldy, Isbister & Co., 1877), I, vii. Further references will be given parenthetically in the text.

46 James R. Hooker, 'Verney Lovett Cameron: a sailor in Central Africa', in *Africa and Its Explorers: Motives, Methods, and Impact,* ed. Robert I. Rotberg (Cambridge, Mass.: Harvard University Press, 1970), p. 264.

47 Robert Brown, *The Story of Africa and Its Explorers*, 4 vols (London: Cassell, 1892–95), II, 266.

48 Brown, *Story of Africa*, II, 267.

49 W. Robert Foran, *African Odyssey*, p. 13.

50 Hooker, 'Verney Lovett Cameron', p. 294.

51 Foran, *African Odyssey*, p. 12.

52 Foran, *African Odyssey*, p. 42.

53 Stanley, *Through the Dark Continent*, pp. 30–1. Further references will be given parenthetically in the text.

54 Joseph Conrad, *Heart of Darkness*, ed. Robert Kimbrough, 3rd ed. (W. W. Norton &

Company, 1988), p. 9.

55 Mary Louise Pratt has termed similar passages, in which an aesthetic and an ideological view of the landscape coincide, the 'monarch-of-all-I-survey' trope. Mary Louise Pratt, *Imperial Eyes: Travel Writing and Transculturation* (London: Routledge, 1992), pp. 204–6. If this kind of labelling is useful, and I'm not sure that it is, then I think the misleading suggestion of regality might better be replaced with something that more accurately reflects the surveyor's hopes for commercial activity; perhaps 'entrepreneur-in-all-I-espy'.

CHAPTER FOUR

'Gone the cry of "Forward, forward"': crisis and narrative

Get Emin

The subject of this chapter[1] is the expedition led by Stanley in the late 1880s to relieve Emin Pasha. The venture embodied and developed many of the features I have discussed so far. I shall use this chapter and the next one to examine some of these concerns in their late-nineteenth-century context with the aim of showing how social and commercial developments affected and were reflected in British attitudes to Africa. In particular, I shall discuss the literary and cultural expressions of the controversy to which the expedition gave rise; crises of class and authority; and the commodification of narrative and explorer. Much of my argument will focus on the production and reception of the expedition and of its accounts. The present chapter deals broadly with production; the next with consumption.

The perception by the protagonists and their audience of their social rank and status provided a focus, at this late stage of the nineteenth century, for the changes in authority that had been occurring in previous years. I use 'authority' in the sense both of command and certainty of vision and expression. The circumstances of the expedition, and the condition of the society from which it was mounted, meant that the established locus of authority was facing considerable challenge. It is to be expected that any threat manifested in behaviour would find its reflection in the various forms of narrative about the expedition. By this I mean not just in the fact of contradictory versions of events, but in the motive to publish and in the form and structure of the texts. Furthermore, the highly visible role of commodities in the expedition, the treatment of narrative as commodity,[2] and the reception of the returning travellers themselves (principally Stanley, but some of his companions also) are not simply a sign of socio-economic developments towards the end of the century, but mark too a shift in the site of power.

The expedition,[3] which lasted from early 1887 to late 1889, had as its apparent motive the rescue of Emin Pasha, by birth Edouard Schnitzer, a German, who in 1878 had been appointed Governor of Equatoria, the southernmost province of Sudan, by General Gordon. The latter's defeat and death at the hands of the Mahdist forces in 1885 and the ensuing evacuation of the Sudan helped establish the conditions for the projection of an image of Emin as an isolated man abandoned by the Egyptian government whose relief would atone for the humiliating failure of the British to save Gordon. In fact, Emin's long-term wish was for Equatoria to be made a British protectorate. His immediate desire was for arms, ammunition and supplies to sustain him at Wadelai. In autumn 1886 public interest in Emin's situation was fostered by his contacts in England, Charles Allen of the Anti-Slavery Society and R. W. Felkin, an Edinburgh doctor. More than £20,000 was raised in support of the expedition, around half of this sum coming from the Egyptian government, and much of the remainder from the Emin Pasha Relief Expedition Committee. The driving force behind the Committee was William Mackinnon,[4] the founder of the British India Steam Navigation Company, and later President of the Imperial British East African Company, the interests and membership of which coincided largely with those of the Relief Committee. Both projects developed together during late 1886. Underlying the proclaimed reasons for the expedition was the hope of commercial gain from the large stock of ivory, estimated at £60,000 worth, believed to be held by Emin, and from a series of land treaties which were to be made with African chiefs.[5] Stanley was also acting for Leopold of Belgium and exploring the possibilities of annexing Equatoria to the Congo.

An attraction of Equatoria was that its position as:

> an abandoned province of Egypt, astride the Nile, made it the most annexable part of the interior. Emin's isolation, his immediate need, and his offer of his province presented an opportunity to enlist Emin himself and to annex his province. Through Emin in Equatoria the whole Lake region might be controlled and its resources exploited and Buganda, at least for the present, could be ignored.[6]

The British government insisted it remain a 'private' expedition because of anxiety over potential embarrassment should there be a repeat of the Gordon fiasco or in case the rescuers should themselves need rescuing. It was agreed that Mackinnon and his colleagues would raise £10,000, which would be matched by the Egyptian government. In Smith's words, 'The British Government saw in Mackinnon's proposal a way to assuage public opinion and to get themselves off the hook'.[7]

Leopold wanted to open up the north-eastern corner of the Congo State and obtain a frontier on the Nile which meant the expense of taking the Congo route, while Mackinnon desired Stanley to take the east coast route so that he could make treaties in the interim. As Mackinnon wanted Stanley to lead the expedition he deferred to Leopold, in whose service Stanley had been until 1885, laying the foundations for the administration of the Congo Free State. Leopold offered the use of the Congo Free State's steamers on the upper river. In short:

> The only way in which the various interests of Leopold, Mackinnon and Stanley could be reconciled was for the expedition to take the Congo route to get to Emin Pasha, but to come back via East Africa. And that was Stanley's plan. In effect, he would serve Leopold on the way out and Mackinnon on the way back.[8]

The route decided upon was to follow the Congo up to its confluence with the Aruwimi River, then up the Aruwimi to the Yambuya, where the rear column was left, through the Ituri forest to Lake Albert, and up the lake towards Emin's headquarters at Wadelai. Stanley argued that to pass through Buganda would be to endanger British and French missionaries there.

Leopold had proposed that Emin should remain Governor of Equatoria under the Congo State. Smith has pointed out that the proposals of Mackinnon and Leopold in 1886 were not incompatible, as behind them was the hope that if Emin were to be assisted to stay in Equatoria Wadelai could become a terminus for the routes into the interior which Stanley's expedition was expected to open up from the Congo State on the one hand and from the East African coast on the other. By 1888, however, Stanley favoured Mackinnon's scheme, still resentful of Leopold's manipulation of him in 1884–86, and, after the terrible nine months' struggle through the Congo to Lake Albert, considered the annexation of Equatoria to the Congo State as not viable.[9]

There followed a mixture of farce and tragedy. Once met with, Emin vacillated embarrassingly and had to be persuaded to accept the relief offered him. This is not altogether surprising since it was unclear whether the aim of the expedition had originally been to aid Emin to stay in or withdraw from Equatoria. Smith, peering through the 'deliberate omissions, the veiled references, and the false trails which Stanley made about this expedition when it was all over – and most obviously and assiduously in his book about it',[10] believes that the Egyptian government favoured Emin's withdrawal and that it was an open question whether Emin (apart from his garrisons) should remain or leave. Smith states that Stanley's 1888 offer to Emin to be placed in the employ of Mackinnon's company was made on Stanley's initiative but within the context of a framework already agreed by Mackinnon and Stanley.

According to Smith, Emin had a low opinion of the Egyptian presence in Equatoria and thought that the area would best be developed when a European occupation began. After the British occupation of Egypt, the rise of the Mahdi, and the fall of Khartoum, Emin believed that it would be only a matter of time before the British occupied Sudan and Equatoria.[11] But Emin and Stanley developed an intense dislike of each other. Smarting at what he saw as the determination to have him abandon his province, Emin wrote of Stanley in his diary:

> For him, everything depends on whether he is able to take me along, for only then, when people could actually see me would his expedition be regarded as totally successful. To Stanley's chagrin, when he went on the expedition to find Livingstone, he experienced what it meant to leave behind in Africa the main object of his expedition. . . . So, here again, we have only egoism under the guise of philanthropy.[12]

There is something in this, especially as regards the Livingstone quest, but Emin too was being egotistical in ignoring the importance Stanley attached to the commercial and political aims of the expedition. Nevertheless, the suggestion that physical evidence of his success was desired by Stanley is indicative of the contemporary cultural crisis over authentication, which I shall be looking at in some detail below. The image of the expedition took a tumble when, at a banquet in the port of Bagamoyo to celebrate the accomplishment of the mission, the short-sighted Pasha fell twenty feet from a window, nearly killing himself. Out of 570 refugees from the Equatorial Province who had been in the expedition's care at Kavalli, only 260 reached Bagamoyo. Two of Stanley's ten white companions died on the expedition. One of them, Major Barttelot, who was much criticised for the severity of his conduct and for his racism, was shot dead by an African porter. The other, Jameson, died, apparently from fever, after rumours that he had solicited, witnessed and sketched, and possibly even participated in, the cannibalistic killing of a young girl. Half of the seven hundred Africans failed, because of desertion or death, to return from the journey. There was strong condemnation of Stanley's judgement and conduct, especially concerning the rear column, which was stranded for several months with no word of Stanley and little aid from Tippu-Tib, the ivory and slave dealer whose support Stanley had enlisted for them.[13] Forming an advance column, Stanley had marched off through the Ituri forest to find Emin, leaving a rear guard camp at Yambuya, under the charge of Barttelot. Barttelot was supposed to wait for the delivery of goods and porters before following Stanley. However, the promised porters failed to arrive. Food grew scarce. A number of men starved. Discipline was brutally enforced as morale declined, and Barttelot's behaviour seems to have become more and more irrational as the months went by without either word from Stanley or the arrival of the porters from Tippu-Tib. After a year of waiting, Barttelot was finally able to move out of the camp in June 1888, but by then one of his fellow officers, John Rose Troup, had been invalided home, and another, Ward, had been sent by Barttelot to the coast to send for instructions from the Relief Committee. In July Barttelot was killed and a few weeks later Jameson died. When, after fourteen months away, Stanley's advance column finally returned and met up with the remnants of the rear column at Banalya he found Bonny, the sergeant, in charge and only around sixty per cent remaining of the 260 or so men who had originally been left. Many of the survivors were pitifully diseased. The horrors and cruelties of these events led to recriminations among several of the officers and their various supporters, with the nature of Stanley's instructions to Barttelot and the latter's interpretation of them forming the focus of many of the charges and counter-charges.

Although the expedition helped map areas of Central Africa and 'discovered' the snow-capped Ruwenzori mountains, and the suffering in the Great Central African forest furnished for Stanley's audience a powerful image of redemption and of the capacity to survive, if not subdue, a hostile environment, the bitter disputes which arose between Stanley and the families of Jameson and Barttelot also saw the controversy widen into a fierce debate (conducted in a variety of print and other cultural forms) about Britain's aims and methods in Africa, with the military and commercial character of the expedition being particularly condemned. Iain Smith ends his book by lending support to the suggestion that the expedition 'occupies an important place in the decline and disappearance of the romantic Victorian conception of exploring expeditions led by determined Europeans through "unknown" continents'.[14] The present chapter and the following one will aim to make good the neglect of textual and cultural factors in examining why this should be so.[15]

The white men who served with Stanley on the expedition were: James Sligo Jameson, grandson of John Jameson of Irish whiskey fame, a naturalist and traveller, a 'fine example of ... the gentleman-amateur';[16] James Mounteney-Jephson, a gentleman whose aunt, the Countess de Noailles, paid £1,000 for him to join the expedition (Jameson had paid a similar sum on his own account); Dr Thomas Heazle Parke, who was recruited in Egypt; Major Edmund Musgrave Barttelot of the 7th Fusiliers; Herbert Ward, a young adventurer who had also been three years in the Congo and who joined the expedition in Africa, having met with it while he was on his way home; Captain Robert Nelson, who had been in Methuen's Horse and had fought in the

Zulu wars; Lieutenant William Grant Stairs, a Canadian serving in the Royal Engineers; John Rose Troup, who had worked for three years with the Congo Free State where he had been a police supervisor; Sergeant William Bonny, who had been in the Army Medical Department; and Stanley's servant William Hoffmann, a cockney of German origin.

The importance of social class was (as ever) inescapable. Bonny had to travel from England in second-class accommodation whilst the others enjoyed a first-class passage. Hoffmann was referred to only twice in Stanley's *In Darkest Africa*, and then not by name, and was mentioned even less often than Bonny in the other officers' narratives.[17] At the other end of the scale, Stanley disclosed that some members of the Relief Committee thought Jephson too 'high class'.[18]

Fear of attacks on authority was palpable, and one of the most obvious symptoms of this was the contracts Stanley had his officers sign, by which they undertook not to publish anything about the expedition until six months after the appearance of the official record. Roger Jones rightly points out that on Stanley's earlier explorations of Africa none of his European companions had survived. His position as sole witness of the scenes he described would now therefore be undermined.[19] Indeed, Dr R. Leslie, the first man to be offered the post of medical officer, had declined to join after objecting to the clause and being refused permission to insert the proviso 'except in the case of my reputation being attacked'.[20] But Jones overlooks the commercial advantages of the contractual silence, which would set up, albeit temporarily, a monopoly of perspective and of narrative as commodity. Truth is to be seen to reside in the official version because it is the only one available, and since this is so it will attract due profits. Thus the material aspects of this exclusiveness are concealed behind the notion of the official record as the authoritative one. This has been recognised in the most recent biography of Stanley by Frank McLynn, who quotes one contemporary commentator as saying:

> Before all things, Stanley was the pressman with an eye to business. We have, up till now, been anxious to demonstrate him no Yankee, but despite himself, a Welshman. I think, at present, we shall all be content to let America claim him.[21]

The crisis of authority

The controversy over the treatment and behaviour of the rear column led to direct challenges of authority in the form of accounts highly critical of Stanley. It is not my purpose here to retell the story of events at Yambuya, as this has been done by many commentators and biographers already; but I want to look at how the erosion of confidence in social command was accompanied by a diminution of faith in the word of the explorer. The threats to social authority made a heavy backdrop to the expedition. The extension of the franchise under the 1884 Reform Act gave, as Weetens notes:

> dramatic political form to the wider cultural and social democratisation which confronted the professional classes with a deeply disturbing problem of social identity, as the boundaries between the lower bourgeoisie and their inferiors became increasingly blurred.[22]

There had been riots in Trafalgar Square in 1886 and large demonstrations of the unemployed in London in 1887, culminating in 'police brutality during the freedom of speech march on "Bloody Sunday", 13 November'.[23] I see this social crisis as wholly bound up with the more general questioning of purpose and language characteristic of turn-of-the-century thought and art. The mood of the time I am looking at is reflected in Tennyson's 'Locksley Hall Sixty Years After', which was published in 1886 but written in 1885, at a time of 'general public nervousness about the fall of Khartoum, renewed socialist agitation and the prospect of Home Rule for Ireland'.[24] Tennyson's poem communicates the worries over pressures for democracy and the strains of imperialism, and asks 'When was age so cramm'd with menace? madness? written, spoken lies?' Social confusion is reflected in linguistic corruption:

> Envy wears the mask of Love, and, laughing sober fact to scorn,
> Cries to Weakest as to Strongest, 'Ye are equals, equal-born.'
> Equal-born? O yes, if yonder hill be level with the flat.
> Charm us, Orator, till the Lion look no larger than the Cat,
> Till the Cat thro' that mirage of overheated language loom
> Larger than the Lion, – Demos end in working its own doom.[25]

However, while some critics have examined some literature with these concerns in mind, I have found no such criticism whatever of explorers and their narratives in this light. Terry Eagleton has remarked on how, by the time of *Heart of Darkness*, 'The confident mid-Victorian pact between producer and consumer has partly collapsed – a collapse reflected in the increasingly problematic status of the writer's productive means, language itself'.[26] But if this is true of Conrad, it is even more true of Stanley, a fact which, so far as I am aware, has been completely neglected in discussions of the Emin Pasha Relief Expedition and of its narratives.

A letter written by Barttelot to his fiancée Mabel Godman in the early stages of the expedition contains the sort of response to Stanley's writing typical of those who were not already opposed to the explorer and to his journalistic style. Barttelot, who informed Godman that he was reading all Stanley's books and finding them 'very interesting', pronounced that they 'are written exactly as he talks himself, straightforward and without much varnish'.[27] Such a declaration reveals an astonishingly naive and inept judgement of literature and character, but, more importantly, attests to a perceived correspondence between the text and the man who wrote it, between the product and the producer. One of the results of the expedition is that such identifications were contested, and the ensuing struggle was often played out around conceptions of heroism.

A surface sign of the social tensions I have mentioned was the claim that certain narratives were unreliable, but beneath this charge there was, I believe, a deep and growing anxiety about the possibilities of veracity and accuracy in language and therefore in writing too. As Jan Gordon has put it:

> fin de siècle art is highly repetitive to the extent that it offers us all surface. This is an art that has self-consciously turned back upon itself, confronted the aesthetics of fatigue and the ontology of boredom. Language, like the Lady of Shalott's tapestry, can no longer appropriate the world. It refers merely to other metaphoric representations; the departure from the archetypal romantic journey is identical to a crisis of language. Structurally the result is a sort of Chinese-box diagram: words and spaces lead us into a confrontation with other words and spaces, never with an identifiable 'world'. . . . The artist, instead of being at the centre of some structural island of art, metaphorically moves to the periphery; this enables him to be everywhere at once, to be both detached and involved, to combine autobiography and art within the frames of a divided existence.[28]

As Barttelot's initial reaction to Stanley's writings indicates, there had been a widespread acceptance – whether genuine or assumed – that the explorers' achievements and personality were embodied within their narratives; that the texts themselves took on the qualities of their authors. Presumably Barttelot aspired to this, and it is a view which underlies Edwin Arnold's praise of Stanley's earlier *Through the Dark Continent*: 'the work itself is an Odyssey of travel, admirable, gallant, unique with a style *sui generis*, like the swing of a traveller's stride'.[29] The narratives, as artefacts, bear the impress of their producers. It is not just that they record the incidents and observations for which their authors have become known, but that they are taken to objectify the human qualities of the hero. In 1904 Marston wrote of Stanley (whom he published):

> His works, in their succession, were received with enthusiasm by the press of almost every political creed or literary pretension: no more

emphatic testimony could be borne to the real greatness of his character. His greatest monument is to be found not only in the books he has written, but on the face of the map of Africa, not long since so largely blank but now covered by the lines of his travel.[30]

Troup and damages

The self-generative properties of the narratives of the expedition demonstrate that the motivation for the production of texts had undergone a change and one which entailed an awkward introspection. The ensuing scrutiny put a tremendous strain upon the identification of product with producer; upon the acceptance of their mutually authenticating structures. In the preface to his book *With Stanley's Rear Column*, John Rose Troup explained that when Stanley gave inaccurate accounts of what had occurred to the rear guard at Yambuya, 'I felt that to defend the honour of myself and my comrades became my duty, especially when our action was condemned in a letter of Mr. Stanley's published April 1889'.[31] The published word came to the defence of a class virtue. Troup was ready to ignore the period of contractual silence because, in his view, Stanley had reneged on his side of the contract as 'he never supplied me with the tent, bed, Winchester rifle, canteen, and a double share of European provisions' (p. vii).

Troup wrote in his defence to the newspapers and, just before the planned publication of his book, Stanley obtained an interim injunction believing, said Troup, that the provisions could have been obtained simply by asking for them. To emphasise that repeated requests had been fruitless, Troup took out a counter-claim for damages. A settlement was reached by which Stanley was to pay costs and Troup to be allowed to publish his book on or after 15 October 1890, before which date none of the other officers should publish their accounts of the expedition.

Such circumstances influenced the structure of the texts. Since the whole expedition was embroiled in controversy, the multiple perspectives acquire a different and more intrusive look than had been the case earlier in the century. They also enable the subject to assume a more conscious position. Troup, whose self-defence depended largely on the assertion that he and the other officers were subordinate to Barttelot and that therefore any blame should be laid at the feet of the Major and of Stanley, includes a stinging attack on Barttelot's racism:

It did not take me long to discover that he had an intense hatred of anything in the shape of a black man, for he made no disguise of this, but frequently mentioned the fact. His hatred was so marked that I was seized with great misgivings concerning his future dealings with them, more

[121]

particularly when he would have to handle Tippu-Tib's men. (p. 145)

Beyond the fact of Troup's motives for revealing his revulsion at Barttelot's attitude, it must be said that Troup, like others who denounced the dead man's race hatred, was confident of securing the sympathies of his audience, or at least of sharing in them. There are two points to be made here. One is that, for a variety of reasons, European behaviour towards and images of blacks were either shifting or being more openly discussed; the second is that Africans were still used within a western-controlled discourse for whites to construct or under-score their own identity.

None the less, the travellers' re-entry into their society has to be negotiated and in the aftermath of the expedition one witnesses the process of that negotiation in textual and cultural terms. A reminder of this comes towards the end of Troup's book with the inclusion of the correspondence between himself and Stanley, with the latter eventually responding to Troup's letter rebuffing Stanley's version of events by telling him his letter is too intemperate and that: 'if you can condense your narrative to two sheets, and not make the mistake of thinking that you defend yourself by attacking Barttelot I may possibly find room in the book, but I really am doubtful' (p. 290). After further exchanges and a meeting the legal agreement referred to in the preface was reached. But the self-reflexive nature of Troup's book underlines the procedures of negotiation and coercion involved in the construction and reception of the narratives. The close of Troup's last letter dramatises the threat to authority. Troup is aggrieved that Stanley has asked him for docu-mentary evidence, which he does not possess, to support statements he has made on oath, while Stanley, charges Troup, is 'totally destitute himself' of documentary evidence to back up his accusations, so that 'Many of your questions contradict each other and some statements you make are contradicted by yourself' (p. 305).

Barttelot: the true English nature

Stanley's perceived contradictions provided a major impulse to the publication of Barttelot's diary and letters, edited by his brother Walter George Barttelot, who in his introductory chapter told his readers that:

> Not a line of this book would ever have been written, not a word of its contents would have been published, if justice, even partially, had been done, or any kindness shown by the leader of the Expedition for the relief of Emin Pasha to the officers left at Yambuya with his impedimenta, his stores, and his sick.
> The story of Major Barttelot's life represents to us a brave English officer

and gentleman, who loved his profession, gloried in the work it gave him to do, and highly prized the only reward he coveted, and sometimes gained, namely, the appreciation and thanks of those under whom he served. He is only an example of the true English nature, and there could be no need to place his actions before the public but for the manner in which his name has been treated by Mr. Stanley since his life was taken by Sanga, a Manyuema porter of Tippu-Tib's, Governor of the Falls Station.[32]

There is a good deal more here than a row between the Barttelots and Stanley. The proud but mournful parading of the late Major's English qualities lines up an opposition to the sense of the newly visible commercialism of the period, reflected in the leadership and sponsorship of the expedition. Barttelot, we are told, sought only the abstract profit of service acknowledged, not the vulgar materialism of money-grabbers. His brother's compulsion to save his 'name' extends to a defence of a class that feels itself in danger because the myths it has constructed and fostered have been openly questioned. The edition of Barttelot's writings is of interest in this context in that its announcement of its origins – Walter Barttelot speaks of his sense of duty in countering the misleading statements made by Stanley and in defending his brother's memory – gives an impression of the discourse of this class being forced into the open by the crass methods of its crudely self-motivated opponents. 'All England', wrote Walter Barttelot, 'was proud of the thought of this gallant Expedition, of the singleness of its aim, and of the integrity and purity of motive displayed by the committee in organizing so chivalrous an enterprise' (p. 6). Words like 'gallant', 'integrity', 'purity', and 'chivalrous' betray such a degree of naivety that they rather suggest the Barttelots had fallen victim to the ideological codes of their own class's construction, while the claim to speak for 'All England' is, as always, a sure indication that those who profess to do so in fact do not. In Barttelot we witness the desperate appeal to the public with whom the officer and gentleman class has suddenly discovered it is out of step. Walter Barttelot writes how:

> I bitterly regret the necessity, which has been forced upon me by Mr. Stanley, to undeceive the public, and to remove the mask which has so well concealed the true features of the Expedition for the relief of Emin Pasha, of which they had formed so lofty an ideal. (p. 6)

It may be true that there was widespread ignorance of the 'real' motives of the expedition, but it was Barttelot's class that most needed undeceiving since it was the one that had been most responsible for nurturing the illusions that had encouraged the venture in the first place. The rude and belated discovery that pecuniary and commercial considerations had been stronger than the trumpet-blasts of national

[123]

honour and chivalry stimulated a frantic appeal to the 'English people, with whom the love of fair play forms a court of honour whose judgment is unimpeachable, and whose justice is world-famed' (p. 10). It was a plea which, like the very publication of the book, looked like a frantic attempt to establish one's credentials, if not an alliance, with a greater public. Even here, however, the address seems to go no further than the middle class. There is little sense of Walter Barttelot appealing directly to the working class as part of the 'English people'. Cutting across this effort is the inbred belief in social superiority, heralded in the opening to the first chapter:

> Edmund Musgrave Barttelot, the second son of Sir Walter B. Barttelot, Bart, C.B., M.P., of Stopham, Sussex, and Harriet, daughter of Sir Christopher Musgrave, Bart., of Edenhall, Cumberland, was born on March 28, 1859, at Hilliers, near Petworth, Sussex. (p. 13)

We are then informed that he attended Rugby and Sandhurst and had served in India, Egypt, Afghanistan, and Cyprus. (I am not claiming that this kind of parading of one's background is new, but that it now acquires a new desperation.)

The form and content of the Barttelot book reflect the tensions which I am discussing. Craving indulgence, Walter Barttelot asks the reader:

> kindly to remember that it is not my aim to write only what will please or interest, but to do a duty to the dead by writing what I have been able to gather of the truth. If the facts recorded in the diary are at times somewhat startling from the manner or brevity of their narration, or from their nature, it will be recollected they were not written down for publication, but for reference for personal use only, and that it was not the intention of my family to publish a word of this pathetic story. (p. 9)

It is far from being a simple matter of straight diary entries however. The text intersperses such entries with letters and editorial commentary, the latter operating both to supply ideological as well as personal justification and to solicit sympathy. At times the editor moves into the present tense, a device which, in offering the illusion of immediacy, aims to place the reader in the officers' situation so that the audience's journey is not just a vicariously physical one but an emotional one too, with emotion working as the route by which empathy is sought:

> The knowledge of their position has not yet fully dawned on the officers of the rear column. ... They are full of foreboding and doubt. ... The monotony of their weekly life is only interrupted by horrible scenes of savage warfare between the cruel natives and their still more cruel and cunning enemies, the Arabs. (p. 174)

Of course the fact that the editor felt it necessary to grope for the reader's sympathy in such a crude way is evidence that the expedition had questioned the consensus between traveller and audience that existed in earlier works. The multivocality of the expedition caused, on most sides, a more deliberate manipulation than had been seen previously. The reception of the officers formed the arena in which various views of Africa and of Britain were played out against one another. The number of narrative breaks to accommodate different types of document and editorial interpolation was a concomitant of this phenomenon but also a reflection of more general doubts in society about authority. The readers may well, and did, derive from episodes meanings different from those intended by the editor.

Barttelot, after writing of 'Aden boys' as the 'scum of the earth' (p. 35), records how he caught one of them trying to cut a hole in one of the water mussocks: 'I pulled him away, when he hit me with his weighted stick. I shot him dead' (p. 36). Obviously sensing that some explanation might be advisable, the killer's brother adds parenthetically: 'Major Barttelot often told me of this adventure; the man hit him twice, and broke the trigger-guard off his pistol and a small bone of the hand' (p. 36). The very presence of the intervention shows that support cannot be taken for granted, and indeed the generally hostile reaction to Barttelot's racial brutality demonstrates that the British readers experienced something of the officer's discomfort when he 'felt like a brute flogging the men to get them on' (p. 79), and when he found he could compare the work of urging them on to 'nothing else but slave-driving' (p. 86), but the readers could achieve the distance that Barttelot could not. The latter, as far as was possible, grew inured to his surroundings, ordering severe punishments, including the execution of the Sudanese Burguri for 'deserting' with a rifle; and overseeing the kidnapping of local women to be ransomed for food. In the main, Barttelot's audience rejected such violence by assuming with some relief the mantle of judge offered to it, or by choosing one of the alternative voices in preference, leaving the officer's brother to insist: 'It was that discipline – so irksome, so miserable, so cruel – that alone saved the camp and the stores' (p. 264). In this respect it could be argued that a result of the oppositions brought out by the debate over responsibility for the rear guard was the general acceptance of commercial enterprise over notions of personal and national honour. (This is borne out by the continued commercial activity in East Africa and the Congo; Cameron's role in the Anglo-Belgian Katanga Company has been mentioned in a previous chapter, and Stairs worked for a rival company after the Emin Pasha expedition.) I don't mean to suggest here that contemporaries saw commercial activity as incompatible with personal and national honour, since indeed the linkage of commerce with Christianity and civilisation is well known; but it is the case nevertheless that those who used the language of chivalry did often try to avoid sullying the concept with material considerations. Given this construction of chivalry and the particular versions of it which underlined some of the discussions of the Emin Pasha Relief Expedition it was inevitable that many of the defenders of Barttelot and Jameson presented their case as one of quietly heroic sacrifice as opposed to personal greed and selfish gain. In turn, it may well be postulated that another outcome was an admission of a materialistic side to heroism. In this light, Walter Barttelot's persistent digs at the Imperial British East Africa Company and at the hidden agenda of the Relief Committee have an air of futility, and his defence of his brother makes both Barttelots and their type seem ignorant and outmoded, clinging to a false ideal:

> He may have had suspicions, but his honourable nature would not allow him to draw the only conclusion, that these two men [Stanley and Tippu-Tib] were playing a deep game, whose secret he must not share, and that he was being blinded by both mutually for some purpose other than the noble object of the Expedition. (p. 325)

In Barttelot's writing, as in the other narratives, Stanley – and by extension the forces he represented – was subject to a strongly critical inspection, the effect of which was to reinforce graphically the growing sense of discord. Damaging passages included the allegation that on one occasion Stanley told the Zanzibaris they were not to obey Stairs and Jephson and should tie them to trees if they tried to order them, and that he challenged Jephson to a fight; and the constant refrain that Stanley disliked Barttelot and was in league with the Arabs against him.

But it is Barttelot and his kin who appear most isolated in their attitudes to race and class. The distance provided by command had become too dangerous:

> I shall be glad to leave because I am surrounded by hatred and treachery. Living among Arabs is not a bed of roses. . . . Bonny is a mixture of conceit, bravery and ignorance; he is most useful with the natives and Arabs; of a slow temperament, he is just suited to them. . . . His continual cry is that he is every bit as good as we are, and must be treated the same. (p. 291)

Barttelot's status makes the air around him too rarefied. In a letter he complains 'it is a disgusting life – nothing to read, no news, nothing to do' (p. 209), and 'It is no good my writing a long letter to you, for I cannot, simply. There is nothing to tell' (p. 210). In life, text, and symbol the traveller's presence in Africa had come to a halt which forced intro-spection and displacement. All three levels are apparent when Walter

Barttelot, writing that kudos is incomprehensible to Stanley, boasted:

> With Major Barttelot it was otherwise; honour to him was more than life,
> and he could say in Shakespeare's words:
>   'Mine honour is my life: both grow in one.
>   Take honour from me, and my life is done.' (p. 324)

The observance of an ideological construct which now seemed to bring no material gain meant that the authority to be vested in its upholding could be fulfilled only in death. In many ways Barttelot's book has the air of being culturally as well as individually posthumous. There was certainly no glory in the Major's death, shot by an African, allegedly Sanga, whose wife he had reprimanded – Bonny and others said he had beaten her – for singing and chanting at night. The identification of Sanga as the killer seems all too summary: Jameson had decided before the court was convened that Sanga was guilty and that the punishment would be death. Barttelot had lost sleep for a second night because of the noise of the Africans' singing and dancing, and it was claimed that a shot had been fired at him earlier, but his death was due, at best, to his racism and cultural intolerance. Several commentators hinted heavily that he had become mentally unstable, which not only let Barttelot's class off the hook but pinned the blame on Africa for being such an unsettling continent.

Jameson and the good name

The editor's note – in this case by the traveller's widow – to Jameson's *Story of the Rear Column* contains, as with the Barttelot book, a statement that the letters and diaries were not intended for publication but that the accusations against the officers of the rear guard make it 'desirable that they should be published in what is practically their original form, with only such alterations as their private nature required'.[33] The inscription to the preface, which latter was written by Jameson's brother Andrew, shows a similar concern too with the defence of one's name, but this time gives it dramatic expression in the form of a quotation from *Othello* which ends:

> But he, that filches from me my good name,
> Robs me of that which not enriches him,
> And makes me poor indeed. (III.iii.163–5; quoted on p. xv)

The concentration on abstract qualities which are judged superior to a crude and grasping materialism is of course an attempt to establish class interests in the form of supposed eternal values which, though challenged, will prevail. Jameson's was a 'chivalrous life' (p. xxxi) we are told, and 'One turns, as in search of a great relief, from this [Stanley's] story of self-seeking, unfairness, and deception to the record of a noble and unselfish life (p. xxiii)'.

Ethel Jameson's determination to preserve as far as possible the form and content of the diary may have been driven by sentimental reasons but it helped transmit the sense of authenticity. Furthermore, she was not free of pecuniary considerations. Offering the diary to the firm of Blackwoods for publication, she wrote: 'I must candidly add that just at present I am not in a position to wish to *lose* by the publication',[34] yet, in a letter finally rejecting the possibility of an arrangement with the company, she seemed to draw the line at conceding, under commercial pressures, structural changes to the narrative, expressing her sorrow that Blackwood seemed to think the diary too repetitive, and insisting that, in obedience to what she was sure would be her husband's wishes, she should keep the original entries much as they were.[35]

Ethel Jameson was moved by the same notions of duty that motivated Walter Barttelot and it is too easy to overlook the influence of such codes and their social origins on the appearance and form of narratives. It is worth recording then that, by and large, Mrs Jameson stood by her intentions. A scrutiny of Jameson's original diaries reveals few notable omissions or alterations.[36] The slight changes serve chiefly to modify the tone of phrases or passages. Thus the published reflection 'It looks strange on Mr. Stanley's part to send him [Barttelot] by himself with the very worst and most rebellious lot in camp' (p. 19) begins in manuscript 'It looks very like a piece of spite on Mr. Stanley's part'.[37]

Authenticity is enhanced by the inclusion in the first chapter of letters from Jameson to his wife because, we are told, he kept no regular diary until the start up the Congo on 19 March 1887. A personal and trusted voice is thus presented. It works to introduce a sense of movement which makes all the more striking the later immobility of the rear guard and frames the later static self. It also solicits a trust for its realism in its details and in its rhythm: 'Nothing but beating niggers with a stick, and lifting their loads on to their heads, and day after day the same disgusting work. It must take a great deal of glory to make up for it all' (p. 30). The realism undercuts mythic expectations of glory. Jameson's diary is one of disillusionment in process. As the lack of incident grows more apparent so the role of writing grows more important in structuring experience and preserving the sense of self through reflection, with the obvious paradox however that in this situation writing, like people, turns in on itself: 'Not a single thing of interest to make a note of. The monotony of this camp life, without one atom of sport or excitement of any kind to relieve it, is becoming perfectly sickening' (p. 168). Entries on flogging as punishment for various offences, including sleeping on sentry duty, theft, and desertion, achieve greater prominence as time goes by. As with Barttelot, one senses that Jameson alternated between inurement and self-loathing. On 7 November 1887, for example, he records that Msa had been given one hundred and fifty lashes, and Bartholomew seventy-five and that he had wanted them instead to be sentenced to hard labour in chains 'as I am sick of flogging' (p. 162), but the overall impression is that such punishments contributed an ever-increasing significance in the routine as a way of imposing oneself on the environment; that, together with writing, they bear one's imprint and offer more authority. Only a month after the last-quoted extract, Jameson describes the flogging of a Sudanese sentry for stealing meat:

> The Soudanese are wonderfully plucky in bearing pain, for although he received 150 strokes, which cut him up very much, he never uttered a sound. . . . Had my first good night's sleep for some time, and woke up quite a new man. (p. 165)

What readers see in Jameson's diary however is the self-destructive end of this stamping of self on one's surroundings; self-destructive because we read Jameson being drawn in by the kinds of images or stereotypes that had been spread by earlier travellers – and were fed by himself – and which formed part of the west's racial ideology. Jameson's relation of anecdotes of cannibalism and his evident interest in the subject grew more frequent[38] until the self-degradation he felt as a result of his part in the midst of the sick, the dying, and the punished merged with the degradation of those around him. Warning signs are probably there when Jameson sketched, skinned, and preserved the head of a black which had been brought to him by an Arab raiding party and which he later sent home. A month later (8 March 1888), Jameson was writing 'Never has life seemed so weary and utterly useless, and yet one can do nothing to alter it' (p. 220). There is, too, a typically late-nineteenth-century decadent attraction in destruction. What would at one time have been a clean picturesque description has now acquired sinister overtones:

> The Arabs had burnt the whole of the village, which now made a beautiful picture, with the smoke and flames rising up from under the dark foliage of the forest, and reflected as in a mirror across the sunlit waters. (p. 204)

Powerlessness, given confirmation too in the fact of the posthumous publication of the writings which had not been intended for publication, could be said to be at the root of the infamous 'cannibalistic' killing. Jameson seems to fall victim to the racial ideology to which he subscribes. His diary account, which his relatives believed exonerated him, and most other observers felt implicated him, has him doubting a tale of African cannibalism told to him by Tippu-Tib, at which stage he was asked for some cloth if he wanted proof. Thinking it to be a jest, Jameson furnished six handkerchiefs, and:

> a man appeared, leading a young girl of about ten years old by the hand, and I then witnessed the most horribly sickening sight I am ever likely to see in my life. He plunged a knife quickly into her breast twice, and she fell on her face, turning over on her side. Three men ran forward, and began to cut up the body of the girl; finally her head was cut off, and not a particle remained, each man taking his piece away down to the river to wash it. . . . Until the last moment, I could not believe they were in earnest. I have heard many stories of this kind since I have been in this country, but never could believe them, and I never would have been such a beast as to witness this, but I could not bring myself to believe that it was anything save a ruse to get money out of me, until the last moment.
> . . . When I went home I tried to make some small sketches of the scene while still fresh in my memory, not that it is ever likely to fade from it. No one here seemed to be in the least bit astonished at it. (p. 291)

Jameson has succumbed to his own culture's racial ideology, his part in this incident costing him his reputation. Especially ghastly to the society which had sent him and which read of the episode – so ghastly that this aspect of it was repressed by the nation's subconscious – was the handing over of the handkerchiefs, for it made the event one of trade. The westerner had exchanged for his cloths a murder which acted out his racial fears and sadistic fantasies.

On this expedition, which, particularly for Jameson and Barttelot, was in their enforced inactivity and confinement so much an anti-expedition, the crisis for Britons was that the essential thing to be written about was the fight to maintain a sense of self, articulating the very phenomenon travel writing had earlier sought to hide through its structural concealment. Structurally and formally now there was greater dispersal and combination.

Jameson, at first admiring Stanley for his ability to beat the men to get them marching, later criticises his leader for humiliating and disturbing him in front of the porters whom Stanley risks dividing by administering punishments. And, telling the same story of Stanley's row with Stairs and Jephson that was related by Barttelot, Jameson concludes: 'I had no idea until today what an extremely dangerous man Stanley was. Could there be anything more inciting to mutiny than what he had told the Zanzibaris?' (p. 48). Exposure of arguments and the revelation of behaviour and procedures which may earlier have been left unreported because of either a monopoly over the story or a consensus between the white protagonists extends the range of responses and uncovers the gaps between expectation and experience, between event and language. Quarrels over dates and information and testimony beg questions about the compact between reader and writer in the genre generally, not just in the immediate case. The expedition has itself become the subject. Extracts from Jameson's diary on African birds (he several times mentions his frustration at having so few opportunities for collecting) are gathered in an appendix on Natural History, separated out from the personal narrative.

Jephson's class

A more concentrated and apparently more integral narrative is James Mounteney-Jephson's *Emin Pasha and the Rebellion at the Equator*.[39] In it Jephson announces his intention not to write on matters and experiences already covered more ably by Stanley and to focus on his part with the advance guard, thereby offering a distinctive tale which will not encroach on Stanley's story and will avoid the main area of controversy. That it is altogether a more comfortable and comforting narrative than the ones I have already discussed is suggested by the inclusion of an introductory letter from Stanley, who remarks:

> Of course you might have begun your narrative at the beginning of our expedition, but I think you have done wisely in not treading out again already threshed corn. You have commenced your story where a great gap occurred in my own narrative, a gap which you alone could fill up. You have told your story with so much modesty, and such absolute truthfulness and loyalty to myself, that I cannot but feel pleased and grateful to you. (p. vi)

The conjunction of truthfulness and loyalty is to be noted and indeed there is little in the book to worry either Stanley or British readers. There is a snide suggestion that Emin Pasha's indecision and pro-crastination, allegedly exacerbated, if not caused, by long residence in the Orient, were to blame for the deaths of Barttelot and Jameson; there is criticism of the Pasha's followers for expecting to be able to have porters transport all their goods and encumbrances on the march to the coast; there is the rebellion which leads to Jephson's imprisonment; and condemnation of the corrupt Egyptian rule. Stanley is praised for being a leader who is prepared to listen patiently to his subordinate officers, but who 'never hesitated, whose word was law, and whose every order was implicitly obeyed . . . [which] was like a tonic coming after the disorder and vacillating policy [of Emin Pasha]' (p. 445). Recognition of authority is accompanied by a smoothly structured text. In his prefatory letter Stanley observes that for Jephson to 'convert [your] rough notes into an intelligent and consecutive narrative required much thought and much labour' (p. v). A physical and intellectual ordering of experience and vision comparable to the activity of exploration itself is implied here, and it gives a reassuring picture to the audience. There are familiar racist gibes: the 'childlike simplicity' (p. 8) of blacks, their absence of malice when they know their floggings are deserved and so on. Stanley's swipe at Barttelot's self-destructive love of kudos is included, but is more than outweighed by the listing of three factors which preserved the officers through the oppressive forest, starvation, the unknown, and illness on the march to the coast:

> First, the love and interest we all had for our work. Second, the implicit trust and confidence we have ever had in our leader. And third, and I think, not least, the strong friendship . . . between Stairs, Nelson, Parke, and myself. (p. 459)

These are virtues which transcend materialism and are contrasted with the selfishness of Emin's party – 'What are your cooking-pots, and angareps, your boxes, chairs, and tables, compared with your life and liberty?' (p. 237), Jephson asks one of them.

Jephson interestingly combines the positive aspects of the Noble Savage view with the hard-edged, self-serving sense of purpose which, as I have shown, dominated later in the century. He gives his opinion that:

> The negro has traits in his character quite apart, and often finer in their way than those of Europeans; it is better to educate and foster those traits, and leave him a negro still with all his own peculiar individuality, but educated and enlightened. Impose and train him, but never try to Europeanize him, – the trial has always proved a failure. (p. 300)

There is a dextrous harmonising of the older, romantic conception with the more obvious materialistic impetus of the newer age. Jephson's narrative, free from damaging incriminations, is a distraction from the British soul-searching and locates authority in 'Trade, [which] it seems to me, will be one of the best and strongest civilizing influences in Africa, for it must develop the resources of the country' (p. 301). And so he appeals: 'Let us raise a new Government [there], firmly built upon the foundation of humanity, justice, and fair trade' (p. 460).

Commercial considerations are bracketed more closely with narrative in Stanley's prefatory letter, which deplores the absence of an international copyright law to protect writers like Jephson and Stanley himself from:

> the cloud of advertising impostors who I doubt not, will buzz around your book as they have buzzed around mine on both sides of the Atlantic with unauthorized imitations, and long extracts with which they had no right to meddle. (p. ix)

Stanley had taken out American citizenship in May 1885 to protect his book royalties when he had learned from his American publisher Harper that a Philadelphia rival was planning a pirated edition of his book on *The Congo and the Founding of its Free State*.[40] (He renounced his American nationality and became a naturalised British citizen in 1892, persuaded by his wife.) There are heavy hints in his letter that he has assisted Jephson in order to protect the latter's rights.

Jephson's thoughts are amplified in his diaries, which were published in 1969.[41] The violence and cruelty are here made more explicit, and include the hanging of 'deserters', the killing of allegedly troublesome Africans and the firing of their villages. He records the display of corpses (in one case of a head on a pole) and acts of mutilation by the expedition to serve as a warning to other Africans. These scenes are intermixed with graphic accounts of Arab conduct and of similar behaviour by the Pasha's people, the latter inspiring feelings of self-remorse in Jephson. Jephson's catalogue of violence and degradation and of disease and starvation is depressing and disturbing, though to do more than simply mention its existence would be beyond the scope of the present chapter. More relevant are the difficulties involving class, race, trade, and temperament that are described. All amount to a struggle for leadership. Scornful of what he sees as the 'stupidity & ignorance' of John Walker, an engineer who spent some time with the expedition, Jephson determines:

> never to work again with one of these middle men who are neither one thing nor the other but either work with people of one's own class or else with the very lower classes with whom one can get on perfectly. (p. 82)

The problem, evidently, is not Walker but the class shifts of which he stands a symbol, just as Bonny's position regarding the officers of the expedition is used emphatically to uphold by contrast their own status. But it is often a violent juxtaposition, which cannot help recreating the loss of control. Jephson describes a shouting match between Nelson and Bonny which turned into a fight, and writes of the discreditable example set by such a display, but the occasion affords an opportunity for a sustained attack on Bonny and his kind:

> Bonny is a most exasperating, low sort of fellow, he is just a sergeant with all the feelings, ideas, & loafing propensities of a typical 'Tommy Atkins' added to this he has an overweening conceit which is quite wonderful seeing that he has absolutely nothing to be conceited about; he has done nothing for the Expedition & is despised by the men. We have treated him much as an equal, being all Europeans together in Africa, & he has come to think that he actually is our equal in every way & so has become spoilt, he is a man none of us have ever liked or trusted, for he is simply dishonest. (p. 364)

[133]

'Typical' British attributes covered by the sobriquet 'Tommy Atkins' are here derided because of a class-based view. Jephson oozes impatience with the inferior who is temporarily granted a show of equality and is ungracious enough to think it genuine. Of course Jephson is worried that the authority of his class is being eroded, otherwise (and the same applies to Barttelot) there would be no need for such an insistent put-down of the alleged inferior. Ambiguity about leadership extends, as we have seen, to Stanley himself. Jephson conveys the sense of ambivalence in a different and striking way which marries to untroublesome virtues the factors he feels cannot be dismissed. The passage starts with Jephson approving the aptness of a description by Murabo, a chief, of Stanley as half a white man and half an Arab. Jephson muses:

> That describes Stanley very well. All the falseness & double dealing, the indifference to breaking his word, the meanness, brutality & greediness, are the Arab side. The wonderful powers of resource, the indomitable energy & strength of mind, the dogged determination to carry through to a successful issue all that he takes in hand, his cleverness in mapping, conversation etc, all belong to the European side. He has two distinct [characters] [sic], one cannot be too much admired & praised the other is contemptible in the extreme. (p. 248)

Delineating Stanley's personality like this, employing racial stereo-types in a racist act of supposed cultural psychology, illustrates the urge to typology struggling against the increasing difficulties of separating out characteristics in a period which sees the complication of ideological constructs. One feels the tension throughout Jephson's narrative. Severe criticism of Stanley is sometimes offset against positive words on Emin and sometimes vice versa. One may expect inconsistencies in a diary covering so many months but it is, I think, a sign of the cultural confusion I have been examining. On the whole the issue is decided in Stanley's favour because he possesses the authority Emin is seen to lack.

In respect of the social and literary contexts of the Emin Pasha Relief Expedition, there is a passage of great interest in Jephson's diary which epitomises the confusion and conflicts, in action, perception, and discourse:

> Stanley always accuses me of being a pessimist & a traveller of the Burtonian school who can see but little to admire either in the country or in the character of the natives, he is quite wrong; I simply see things as they are & speak of them as they are, he writes flowery descriptions of King's palaces, court pages etc, of colonels, generals & regiments, of pomp & show, & gives people at home a most false idea. . . . I think people like Stanley who write in that absurdly exaggerated style do a great deal of harm in Africa, people who do not know their style come out expecting to

find all these things & go away disappointed. All this talk of Kings & emperors & princes of the royal blood, with their residences, courts & palaces sounds all very fine in books of travel, but it is nothing but bosh & it conveys a very false idea to the people for whose instruction the book is published. (p. 390)

Perceptual and stylistic differences in this case have their origins in class (gentlemanly reserve against historical romance and popular journalism) and in the chronological shifts that make the emergent trends of greater realism an increasingly dominant mode; Stanley's would soon be seen as a residual form. Anti-climactic experiences of the kind evoked by Jephson fit into the general pattern of the character and reception of the expedition. It is a more pervasive, less personal attack than the one launched by Burton and Macqueen on Speke's exaggerated language. Jephson's self-professed down-to-earth approach is seen too in his advocacy of miscegenation to produce a mixed race of European Africans to populate and civilise Central Africa, a proposal which is hushed in the published narrative. His hard-edged prose, mostly free from Stanley's romance and exaggeration, uncovers practicalities of economic influence. At one point, explaining how the party has stolen cattle from the Africans, who can redeem their property by transporting loads for the expedition, he suggests this as an arrangement more favourable to the blacks than any they would get from traditional enemies because 'until now they have never been payed for labour & did not know it had any market value' (p. 340). The Africans are used as commodities in other ways too, with Jephson writing that Stanley would capture them and hold them in chains for a few days until he got from them the information he wished and would then release them.

The doctor

Like Jephson's *Emin Pasha*, Parke's book gives the appearance of contributing to the design of an overall narrative.[42] His preface announces that he has made no changes from his note-books apart from those concerned with syntax, orthography and diagnoses of disease, and that:

The remainder of the text I regard as supplementary, in some measure to Mr. Stanley's volumes. Excepting 'Darkest Africa,' no other journal of the entire course of the expedition has been published, and no account of our experiences at Ipoto and Fort Bodo has hitherto seen the light in any shape. (p. v)

As surgeon, Parke's descriptions of the horrors of the journey – the discovery of three children, two of them still living, impaled on spears; the maggots that get into one's boots; the river which provides their

[135]

drinking water filled with excrement; the illnesses, the starvation, punishments, and killings – are related in a more matter-of-fact way than by some of his companions, and are often distanced by a tone of detached irony and dry humour.

If, as I have remarked, one of the traits of the expedition was the multiple perspectives it offered, then in the case of Parke his is a viewpoint which carries another kind of authority: that provided by the supposed objectivity of science. Often this supplies restorative powers as when Parke treats Stairs for his arrow wound and Stanley for near-fatal sub-acute gastritis.[43] Also impressed upon the reader is the power of the western discourse to continue at times of incapacity to some of its practitioners. Just as impressive is the power of self-diagnosis, as when Parke voices his certainty that he is suffering from blood-poisoning as a result of handling other men's ulcers, and of course the periods of silence when he is ill are covered by the other officers' records (though Parke does remind us that he met Ward only once and Troup not at all). Observations like Parke's bear a technical and presumed dispassionate air that validates and, when on occasion combined with emotion, emphasises the poignancy and misery of parts of the expedition. An example occurs with the arrival of Nelson from 'Starvation Camp':

> Poor fellow! he arrived here this evening about 3 P.M.: a living skeleton, with hollow cheeks, sunken eyes, and bearing every trait of the extremest physical depression. I felt choking with emotion to see him in this state – a photographic record of the horrors which he has outlived. (p. 133)

Choking emotion at a photographic record neatly shows the impact of joining the two discourses and could be said to reveal the felt need for both a technical, impersonal response and a 'human', emotional reaction to experience.

More direct efforts of this type of discourse upon the transmission of racial stereotypes make themselves felt when Parke, with the authority of rational, scientific analysis behind him, turns his attention to racial comment: 'they have no forethought – none: the observation that the black man at any age is still but a grown-up child is, in my experience, critically accurate' (p. 247).

All the personal and scientific authority of Parke vests leadership in Stanley, who he acknowledges may have annoying and alienating traits, but whom 'one feels compelled to respect and admire' (p. 369). Parke holds up for his readers the desirability and benefit of submitting to the absolute leadership of Stanley:

> When difficulties and hardships came thick and fast upon us and around us, there was something approaching the sublime in the strength with which the iron will of our leader enabled him to oppose, and in the

readiness of resource with which he was so frequently able to overcome, or elude them. (p. 512)

There is probably much here of the scientific and the socially unstable finding settlement and unity in the shape of a figure of almost inhuman strength. It is a short step, and one that is duly taken, to extolling the advantages of such authoritarian rule over other cultures or 'races', and Parke does this by insisting that Stanley's treatment of the porters was 'absolutely necessary to maintain the discipline on which the very existence of the Expedition, and of its officers, depended' (p. 513). And from there one reaches the convenient paradox that the hard leader is the one that is best for his subjects. It is in this context that one should read Parke's version of a statement that in the mouths of his companions was a grudge: 'he was always inclined to favour the black man in preference to the white' (p. 513).

Ward: the adventurer

Herbert Ward's narrative, *My Life with Stanley's Rear Guard*, was published in 1891. His *Five Years with the Congo Cannibals* had already appeared and won the favour of, among other journals, the *Lady's Pictorial*, whose reviewer found:

> I very much prefer *Five Years with the Congo Cannibals* to *In Darkest Africa*. Mr. Ward tells his story in a simple, unaffected style; he indulges in no rhapsodies; he poses as neither prophet, martyr, nor saint.[44]

In his introduction to *My Life with Stanley's Rear Guard*, Ward explains that Stanley had privately suggested to him the previous July that he should prepare a small volume of the kind. Ward says that he did not wish to, that the rear guard was a failure, that something could be said on all sides, and that the subject was best left alone. Having been dragged unwillingly into the quarrel, however, he had decided to publish:

> a picture of my life as it really was at Yambuya, avoiding all controversy in my narrative; and at the close to deal, in a calm and impartial way, with the different matters in dispute, as they affect myself. (p. viii)

This statement is a shrewd one. Evident tact is buttressed by a movement that resists charges of vulgar self-interest whilst avoiding the stand-offishness of the upper classes. His reported motives for joining the expedition similarly present him as a kind of honest, disinterested gentleman and amateur: 'For glory or profit I had no heed; but for sport and adventure I was keen and excited' (p. 3). Feeling pressed to tell his story, Ward aims to impress us with his dignity. Stanley had been quoted by the *New York Tribune* as having, in a New York lecture on 3 December 1890, blamed the wrecking of the rear column on the 'irresolution, neglect, and indifference of the officers' (p. 150). He had also insinuated that there was immorality in the camp at Yambuya and had accused Ward of misappropriating brass rods (the currency of the region). Ward points out in his own defence that he left the area on 28 March 1888.

Ward was born in London in 1863 and had travelled in New Zealand, Australia and Borneo before working in Africa from 1884 for the Congo Free State and then for the Sanford Exploring Company, an American trading concession in the Congo. His narrative, like those of his colleagues, reveals challenges to authority and signs of social shifts as authority is newly asserted. Ward's own attempt to establish command would, according to his own account, have had consequences fatal to himself. Convinced that light work encouraged indiscipline and laziness, he decided to put a halt to what he perceived as demoralisation by making an example of 'one black – a regular scoundrel – who completely ignored orders, and altogether placed our authority at defiance' (p. 16). When the man ignored a warning to turn up on parade and was found to be absent from the camp, Ward ordered him, on his return that evening, to be flogged. The man shook off those who tried to seize him, and Ward saw that:

> The moment was critical, and I realised that, if I was to maintain my authority, I should have to assert it with my own right arm. I went for him, as the phrase is, and we closed with one another, the men grouped around watching the result. The mutineer was possessed of a club, and had me manifestly at a disadvantage. In the fight which ensued, my foot caught in a tent-peg, and I fell back on the ground. I was at his mercy, when Bonny, rushing forward, clubbed the man with his musket, and he was secured as prisoner. My original instructions were subsequently carried out, and this mutinous spirit was quelled. (p. 17)

The temptation to assert that Bonny's rescue of Ward is an overturning of western class order must be measured by Ward's lack of embarrassment in telling the story. It cannot be disputed that Bonny exercises the crucial power in this anecdote, but his strength restores and is in the service of Ward. Bonny's brute force saves the day. Yet even without much knowledge of Bonny's controversial role in the expedition, one senses in the episode, I think, a feeling of unease about the telling intervention of the sergeant. Ward's helplessness is so pronounced that we are left with the impression that he is not just under threat from the black 'mutineer' but is equally at the mercy of Bonny. The relief Ward feels at being saved by the sergeant is so great that it is surely not unreasonable to see this also as a larger image of the upper- and middle-classes' sense of vulnerability at that time.

Once arrived at Yambuya to join the rear guard, Ward was 'enabled to devote myself to a study of my new companions, and the way in which African life affected their views and dispositions' (p. 30). This is an unusual acknowledgement of the effect Africa could have upon the white traveller, whose identity, more often than not, was regarded as stable. Ward contrasts himself – 'I, who had roughed it all the world over, had the influence upon me which came of much adventure, and that cosmopolitanism which results from being vis-à-vis to every phase of life' – with Barttelot, who saw things 'through the strict, stern, rigid spectacles of discipline and with the autocratic manner of a British officer' (pp. 30–1). Ward portrays himself as knowing two or three African languages and possessing 'that knowledge of native methods which could only be acquired by residence amongst the people', while Barttelot was ignorant of 'African manners and speech' (p. 31), and was, therefore, for ever suspicious. The 'contempt and disdain natural to the highly strung officer who believed nothing was equal to the British soldier, gained full and unfortunate sway', but Ward's complaints against Barttelot ought not to lead us into a rousing approval of Ward's own racial attitudes, for he judges that the Major was 'completely at sea when dealing with the *black whose word is so frequently a lie*' (p. 31, my emphasis).

Nevertheless, Ward saw some good in Barttelot and commented on his boundless affection for his father, whom he often referred to, we are told, as the 'dear old Guv'nor' (p. 32), a term of endearment which nicely illustrates the attraction of submission to the rule of patriarchy: affection for the father combined with an echo of authority at work. (I am thinking of 'Guv'nor' in the sense of one's employer.) Ward describes Barttelot as 'British, too, to the finger tips in the matter of his tastes' (p. 32). There is, however, in Ward's epitaph for Barttelot a strong impression of an England that has passed away. Ward seems able to stand back and find a perspective on Barttelot that hints also at the fate of Britain:

> His talk was a breath from the country-lanes and pleasant fields; his stories constantly those of the hunting-field; and as one's recollections travel in sorrow to that lonely grave in the primæval forest, one cannot help the saddening thought, that better far would it have been if the glories of the chase he loved so well had held him fast; rather than the unhappy influence which drew him on to death at the hands of the assassin's rifle, and a grave in an African desert. (p. 32)

The metaphor of Barttelot's talk parallels the wished-for perception of the mark of the producer in the product that I have discussed above.

Here it is a much more fixed, even imprisoning presence that would have the Major stay at home in his country lanes.

Jameson is described by Ward as 'one of nature's noblemen' (p. 33), which is quite typical of how qualities are naturalised in order to transcend collapsing class barriers. Although this naturalisation can perform a radical function, insisting upon equality, it can also – and often did – act in a conservative way by refining hegemonic virtues and pulling exemplars within the circle of influence of the ruling class.

Stanley and the book

Stanley's book itself proclaims its status as commodity, both embodying and shaped by post-industrial western features connected with the value of time and space. The author's and publisher's note to the work announces:

> It may safely be asserted, without fear of the assertion being questioned, that no work of travel of this magnitude was ever before produced in so short a space of time; it has taxed to the utmost the vast resources of Messrs. CLOWES and SONS' Printing Establishment; and two of the largest binderies in London, those of Messrs. Burn, of Hatton Garden, and Messrs. Leighton, Son, and Hodge, of New Street Square, E.C., have scarcely been equal to the demands made upon them. The publishers' aim throughout has been to produce workmanship of the very best kind: any deficiencies that may be discovered must be attributed to their earnest endeavour to meet as speedily as possible the extraordinary and unprecedented demand, that has been made upon them by the public.[45]

More than most other books it makes reference to the physical and mechanical industry behind its production, but not at the expense of the commercial or spiritual. A prefatory letter dedicates the book to Mackinnon, describing it as the Official Report of the expedition, and containing the first of many tributes to the divinity:

> Constrained at the darkest hour to humbly confess that without God's help I was helpless, I vowed a vow in the forest solitudes that I would confess His aid before men. . . . In this physical and mental distress I besought God to give me back my people. Nine hours later we were exulting with a rapturous joy. In full view of all was the crimson flag with the crescent, and beneath its waving folds was the long-lost Rear Column. (p. 1)

Supplications to God suggest, when answered, a special relationship and endow the suppliant with, if not a halo, an aura of supernatural favour. It is a motif often repeated in *In Darkest Africa* and it works to bolster with spiritual power the secular and commercial strengths that have gone into the expedition and its technologically-aided report. In that respect it aims to remedy a perceived lack in the spirit of the age. Stanley plays as much as he can for the spiritual authority which will shore up the deficiencies or vacuum exposed by the public quarrels over the expedition. On one occasion Stanley records himself reading before bed the lines from Deuteronomy in which Moses exhorts Joshua: 'Be strong and of a good courage; fear not, nor be afraid of them: for the Lord thy God, He it is that doth go with thee; He will not fail thee, nor forsake thee' (p. 181). On questioning the voice which he then hears repeating the advice, the words are amplified: 'Advance, and be confident, for I will give this people and this land unto thee' (p. 182). For those readers not put off by Stanley's presumptuous tone, the idea of his being watched over by a communicative deity lends credence to his pronouncements on worldly matters, such as his criticism of the rear guard for not marching out of Yambuya; and it makes Barttelot appear sacrilegious in sending Stanley's goods to Bangala: 'He reduces me to absolute nakedness' (p. 292).

Discipline assumes a biblical justification too as Stanley plays his Old Testament role, harnessing it for the benefit of material culture:

> An unreflecting spectator hovering near our line of march might think we were unnecessarily cruel; but the application of a few cuts to the confirmed stragglers secures eighteen hours' rest to about 800 people and their officers, saves the goods from being robbed – for frequently these dawdlers lag behind purposely for such intentions – and the day ends happily for all, and the morrow's journey has no horrors for us. (p. 54)

God seems hand in hand with Stanley when he orders the hanging of one 'deserter' and then, after portraying himself as persuading the head chief Rashid of the value of mercy and repentance, he arranges a macabre charade in which the noose is placed around the neck of the second of three 'deserters', who is then pardoned after a pre-planned intercession by Rashid's fellow chiefs. When, Stanley writes, many cry with emotion, including the prisoner, Stanley shakes hands with him and declares 'It is God's work, thank Him' (p. 129). This last attribution is not especially convincing after Stanley has shown in such detail his own part in arranging the whole episode. Divine judgement is evidently more important than the verdict since later the hanging of Juma, a cook, for stealing rifles is reported in a single sentence.

In Darkest Africa is perhaps most often remembered and commented upon for its description of the Ituri forest. I shall not discuss this in great detail here as it has been examined elsewhere,[46] but I do wish to consider it in the context of authority. The first level of authority is provided by the primeval quality of the forest and, consequently, of

Stanley's status in being the first white man to penetrate it: 'it is an absolutely unknown region opened to the gaze and knowledge of civilized men for the first time since the waters disappeared and were gathered into the seas, and the earth became dry land' (p. 87). The unprecedented nature of Stanley's encounter with the forest sees him deliberately exploiting the discourse he employs for the endowment of his text with uniqueness:

> I promise to be as little tedious as possible, though there is no other manuscript or missal, printed book or pamphlet, this spring of the year of our Lord 1890, that contains any account of this region of horrors other than this book of mine. (p. 87)

In an age of mass-production, whose facilities in the production of *In Darkest Africa* are widely advertised, Stanley hopes to invest his book – as well as the narrative – with individuality,[47] and part of this involves the request of a compact with each reader: 'Beseeching the reader's patience' (p. 87).

Images of penetration have yielded to recent critics sexual readings but Stanley was well aware of his metaphors and utilises the idea of penetration for commercial thrusts. Regarding the river and the 'long unbroken forest frontage', he writes that: 'Nature in this region seems to be waiting the long expected trumpet-call of civilization', for 'Nature, despite her immeasurably long ages of sleep, indicates no agedness, so old, incredibly old, she is still a virgin locked in innocent repose'. Stanley's meaning becomes more explicit: 'What expansive wastes of rich productive land lie in this region unheeded by man! Populous though the river banks are, they are but slightly disturbed by labour' (p. 96).

Pertinent to the question of authority is the observation by Peter Knox-Shaw that in the forest scene, 'self-sufficient and self-generated', it is the absence of man rather than the presence of God that is felt. Knox-Shaw makes the important point that the 'sole creator here is the perceiver'.[48] And, as he indicates, we can witness this in Stanley's mode of description, such as when he asks his readers for their active imagination:

> Then from tree to tree run cables from two inches to fifteen inches in diameter . . . fold them round the trees in great tight coils . . . let them flower and leaf luxuriantly . . . let slender cords hang down also in tassels. (pp. 349–50)

When Stanley invites: 'Now let us look at this great forest, not for a scientific analysis of its woods and productions, but to get a real idea of what it is like' (p. 349), he sets up an opposition of discourses. He repeats the phrase 'the race for air and light' in giving a social Darwinian account of the forest. And then he compares the scenes with ones from civilisation:

the forest is typical of the life of humanity. No single glance can be taken of it without becoming conscious that decay, and death, and life, are at work there as with us. I never could cast a leisurely look at it but I found myself, unconsciously, wondering at some feature which reminded me of some scene in the civilized world. It has suggested a morning when I went to see the human tide flowing into the City over London Bridge between half-past seven and half-past eight, where I saw the pale, overworked, dwarfed, stoop-shouldered, on their way to their dismal struggle for existence. (p. 354)

And, with a louder tone of subjectivity:

And as there is nothing so ugly and distasteful to me as the mob of a Derby day, so there is nothing so ugly in forest nature as when I am reminded of it by the visible selfish rush towards the sky in a clearing, after it has been abandoned a few years. Hark! the bell strikes, the race is about to begin. I seem to hear the uproar of the rush, the fierce, heartless jostling and trampling, the cry, 'Self, for self, the devil take the weakest!' To see the white-hot excitement, the noisy fume and flutter, the curious inequalities of vigour, and the shameless disregard for order and decency! (p. 355)

Stanley's disenchantment with Emin Pasha resulted in his presenting himself as a kind of spiritual romantic in contrast to the Pasha's alleged cold materialistic science. It makes for an interesting clash of discourses and, whether intentionally or not, provides a deflection or relief from the commercial and political interests Stanley was actually serving and from the image of conquistador which was frequently applied to him on and after this expedition. Stanley sees a way of projecting himself as a sensitive human being in contrast to cold men of science, thus again juggling with terms of authority:

The Pasha is in his proper element as naturalist and meteorologist. . . . His love of science borders on fanaticism. I have attempted to discover during our daily chats whether he was Christian or Moslem, Jew or Pagan, and I rather suspect that he is nothing more than a Materialist. . . . [Such men] strike me as being somewhat unsympathetic, and capable of only cold friendship, coolly indifferent to the warmer human feelings . . . I think they are more apt to feel an affection for one's bleached skull and frame of unsightly bones, than for what is divine within a man. (p. 402)

Stanley is neatly working towards a depiction of the Pasha as an absent-minded scientist whose observations and classificatory systems are inferior to Stanley's interior, more human, kind of perception:

We have some dwarfs in the camp. The Pasha wished to measure their skulls; I devoted my observations to their inner nature. . . .
. . . He knows their names, their families, their tribes, their customs; and little as I have been with them, I think I know their natures. (p. 404)

The Pasha's renowned short-sightedness is used to paint him as hopelessly out of touch with the mood and condition of his people: 'we observe the Pasha, serene and tranquil, encircled by wrangling rebels, and yet all along apparently unconscious of the atmosphere of perfidy in which he lives – at least more inclined to resignation than resistance' (p. 444), and this myopic self-satisfaction is in turn employed as a feature which distinguishes a certain view of Africa from Stanley's, which latter now assumes the authority of a penetrative gaze. People like Emin, avers Stanley:

will never reflect that work in this world must not consist entirely of the storage in museums of skulls, and birds, and insects; that the continent of Africa was never meant by the all-bounteous Creator to be merely a botanical reserve, or an entomological museum.
Every man I saw, giant or dwarf, only deepened the belief that Africa had other claims on man, and every feature of the glorious land only impressed me the more that there was a crying need for immediate relief and assistance from civilization. (p. 463)

Stanley self-consciously relates his writing of the book in Cairo. The process is seen very much in terms of production, of manufacturing from the raw material of experience a shaped and ordered product which will bear the impress of its producer.

If the Emin Pasha Relief Expedition resulted in an intense scrutiny of text as the record of experience and perception, it also led to an unprecedented attention to the mechanics of production, including the manufacturing and marketing of the product as a commodity. Stanley's access to the mind of the Creator is complemented by his own role as a more mundane artificer. A factor linking both these developments was the nineteenth-century concern with the individual. Just as the bitter controversy over the conduct of the rear guard officers and Stanley's treatment of them focused on personal character and the written account of the individual's actions, so attempts to smoothe over the divisive disputes would seek to absorb them within a greater confluence of a more forceful identity.

This can be seen in Edward Marston's booklet *How Stanley Wrote 'In Darkest Africa': A Trip to Cairo and Back*,[49] ostensibly an account by Stanley's publisher of the writing and publication of *In Darkest Africa*, but having under its surface a deeper ideological significance. Seizing on the 'special and peculiar interest' attached to Stanley, Marston sets about describing something of the 'method of writing, and the daily life' of the explorer as he laboured at the book in Cairo, declaring that 'probably no book has ever been more eagerly looked for in every part of the civilised world, and in many languages, than the one which Mr. Stanley lately finished'.[50] Stanley's importance established, Marston proceeds to invest the former's text with the qualities of exploration. This seems necessary to validate the book's signature; to stamp the text with the mark of its producer. Thus Marston emphasises the self-denial and disciplined labour that both men would have characterise the writing of *In Darkest Africa*, but which we also know to have been presented as prominent features of Stanley's marches:

> As a rule he shut himself up in his bedroom, and there he wrote from early morning till late at night, and woe betide any one who ventured unasked into this sanctum. . . . His whole heart and soul were centred on his work. He had set himself a certain task, and he had determined to complete it to the exclusion of every other object in life. He said of himself, 'I have so many pages to write. I know that if I do not complete this work by a certain time, when other and imperative duties are imposed upon me, I shall never complete it at all'.[51]

Cairo, in many ways, acts as a kind of half-way house between the darkness of Africa and the lightness of civilisation, and it is interesting therefore to look at the space it affords for a working out of the differences between the two worlds, with the returning explorer using it to facilitate the representation of the one to the other. This space, I would argue, sees the meeting of African experience with western modes of production and transmission. Hence the severe consciousness of the pressures of time and the demands of other tasks which will disrupt the patterning of experience if the latter is not controlled and contained. From the passage just quoted one can see that the production of writing becomes an individual act of labour, the routine of which is shaped by capitalistic concerns of time and quantity, the one being measured by the other. Not only is Stanley projected in Marston's text as a professional author (literary figures present at his publisher's party in London on 26 June 1890 include Thomas Hardy, G. A. Henty and Bram Stoker), but he is viewed as an employer. Quoting from his own speech at the party Marston suggests that having written about eight thousand words per day for fifty days and his book appearing in at least ten different European countries and languages:

> Mr. Stanley may comfort himself with the reflection that during the last four months his fifty days' labour of brain and pen has given employment to an army of probably seven thousand men and at least as many women and girls, and probably the aggregate weight of all the editions which will

be issued simultaneously on Saturday will exceed three hundred tons.[52]

Such a productive and profitable relationship marks more than the rewarding combination of brain and pen; it signifies too the incorporation of the explorer into western industrial capitalism as Stanley, through his creative labour, transforms the raw material of African experience into a commodity which, under mass production, will employ many others as well. His re-entry as individual and producer into western culture (assisted by advertising) is assured. Stanley highlights the difficulties of re-entry into society partly because he is apparently more interested in the site of transference, but partly because the focus obscures the more important and controversial scene of activity: the immersion of the white into Africa. The explorer must be seen to return or he is lost, and he must find his route back into European society because African culture is to be made subordinate to it. This is not to say that the image of Africa ceases to perform one of its enduring functions:

> In Africa, where I am free of newspapers, the mind has scope in which to revolve, virtuously content. Civilisation never looks more lovely than when surrounded by barbarism; and yet, strange to say, barbarism never looks so inviting to me as when I am surrounded by civilisation.[53]

But it is to suggest that in concentrating on the temporary silence and confusion he encounters in the attempt to fit the African discourse within the literate white one he draws attention to the means of resolution. In the *Autobiography* it is said that the immediate block he experienced was removed by the relief of his feelings in writing the forest chapter and then the march from Yambuya. In the text of *In Darkest Africa* we are given a slightly different version. There he writes:

> On January 25th I seized my pen to do a day's work. But I knew not how to begin. Like Elihu, my memory was full of matter, and I desired to write that I might be refreshed; but there was no vent. My right hand had forgotten its cunning, and the art of composition was lost by long disuse. Wherefore, putting firm restraint against the crowds of reminiscences that clamoured for issue, I let slip one after another with powerful deliberation into the light, and thus, while one day my pen would fairly race over the paper at the rate of nine folios an hour, at other times it could scarcely frame 100 words. But finally, after fifty days' close labour, in obedience to an irresistible impulse, I have succeeded in reaching this page 903 of foolscap manuscript, besides writing 400 letters and about 100 telegrams, and am compelled from over-weariness to beg the reader's permission to conclude.[54]

It is a lengthy quotation but it contains images that clarify the process of cultural assimilation. Africa threatens to prevent labour (the act of writing). Literature as industry and art has been neglected and, here, there is more of an emphasis on the continuing exercise of self-discipline. Productivity signals the expressive and material return of the traveller to the industrialised culture. The silence anticipated at the end of the above passage is, suitably, one of satiety and the result of a compact between the author and the reader, and is thus in complete contrast to the frustration of the confused silence enforced upon him earlier by Africa. The crucial point, then, is that although Africa has supplied Stanley with the raw impressions and sensations that create a mass of memories these cannot be directed or coherently uttered until he is seen to enter once again into a literate society. Disciplined reflection on his experiences empowers him to write. In a paradigm of the economic relationship, Africa contributes the raw materials, the west the craftsmanship and tools to finish them in production and introduce them to the market. In this sense Stanley, like Tennyson's Ulysses, engages in 'an imperialism of the imagination . . . he is the colonizer who requires ever more remote margins to sustain his enterprise'.[55]

Furthermore, whilst *In Darkest Africa* is, more signally than any other record of exploration or travel in Africa, a commodity, Stanley, in the above passage, has sought to authenticate it by conveying the sense of labour that has gone into its creation; a kind of labour that is meant to reflect the trials of the expedition, hence the over-weariness. The idea of irresistible impulse – a sort of unconscious inspiration – ordering memory through the medium of Stanley enhances the notion of traveller as an agent for the divine, and it is fitting that this, the final chapter, should close with the words:

THE THANKS BE TO GOD FOR EVER AND EVER. AMEN. (p. 578)

The effect of the passage is thus neatly to bestow traditional authority upon the modern; to grant a divine blessing upon commercialism.

The thanks to God come after Stanley has bid 'Good-night' to Emin and Casati, to Gentlemen of the Relief Committee, and to his companions (of whom he mentions Stairs, Jephson, Nelson, Parke, and Bonny), and has quoted, in adapted form, from Browning's 'Epilogue to Asolando'. The effect is to emphasise divine and cultural authority by portraying Stanley as servant. The supposed reality of his voice is reinforced by his address to the individual reader, whose permission to conclude he asks. Author and reader share now the experience and the record, the raw materials and the product: 'Some scenes of the wonderful land of Inner Africa, through which we have travelled together, must for ever cling to our memories' (p. 577).

Notes

1 The quotation in the title of this chapter is from Tennyson's 'Locksley Hall Sixty Years After', *The Works of Alfred Lord Tennyson Poet Laureate* (London: Macmillan, 1893), p. 563.

2 For a brief but fine discussion of writing as property at this time see John Goode's account of the Society of Authors. John Goode, 'The decadent writer as producer', in *Decadence and the 1890s*, ed. Ian Fletcher (London: Edward Arnold, 1979), pp. 109–29.

3 For recent histories of the expedition see Tony Gould, *In Limbo: The Story of Stanley's Rear Column* (London: Hamish Hamilton, 1979); Roger Jones, *The Rescue of Emin Pasha: The Story of Henry M. Stanley and the Emin Pasha Relief Expedition, 1887–1889* (London: History Book Club, 1972); Iain R. Smith, *The Emin Pasha Relief Expedition 1886–1890* (Oxford at the Clarendon Press, 1972). Smith's is by far the best account, in both detail and criticism.

4 On Mackinnon see John S. Galbraith, *Mackinnon and East Africa 1878–1895: A Study in the 'New Imperialism'* (Cambridge: Cambridge University Press, 1972). It is Galbraith's assessment that 'Mackinnon craved identification with great causes; his employment of his wealth in the development of Africa enabled him to experience excitement which he had never known in his earlier years. . . . Mackinnon thought of the Imperial British East African Company as a vehicle for the realization of Imperial objectives; it was also a vehicle for his realization of himself'. (pp. 72–3).

5 On the dubious status of these treaties see Smith, *Emin Pasha*. Smith asserts that they were initially only oral agreements and are best regarded as '*post-facto* memoranda constructed by Stanley of certain ceremonies of friendship and blood-brotherhood' (pp. 267–8).

  On the relationship between ivory and imperialism see John M. MacKenzie, *The Empire of Nature: Hunting, Conservation and British Imperialism* (Manchester: Manchester University Press, 1988), especially pp. 121 and 125–6. MacKenzie notes that 'ivory acted as the first lure to the interior . . . Later ivory was used as a subsidy to underpin other endeavours' (p. 121). See also R. W. Beachey, 'The East African ivory trade in the nineteenth century', *Journal of African History* 8, 2 (1967), 269–90.

6 Smith, *Emin Pasha*, p. 53.

7 Smith, *Emin Pasha*, p. 60. On the government's anxieties see Smith, p. 59.

8 Gould, *In Limbo*, p. xviii.

9 Smith, *Emin Pasha*, pp. 83; 158.

10 Smith, *Emin Pasha*, p. 62.

11 Smith, *Emin Pasha*, pp. 62–3; 142.

12 Quoted in Smith, *Emin Pasha*, p. 241.

13 By an agreement Tippu-Tib was to become Governor of the Stanley Falls district on behalf of the Congo Free State at a salary of £30 per month and would suppress slave-raiding in the district under his control (but by implication was free to carry out his own raids elsewhere), and was contracted to supply the expedition with porters. (See Jones, *The Rescue*, p. 95.)

14 Smith, *Emin Pasha*, p. 299.

15 The literature, published and unpublished, on and of the expedition is extensive, and in these two chapters I draw on only a fraction of the sources I have consulted. I trust that my criteria and my concerns here are clear enough. I intend to produce further studies of various aspects of the expedition in the future.

16 Gould, *In Limbo*, p. 7.

17 Jones, *The Rescue*, note 10, p. 124. John Bierman, noting that Stanley dismissed Hoffmann four times during the expedition, only to take him back each time and that a court-martial document records the accusation that he was 'filthy in his person', conjectures he was guilty of gross sexual indecency. See John Bierman, *Dark Safari: The Life Behind the Legend of Henry Morton Stanley* (London: Hodder & Stoughton, 1991), pp. 329–30. There may well be something in this, but it does not explain the silence on Hoffmann observed in the contemporaneous diary and journal entries right from the start. Frank McLynn, on the other hand, believes, from the evidence of

Stanley's unpublished journal, that Hoffmann was disciplined for his kleptomania. See
Frank McLynn, *Stanley: Sorcerer's Apprentice* (London: Constable, 1991), p. 299.
Offering a third view, Wim Neetens has suggested to me that the near invisibility of
Hoffmann may have much to do with the way in which the urban poor were depicted
(if at all) as members of another race. My own feeling is that this latter fact provides the
framework by which any misdemeanour committed by Hoffmann further obscures
him from sight. It is also likely too much attention on the servant's role would
lessen the impact of Stanley's rise from workhouse orphan.

18 Henry M. Stanley, *In Darkest Africa or the Quest, Rescue and Retreat of Emin
Governor of Equatoria*, new edition (London: Sampson Low, Marston & Company
Limited, [1890] 1893), p. 28.
19 Jones, *The Rescue*, pp. 73–4.
20 See Jones, *The Rescue*, p. 93.
21 From *Land and Water*, 1 November 1890. Quoted in McLynn, *Sorcerer's Apprentice*,
note 7, pp. 466–7. See also p. 344.
22 Wim Neetens, *Writing and Democracy: Literature, Politics and Culture in Transition* (London: Harvester Wheatsheaf, 1991), p. 37.
23 Neetens, *Writing and Democracy*, p. 141.
24 Alan Sinfield, *Alfred Tennyson* (Oxford: Basil Blackwell, 1986), p. 152.
25 Tennyson, 'Locksley Hall Sixty Years After', *The Works of Alfred Lord Tennyson*, p.
563.
26 Terry Eagleton, *Criticism and Ideology: A Study in Marxist Literary Theory*
(London: Verso, [1976] 1978), p. 136.
27 15 February 1887, quoted in Gould, *In Limbo*, p. 4.
28 Jan B. Gordon, '"Decadent spaces": notes for a phenomenology of the fin de siècle', in
Decadence and the 1890s, ed. Ian Fletcher (London: Edward Arnold, 1979), pp. 32–3.
29 Quoted in Edward Marston, *After Work: Fragments from the Workshop of an Old
Publisher* (London: William Heinemann, 1904), pp. 226–7.
30 Marston, *After Work*, p. 200.
31 J. Rose Troup, *With Stanley's Rear Column* (London: Chapman & Hall, Limited,
1890), p. vii. Further citations will be given parenthetically in the text.
32 Walter George Barttelot, *The Life of Edmund Musgrave Barttelot*, 3rd ed. (London:
Richard Bentley & Son, 1890), p. 1. Further page references will be given
parenthetically in the text.
33 Mrs J. S. Jameson, ed., *Story of the Rear Column of the Emin Pasha Relief Expedition
by the late James S. Jameson, Naturalist to the Expedition* (London: R. H. Porter,
1890), p. xiii. Further page references will be given parenthetically in the text.
34 Ethel Jameson to Blackwood, 1 July 1890. Blackwood Papers 4553, National Library of
Scotland, Edinburgh. (Hereafter, Blackwood Papers, NLS.)
35 Ethel Jameson to Blackwood, 8 August 1890. Blackwood Papers 4553, NLS.
36 These are held in the Pitt Rivers Museum, Oxford. The two volumes of the manuscript
journal were written in diary form on pages previously blank, allowing Jameson to
allot whatever space he wished for each day's entry. Some of the material was taken
from notes first made in a rough diary, but these were often copied.
   It is of course significant that the pages describing the cannibalism scene have been
cut out of Jameson's notebook and torn from his diary. Given the consistency of
reasonably faithful publication of the rest of his diary, we may assume that the pages
were removed through family sensitivity – or possibly Stanley's as the diaries were in
his possession before, under the threat of legal action, he released them to the family –
rather than through a wish to suppress a substantially different account from that
which appeared in the published narrative. An important feature none the less is the
continued silence this effects.
37 Manuscript entry for 9 April 1887.
38 See, for example, pages 31, 54, and 59 of his published narrative.
39 A. J. Mounteney-Jephson, *Emin Pasha and the Rebellion at the Equator: A Story of
Nine Months' Experiences in the Last of the Soudan Provinces* with the revision and
co-operation of Henry M. Stanley, 3rd ed. (London: Sampson Low, Marston, Searle &

Rivington, 1890; reprint ed., New York: Negro Universities Press, 1969). Page references will be given parenthetically in the text.

40 McLynn, *Sorcerer's Apprentice*, p. 114.

41 Dorothy Middleton, ed., *The Diary of A. J. Mounteney-Jephson: Emin Pasha Relief Expedition 1887–1889* (Cambridge: for the Hakluyt Society, 1969). Page references will be given parenthetically in the text.

42 Thomas Heazle Parke, *My Personal Experiences in Equatorial Africa as Medical Officer of the Emin Pasha Relief Expedition* (London: Sampson Low, Marston & Company, 1891). Page references will be given parenthetically in the text.

43 On the connection between writing and medicine in Parke's narrative see Tim Youngs, 'The medical officer's diary; travel and travail with the self in Africa', in *Representing Others*, ed. Mick Gidley (Exeter: University of Exeter Press, 1992), pp. 25–36.

44 Advertisement facing the title page of Herbert Ward, *My Life with Stanley's Rear Guard* (London: Chatto & Windus, 1891). Further references to *My Life* will be given parenthetically in the text.

45 Henry M. Stanley, *In Darkest Africa*, pp. iii-iv. Further page references will be given parenthetically in the text.

46 See for example Peter Knox-Shaw, 'The explorer, and views of creation', *English Studies in Africa* 27, 1 (1984), 1–26.

47 On the loss of 'aura' of the work of art see Walter Benjamin, 'The work of art in the age of mechanical reproduction', in *Illuminations*, ed. Hannah Arendt, trans. Harry Zohn (London: Fontana, 1973), pp. 219–53.

48 Peter Knox-Shaw, 'The Explorer', 10.

49 Edward Marston, *How Stanley Wrote 'In Darkest Africa': A Trip to Cairo and Back* (London: Sampson Low, Marston, Searle & Rivington, 1890). This book added to and revised an article which first appeared in *Scribner's Magazine* in August 1890. It should be noted that the title and structure of the book provided Marston with a minor travel narrative of his own.

50 Marston, *How Stanley Wrote*, pp. 1–2.

51 Marston, *How Stanley Wrote*, p. 16.

52 Marston, *How Stanley Wrote*, p. 74. Stanley's autobiography has him completing the manuscript, after rewriting some chapters, on the eighty-fifth day. Dorothy Stanley, ed., *The Autobiography of Sir Henry Morton Stanley* (London: Sampson, Marston and Co. Ltd., 1909), p. 411.

53 Dorothy Stanley, ed., *The Autobiography*, p. 528.

54 Stanley, *In Darkest Africa*, p. 577.

55 The description is Sinfield's. Alan Sinfield, *Alfred Tennyson*, p. 53.

CHAPTER FIVE

Consuming Stanley

The press

A concomitant of the disputes surrounding the aftermath of the Emin Pasha Relief Expedition was a series of acrimonious exchanges over property rights. Claims of ownership were fought in a manner that reveals an intensified drive towards the acquisition of the record or testimony of experience. Besides Stanley's contractually imposed silencing of his colleagues for six months, there were declarations of proprietorship linked closely with the commercial interests behind the expedition. Leopold himself, in 1906, drew upon ideas of proprietorship and authorship in describing his relation to the Congo:

> The Congo has been, and could have been, nothing but a personal undertaking. There is no more legitimate or respectable right than that of an author over his own work, the fruit of his labour. . . . My rights over the Congo are to be shared with none: they are the fruit of my own struggles and expenditure.[1]

A more direct example is a letter from de Winton, secretary of the Emin Pasha Relief Committee, to the publisher Blackwoods protesting at the proposed title of a projected book by Werner, who had visited the rear guard camp while working as an engineer on a steamer in the service of the Congo Free State. De Winton writes that he has learnt of Blackwoods' intention to publish later that month Werner's book, 'purporting from its title to be a history of the Emin Relief Expedition under the leadership of Mr. H. M. Stanley'. Pointing out that 'the title is misleading and calculated to deceive the public as well as to infringe upon the rights of the Committee and of the distinguished traveller in charge of the Expedition', de Winton denies any connection between the expedition and Werner, who, therefore, 'has consequently no warrant to use it as a title for his book'. Thus, de Winton tells Blackwoods, not only is Werner's information inauthentic, but 'you will see your way to removing from the title of that gentleman's book a reference to which the writer can have no claims'.[2] It may be a sign of the duplicitous masking so characteristic of the expedition that de Winton, complaining of Werner's lack of courtesy in failing to provide the Committee with advance notice of his title, projects financial considerations on to Werner, separating out and retaining for the Committee the moral high ground: 'Such a procedure on his part can only lead to the conclusion that the title adopted by him was intended to increase the sale of his work'.[3]

There is clearly a conflation here of financial gain and honour. De Winton suggests that in Werner's case the two concerns are incompatible. At the same time, the Committee is obscuring its own material interests through an appeal to codes of gentlemanly conduct. This kind of behaviour is a feature of many of the activities associated with the expedition.

The projection of a sole voice of authority is especially evident in contemporary newspaper coverage of the expedition, in which the exercise of power in the interests of undisputed property is evident in two main facets. First, there was the arrangement between the Emin Pasha Relief Committee and a group of newspapers on the publication of letters and reports from the officers. The correspondence of the Committee, held in the Mackinnon Papers at the School of Oriental and African Studies in London, reveals many troubled exchanges in connection with the matter. These mostly concern the failure of certain parties to observe the agreement that had been made to publish relevant material simultaneously.[4] Thus, at the end of March 1887, the *Daily Telegraph* announced to the Committee that, after the appearance in *The Times* of two signed letters from Stanley, following on from the explorer's dispatch to that paper of exclusive telegrams, the *Telegraph* was withdrawing from the arrangement that had been made for it to receive copies of letters and telegrams from Stanley for simultaneous publication with *The Times*, *Standard*, and *Scotsman*.[5] At the end of the following year, owing no doubt to the mounting interest in the expedition, Edwin Arnold informed Mackinnon that the *Daily Telegraph* wished to re-enter the agreement.[6] But similar complaints followed. In 1889 Buckle of *The Times* wrote of his great surprise at finding a letter from Stanley published in full in London by the *New York Herald*;[7] and on the same day the *Standard* complained of the publication of a map in the *Daily News* and of Stanley's letters in the *Scotsman*.[8]

This affair led to a crisis. Charles Cooper of the *Scotsman* denied to Sir Francis de Winton that there was any breach of faith or of copyright,[9] but, a day later, Bruce apologised to the *Standard*, explaining that he had believed himself a free agent in passing Stanley's letters on to Cooper.[10] Indeed, the dispute over access to the property – which by this stage the written records of the expedition had demonstrably become – would even seem to have threatened de Winton's position, for on 7 April Bruce told him to abandon all idea of resigning as Secretary of the Committee, a thought he must have seriously entertained.[11] Nevertheless, on 9 April, the *Daily Telegraph* again voiced its grievance at prior publication by *The Times* of more Stanley letters and in the next month Arnold finally withdrew his paper from the arrangement 'which has been productive of no advantage'.[12]

In June the *Telegraph*'s place was taken by the *Yorkshire Post*, which declared: 'the interest in Mr. Stanley and companions is by no means confined to London, and is, as a fact, quite as keen in Yorkshire as it can possibly be in town'.[13] Support for this announcement of provincial interest is seen in the payment in late November 1889 of £200 by the *Manchester Guardian* for exclusive rights in Lancashire, or at least Manchester, to the publication of Stanley's letters and dispatches to the Committee.[14] The Committee's troubles were far from over. For example, in the same month Edward Lloyd of the *Daily Chronicle* wrote to Mackinnon asking how it was that in all the daily papers that morning except his own there had been published some 'Stanley Correspondence', and asserting: 'if you omitted to send such an important matter I want to be in a position to put myself right with the public'.[15]

The impression to emerge from the dealings of the Committee with the press is of the marketable value of a figure of national interest and therefore, by the processes already identified, of truth itself. To say this is not to propose a naive or absolutist faith in the indivisibility of 'truth', but, quite simply, to recognise that commercial considerations unquestionably shaped the presentation of the expedition and its image. The concern noted above with simultaneous publication of the Stanley material within the syndicate concentrates attention on an individual voice of authority which speaks for the group and, through the interest in that voice, perhaps for the nation. This process exhibits a control of voice, both in the content and timing of its public utterance. Mackinnon, for instance, writing to McDermott in December 1889, encloses the principal part of a letter from Stanley to de Winton and asks that it be typed and copies sent to the papers. Mackinnon retains the original 'as I have dropped out here & there parts of it that I thought it wd. [*sic*] do no good to publish'.[16]

We have here then the manipulation of the traveller's writings by vested political and financial interests. Institutional barriers are erected between Stanley and his readers. Stanley is made to appear as if he is speaking to, if not for, the nation, and his voice is therefore subject to some controls. There is a much more organised mediation between author and readership than we have seen earlier in the century and it is characterised by the desire to acquire the voice as commodity, one that will yield further returns.[17] This is seen quite clearly in a letter from Edmund Gosse to Lord Wolseley in which Gosse relays from a publisher an offer to Stanley of £3000 plus fifteen per cent royalties over fifteen thousand copies for 'a work similar in length and character to *Through the Dark Continent*'. Crucially for the argument being made here, Gosse adds:

> Should Mr Stanley be inclined to consider this offer, it is most desirable ... that as little of his narrative as is consonant with his obligations in other quarters should find its way to the newspaper press.
>
> Permit me to suggest that such matter as must unavoidably be published might substantially advantage Mr. Stanley if he, or his representatives, would authorize its first newspaper publication through my friends.[18]

This, then, exemplifies one of the principal features of the exercise of power over the written record of the expedition in the interests of financial gain. The object is the influence that can be brought to bear upon Stanley's individual but also official record of the expedition.

The second feature displays a similar purpose but entails the suppression of alternative accounts. Thus Mackinnon in July 1888 expresses to de Winton his annoyance at Herbert Ward's part in circulating reports of the expedition to the public, and condemns the action as a breach of Ward's engagement with Stanley.[19] In March 1888 de Winton stopped for the time being payment of Troup's salary because of the publication of the latter's correspondence in the *Whitehall Review*, even though the letters had been given to the press by Troup's brother, and in May 1889 solicitors recommended to de Winton that a writ be served on Troup in order to secure an injunction delaying the publication of his book.[20] This second aspect of control has to do therefore with the attempt to protect the sole official voice from challenge and it includes quite literally the buying of silence.

But the conditions of the final decade of the nineteenth century and of the Emin Pasha Relief Expedition were such that the multiplicity of voices, often contradictory, strove to break the monopoly on utterance. The task facing the Establishment was to transform them to its own advantage and to pull from the entanglement of conflicting noises a coherent line which could be proffered as the overriding national image. The narratives which were spawned by the expedition thus fed into a larger controversy over the English role in Africa – and by implication in imperial affairs – and over the rights of certain sections of society to speak for the nation. Because of the organisation around the expedition and its institutional connections the writings from it met with a much more self-conscious response than previously in the century.

It is, frankly, almost impossible to offer a definitive view on how far the character of and responses to the Emin Pasha Relief Expedition were determined by its social and cultural context and how much they were due to what some might hold to be the unique nature of the expedition. But my own conclusion is that most of the factors which might have made the expedition unprecedented were ones which are attributable to the concerns and features of the time. Thus, although I recognise there are dangers in making claims for the social significance of the expedition (compared, say, with dissimilar expeditions in earlier years), it seems to me undeniable that the questions of class, authority, language, and commerce which were at the heart of the conduct and the discussions of the expedition are so much in keeping with the apprehension and expression of such matters in the literature (factual and fictional) of the last fifteen years or so of the century, that certain observations about the relation of the expedition to its time can reasonably be made.

Perhaps the best way of gauging the climate is to scrutinise some of the newspaper comment, for the press was loud in debating and judging the issues arising from the expedition and in offering itself as an arena in which the public drama could be enacted. In so doing it also inserted a mediating layer between the public and the literature of the expedition. It could be argued that the high visibility of this layer, constituting a perceptible, quasi-official intervention of a kind not so apparent earlier, had much to do with social flux in combination with the genuinely popular interest in Stanley. The unease felt about the social composition of the expedition, with Stanley, of dubious background, assuming command over British officers and gentlemen, reflects the larger social movements and uncertainties of the time. And it makes for a revealing commentary on the relationship between attitudes to 'race' and class. Then, as now, the *Daily Telegraph* provides a useful example. The newspaper claimed in November 1890 that none of the surviving officers of the rear guard had supported Stanley in his more serious allegations against Barttelot, nor had they agreed with him on the possibility of an advance. The comment continues:

> They were on the spot; he was at a distance. They are English gentlemen; he repeats the malignant gossip of anonymous and irresponsible natives, many of whom have no idea whatever of the moral distinction between truth and falsehood.[21]

We would seem to be presented with an uncomplicated confirmation of the moral and perceptual superiority of English gentlemen over the 'natives', with whom the debased Stanley is identified. But the news-paper's comment goes on to outline the difficulty of disentangling the facts and then, very interestingly, uses the standards of an assumed past to criticise the then contemporary African explorers:

> It may be that to penetrate Africa a man must be courageous, resolute, enduring, and 'as hard as nails'; it may also be necessary that he should strike, flog, and occasionally hang indolent or treacherous natives under his command. Yet who gave unofficial and individual Englishmen the moral right to treat all Africans, from chiefs to tribesmen, as beasts of burden, to be kicked, cuffed, and killed, in order that this or that explorer may make money or reputation? The best missionaries – LIVINGSTONE, for example, – got on without brutality. Some of the greatest African travellers have not needed the rope and the stick. Why, then, should it be taken for granted that MR. STANLEY or MAJOR BARTTELOT should be entrusted with powers of life or death?[22]

And the paper condemns the expedition as 'a comedy of errors'. It would be mistaken however to take this attack on the present-day explorer as an outspoken criticism of imperialism and racism. It is the highly visible cruelty that disturbs.

The appeal to the golden age of Livingstone disguises both the means by which his society sought commercially and psychologically to exploit the Africans for its own ends and, ironically, Stanley's own role in constructing the myth of the benevolent selfless missionary.[23] In truth, what the tone of the paper's lament reveals is a class-based reaction against the kind of money-making that it dismisses as grubby because it cannot, under the circumstances, be altogether hidden under the cloak of a humanitarian and religious mission as had been possible earlier. It is, largely, the vulgar methods of the self-made man that rankle. What troubles the *Daily Telegraph* so much, I think, is the mutual dependency of the expedition and society, and the accountability fostered by the semi-official status given the expedition by public opinion and tacit government support. There is something desperate in the branding of the expedition's members 'unofficial and individual Englishmen'; a realisation that the contract of support and interest offered by the public has made the activities of Stanley and his party uncomfortably close; has, indeed, made reading the records of the expedition an immediate and dirty affair. The sense of social divisions could not but be felt once the officers themselves questioned the motives and conduct of the expedition. The *Times Weekly Edition* carried an interview with John Rose Troup from Boston and reported him as saying:

> Mr. Stanley is a great explorer, but he went into this Emin Relief Expedi-tion for fame and what he could get out of it. He has no more philanthropy

than my boot. I will go further and say that the expedition was in the nature of a speculation, and not a philanthropic relief movement. The capitalists backing it were after the ivory which Emin Pasha was supposed to have collected. The officers of the expedition were promised certain shares in the expected big supply of ivory as a reward for their services. The release of Emin Pasha was a secondary consideration entirely.[24]

When massive public and newspaper interest has followed the expedition a criticism of this kind must inevitably lead to an examination of the motives and conduct of the nation itself. The travellers' writings therefore come under a scrutiny whose conscious intensity may not have been matched earlier in the century. There was suddenly a search for evidence. Different officers' accounts were deliberately judged one against the other. Verification was sought in the compatibility of two or more versions and this meant that the criteria by which formerly an individual's narrative was accepted were now forcibly made the subject of enquiry. The travellers themselves were now explored. This marked no progression of values, however. The self-questioning which greeted the accounts of the expedition was in accord with the intellectual and aesthetic concerns of the time. Africa was still used to construct Britain's image of itself. What had changed was the sense of crisis within Britain.

On 8 November 1890 *The Times* carried a statement by Stanley, dictated to its New York correspondent, in which the explorer defended himself and laid further charges against Barttelot, including the accusation that the latter had given a ten-year-old boy, Soudi, a heavy kick from which the youngster had died. Commenting on this and the other charges, the paper declared:

> it would be altogether premature as yet to attempt to pronounce judgment in a controversy where the issues are so confused and confusing, and the evidence is so conflicting and so inconclusive, that a satisfactory settlement could only be obtained by a strict and exhaustive judicial investigation.[25]

The individual voices of earlier travellers which might stand or fall on their own merits would appear to have been lost. This is not to ignore, say, the arguments between Speke and Burton, but to argue that the institutional and quasi-official apparatus surrounding the expedition gave disputes between individuals a more national significance.

National feeling would not have been comforted by Bonny's statement carried by *The Times* on 10 November, in which the Sergeant confirmed that Barttelot had sentenced interpreter John Henry to three hundred lashes, and added: 'This scene was the most horrible I ever saw. Mortification set in, the man's flesh fell off in pieces on to the ground, and his body swelled to twice its ordinary size. Within 24 hours John Henry died.'

Furthermore, Bonny accused Barttelot of having killed, the day before the Major's own murder, a Manyuema whom he suspected of having shot at him and whom, said Bonny, Barttelot 'prodded quite 30 times with his steel-pointed cypress staff, and finished up by beating the man's brains out before the eyes of all in the village'. Whites' heteroglossia on this expedition is evident in Bonny's self-reported reaction to Barttelot's act. He claims to have saved the officer's life: 'It was only by knocking him down myself that the natives held back, for then they thought I meant punishing him'.[26] Bonny offers his view of white-black relations as more perceptive than the Major's. He not only recoils from the officer's cruelty but has to act to save him from the consequences of it. Bonny is capable of reading the blacks' intentions where Barttelot is unable to, through either ignorance or haughtiness. Bonny's class position is greatly relevant to his situation. He employs it to insert himself between the white officer and the subordinate or outsider blacks.[27] This manoeuvre provoked fierce criticism of his role from officers and gentlemen back in England. All the same, his expressed belief that Barttelot was insane was far from dismissed by *The Times*, for it provided a way of accounting for the behaviour of the man without necessarily indicting the society from which he came.

A consequence of the dispute of which this was a part was that the narratives spilled over into the newspapers. Episodes recounted in the travellers' books were compared with the versions of those episodes that appeared in the papers. And this had an effect on the response to the structure and content of the books. More tangible pressure was put upon writers and the public than was experienced by previous travellers. On the matter of Barttelot's alleged cruelty and Jameson's alleged cannibalism, *The Times* pronounced:

> We must again insist, for the sake of the good fame, not only of the parties themselves, but of the British nation, to which they belong, and whose reputation the atrocities charged to their account will cloud, that the whole mystery of this dreadful business should be cleared up. It becomes the duty of MR. WALTER BARTTELOT to print the expunged portions of his brother's diary, and the forthcoming diary of MR. JAMESON, which his widow is about to publish, ought to be free from any *lacunæ* whatever.[28]

The plurality of actors and voices allows a choice to be made between them, a choice which can be turned to one's advantage by signifying one's difference from the options one rejects. It is no exaggeration to say that the increase in voices is in keeping with the greater specialisation and differentiation of a society more technologically advanced than in previous decades. The consumers are apparently free to opt for the line they wish and to shape their own identity through the option. A result of the expedition was to intensify contrasting modes, making the matter of self-identification more complex than before. No longer was it simply a matter of distinguishing oneself from the Africans or from features of one's home country. There was now the possibility of a more sophisti-cated range of disavowals, perhaps recognising the inescapable diversity of social interests by the 1890s. It is also important that at this time the newspapers and reviews were offering differing political lines as the nature of their constituencies changed.[29]

The Times, reviewing Jameson's diary in December 1890, declared plaintively that 'The publication of this volume completes the melancholy cycle of the tragedy of Mr. Stanley's Rear Column', and went on to convey with painful clarity the atmosphere of distress in which the venture and its writings were received:

> If no controversy had arisen we doubt if much was to be gained by the publication of these letters and diaries. The depressing and distressing story of the Rear Column, however told, is very melancholy reading. It is a story of failure, of sickness, of despondency, of barbarities and severities which if necessary are a condemnation in themselves of the expedition of which the Rear Column was an essential part, and if unnecessary are a disgrace to the English name.[30]

The whites' faults are personalised so that, for example, Barttelot's lack of self-control which accounted for his inability to govern other men incriminates Stanley for choosing him in the first place. An attempt in some quarters to unite the country in its view of one or more of the officers had been apparent long before this. When news of Barttelot's death had first been circulated the *Standard* had announced:

> The intelligence . . . will be received by *all classes of Englishmen* with feelings of no ordinary concern. . . . There are very few who will not associate with their regret for his untimely end profound sympathy for his bereaved father. In an age when political enemies too often embitter even the relations of private life, SIR WALTER BARTTELOT, though the staunchest and most outspoken of Conservatives, enjoys the esteem of men of all Parties and of all schools.[31]

The *Spectator* desperately engaged in a kind of damage-limitation exercise, solemnly announcing 'We believe the Barttelot story – though we hold the Major irresponsible – and we do not believe the Jameson story'. Barttelot, the paper said, was insane, but the accusation against Jameson was too incredible to be believed even if supported by his own words, for '*No* evidence is sufficient to prove such a charge against any educated European whatsoever'. With a touching faith in the rectitude of its countrymen, the paper elaborated on its defence of Jameson against the attack made on him: 'It is not true, because moral impossibilities exist, and the crime alleged in this story is one of them, and one of the least believable we ever remember to have seen'.

To the *Spectator*, for Stanley even to have raised the matter of Jameson's alleged deeds was unforgivable because it could:

> have no possible effect except to raise in the public mind a feeling that Africa is a sort of tropical hell where any crime is possible, and that as the Arctic regions seem to freeze wickedness out of their explorers, so Africa seems to heat every evil passion into a blazing fire.[32]

The lawlessness in which explorers find themselves, asserts the paper, and the lack of accountability to opinion ('they are themselves, as a rule, the reporters to Europe of their own deeds') encourages them, when by 'a law of selection' they are 'almost inevitably men at once of reckless courage, of indurated hearts, and of the true domineering temper, the temper which will slay rather than suffer its will to be unfruitful', to act rashly and with severity.

Concern is still not felt for the Africans. Rather, the preoccupation is with what their treatment by whites discloses of the latter. Africa and its people are to blame for provoking unwanted behaviour in the British explorers, of whom:

> Some . . . regard the race with kindly contempt, and some with malignant contempt, but with almost all contempt is the substratum of their thoughts. We are not great believers in Negroes, and do not say that they do not deserve the special feeling which alike in America and Africa, they appear to inspire in almost all white men . . . but the feeling accentuates frightfully the natural white disposition towards tyranny.[33]

Elsewhere, the extent and coverage of the disputes led some to call for an end to public debate over the affair. If reports of African travel had originally been a distraction, they were now too close to domestic problems for comfort. Maintaining some detachment, the *New York Herald* judged that:

> The controversy over the Emin Expedition has now reached a point at which the great body of the public will give it up. It is of no use attempting to follow it any further. The average reader might as well try to explore Africa on his own account as to decide the exact amount of blame which ought to be attached to all the persons in the present dispute.

Significantly, though, and by no means alone, the paper felt strongly that 'these terrible charges and counter-charges . . . have killed "African Exploration" as a profession'.[34] This feeling, I would suggest, is characteristic of the *zeitgeist* anyway, but it does show that images and experiences of Africa were as much affected by *fin de siècle* sentiment as were other parts of the culture. If part of the 1890s aesthetic involved the sensation and depiction of decadence and ennui, leading to self- or interior examination, then the writings on the Emin Pasha controversy can be seen to occupy a similar role. This is true too of the reaction against the events. In art and politics the inward gaze, especially one which employed the detail of realism, disturbed, and there was a determined – one might say rearguard – attempt to deflect it elsewhere. Just as impressions of Ireland had been exported to Africa, so now could the Irish be used to shield the dominant culture from further harmful attention. The *Liverpool Post*, not surprisingly, was one of many newspapers to seize upon an Irish element as a distraction. Urging Stanley 'in the name of decency to let the matter rest', the paper wrote that 'The Parnell episode came as an interesting, if not a gratifying, relief to the daily tale of horrors with which Mr. Stanley appalled the sensitive and gratified the morbid'.[35] To dwell on the newspaper comment is to get some idea of the environment which the narratives, when published in book form, entered. More than content is at issue, for the terms of the debate, I would contend, affected the response to the very structure of those narratives. That response can be related to reactions to diaries, journals, and other autobiographical forms more generally. For example, reviewing Troup's book, the *Daily Graphic* thought:

> Lieutenant Troup has exercised a wise discretion in preserving, as far as possible, the record written at the time while everything was fresh in his memory. No narrative, however picturesque, possesses the *vraisemblance* which attaches to a diary.[36]

The paper did concede though that the publication was not 'complete' (Troup having excised references to purely personal affairs). The latter fact weighed much more heavily with the *Observer*, for which:

> Mr. Troup's book is full of strange gaps, and his diaries, like those of Major Barttelot, consist for the most part not of any records that can be useful to science or civilisation, but merely of registers of the deaths and floggings of the men [and?] of the dinners the officers were eating while their troops were starving.[37]

This is civilisation refusing to acknowledge its nature and signalling thereby the kind of writing that is unacceptable to it. What I want to take from this is some sense of the implications for the relationship between textual form and content. The conjunction exercised the minds of several reviewers. The *Saturday Review*, which covered Troup's book some months later, criticised its excisions and then mused:

[161]

A still worse fault, perhaps, is that it is half original diary and half ratiocination, not only after the event, but after the discussions about the event – ratiocination, moreover, in which we do not know that Mr. Troup shows himself an invariably good reasoner.[38]

The suspicion of retrospection revealed here validates the immediacy of the spontaneous account, which, the argument surely goes, must be true because it was written *there*. All that I have said shows that the deep beliefs were a good deal more complex than this, but the *Saturday Review*'s apparently naive wish for a pure form and an uncomplicated truth is significant as an expression of feeling in the last decade of the century; as a kind of purposeful nostalgia for what really never was so that the present can be bemoaned. There was a difference of emphasis in the thoughts of the *National Observer*,[39] which saw the controversy as having not only shaped the appearance of the book, but as being its *raison d'être*:

> Take away what may be called the controversial part, and you take away well-nigh everything tangible in the book, and the very reason for its existence. Preface, introduction, and appendices are but rounds in a long turn-up between Mr. Troup and his leader.

The stress may be different, but the sentiments would seem to be pretty much the same as those felt by the *Saturday Review*. A case may be put forward for claiming that the preface, introduction, and appendices bore a kind of structural energy that had been displaced from the conventional pattern of the chronological, linear narrative, and that this diversion was a technical reflection of the frustrations and relative immobility which beset the members of the expedition. The *National Observer* proposed that:

> it would have been better to struggle on and even die in the forest than to eat their hearts out at Yambuya; for them the tragedy of the rear column would not have lacked that touch of the heroic for which we search its history in vain.

It is not a great surprise to find this twittering urge to glorious death in the pages of the *National Observer*, for its editor was the poet W. E. Henley (1849–1903) who, like Kipling, would constantly invoke 'the Virgin of the Sword, the Red Angel of war, the Lord God of Battles, or the Lord of our far-flung battle-line', and who was 'as gruesomely jingoistic as Kipling at his worst'.[40] His poem, 'England, My England', for example, includes the stanza:

Ever the faith endures,
England, my England: –
'Take and break us: we are yours,
  England, my own!

Life is good, and joy runs high
Between English earth and sky:
Death is death; but we shall die
To the Song on your bugles blown,
England –
To the stars on your bugles blown!'[41]

Stanley had not obeyed the bugles and there is plainly a feeling that had the physical movement called for by the *National Observer* occurred it would have facilitated a literary progression of heroic action which need not have seen a dissipation of energy into structural accoutrements that carried inward-looking defences and recriminatory statements. The unproductiveness the audience felt to be a characteristic of the efforts surrounding the contributions to the debate is noted by many, and there would appear to be an attempt to hold this structural aimlessness within the expedition literature itself rather than admitting it to be a feature more widely suited to social trends. On the publication of Troup's book, the fifth on the expedition to appear, the *Daily News* remarked 'Twenty books will leave us as powerless as we were at the outset to judge this melancholy quarrel on its merits' and laid down its own route to productivity:

> Let us all try to forget that the Rear Guard suffered and died, and only remember that the more fortunate, but perhaps not more heroic, column in advance crossed Africa from sea to sea, and performed one of the most daring exploits of pure adventure in the history of our time.[42]

A selective memory and carefully directed vision are encouraged. Let's not talk the country down by recalling the facts. There is a touching effort to distil from the mess a harmless and worthy achievement of 'pure' adventure (perhaps complementing the yearning for a simple form noted above), while the grand sweep of history 'of our time' possibly gives the game away.

Another means of dealing with the lack of usefulness of the literature was to personalise it. A couple of cartoons from the period illustrate very clearly the two main kinds of response to the expedition and its narratives. One, from *Rare Bits* (Fig. 6),[43] depicts Stanley as a goalkeeper desperately trying and, it seems, failing to keep his goal intact against attacks from books authored by his former companions. The goalposts are marked 'Public Opinion', an inscription which works to indivi- dualise the event by placing on Stanley the onus to carry public opinion with him.

On the other hand, *John Bull* carried a cartoon in which John Bull throws a light on Stanley who stands on his book *In Darkest Africa* in front of an obscured forest scene in which one can discern shadowy

Figure 6 'Stanley's Hot Goal'. *Rare Bits*, 15 November 1890.

figures of a skeleton and of men hanging from trees (Fig. 7).[44] In front of Stanley are the impediments of 'reports, rumours, criticisms, queries, allegations and charges'. John Bull stands this side of them and is captioned demanding 'Step down Stanley and let me see behind you!'. John Bull, as one would expect of the character, is portrayed as representing the national interest.[45]

The *Agnostic Journal* was anxious to see its country behaving rightfully but offered a radically different analysis of the situation. Its commentator, R. L. Travers, under the heading of 'Poor Africa!' saw the expedition as the summation of all arguments against Britain's imperial role. Asking if Britain felt 'justified in being a thief and a robber under the plea that she has not sufficient space for her ever-increasing masses of miserable, abortionate burlesques on humanity?', Travers followed up this temperate question by listing England's colonies in Africa and commenting: 'Truly a goodly array of possessions, in all of which she is civilising her black subjects out of existence'. It is true that Travers, no less than other commentators, manipulated the image of Africa and used its people as objects with which to construct and advance his argument for a hands-off role for England (taking as his rule not so much the Noble Savage as the ignoble Briton), but all the same his view of England and of the civilisation which it claims to embody and promote is greatly at odds with that of those contemporaries who shared in the attack on the expedition.

> Stanley is to-day the direst enemy the African ever knew. He is the forerunner in the centre of the continent of civilisation, which is, as I have frequently shown, the hell-hound of all savage races. The Stanley expedition was supposed to have been fitted out in the cause of philanthropy. I may mention that I never believed the miserable pretence; but now the world has good proof that the leader's objects were mammon and ambition, while the aim of the speculators in it was solely to make money.[46]

Travers's was not a lone voice. Similar sentiments were expressed two years earlier in *Truth* in a poem about the expedition, published shortly after Barttelot's death. Technically the poem is atrocious (and, indeed, that may be a safety-valve, taking pressure away from any real radical force it might otherwise have carried), but the attitude it reflects is a further sign of the *fin de siècle* feeling which met the expedition. The poem lamented that:

> as a fact, we often find our Bold Explorers now
> Are Bloodshed as their chief ally too ready to avow;
> And, 'stead of that diplomacy and skill which once were shown,
> On sword and rifle-bullet now dependence place alone.

[165]

Figure 7 John Bull and Stanley. *John Bull*, 22 November 1890.

Purpose, as well as methods, is condemned:

> They uninvited make their way to lands that want them not,
> Carry for claims of ownership or justice not a jot;
> And, trampling with rough recklessness on savage creeds and rites,
> Hoist England's ensign o'er the land their terrorism blights.

The conclusion was unambiguous:

> England, at least, must countenance such murderous raids no more,
> Nor honour sham explorers who, when they'd a land explore,
> Gather a venal, cut-throat gang, too vicious to control,
> And march through rapine, fire, and blood, to gain their useless goal![47]

The poem, like so many other commentaries, compares the calamitous contemporary conditions with an uncorrupted golden age, but there does seem to be here a genuine, rather than simply generic, distaste for the present state of things. That the emphasis is on violence and destruction is characteristic of the tenor of much writing towards the close of the century; that Stanley and his fellows should be seen as in some way counterfeit is characteristic not just of the sentiment that some kind of real quality of personality has been lost, but epitomises too the worry that the loss is due at least in part to the irreversible onset of mass production and the growth of brand names and their promotion which accompanied it.

Public opinion and the sham explorer

Travel literature is received in these later years not as the playful manipulation of constructs and mores, but, in common with works of 'fiction' too (in particular those of naturalism), is deemed to display the morality of its practitioners. And so, even when Stanley is attacked it is from the same premise as that held by Barttelot, Edwin Arnold, and Edward Marston. Harry Quilter, who in May 1888 had founded the *Universal Review*, was an especially vocal critic of Stanley's role in the Emin Pasha Relief Expedition, and wrote sadly of the explorer's books:

> there is perhaps no modest or honourable Englishman who has not felt a touch of shame in reading these narratives at the boastfulness and arrogance of the writer, and at the peculiarly unpleasant dealing, and religious sentiment which characterise Mr. Stanley's actions as they are depicted in Mr. Stanley's own words.[48]

Such feelings appeal to anti-Americanism and class prejudice, but, it is claimed, they emanate from the perception of a match of the man with his writing.

The same uncomplicated belief in the reflection of the qualities of authors in their work is evident in the editorial commentaries on the diaries of Barttelot and Jameson, both published posthumously, edited by relatives of the dead men, and not originally intended for publication. Their appearance was due to a faith in the private document. For Barttelot's brother: 'the diaries and letters direct from the hands of the dead form evidence of supreme value. . . . They have not been able to alter or add a tittle to what was written at the time'.[49] And from Jameson's brother came a more elaborate declaration of the same tenet:

> A man's diary is a self-revelation. His true personality is as certain to present itself continually as the refrain in a theme of music. No man lies to himself, when night after night, as his work is done, he sits down to write out the story of his life from day to day; and the life which Jameson reveals to us in his Diary is one whose keynote is duty, kindliness, and hard work.[50]

The idea of the private space revealing true personal worth is a comforting facet of bourgeois ideology, fostering the myth of a self essentially unaffected by socialisation and cultural value. People such as Quilter and the brothers of the dead officers used this concept against Stanley, pitting private thoughts against public posturing, as they saw it. Quilter described Stanley as 'using every device of journalistic exaggeration to wound the feelings of their relatives, their comrades, and their friends'.[51] Their defence, based on trenchant if pained affirmation of British qualities, seems modified nevertheless by the sense of newer forces. Andrew Jameson emphasised hard work (performed by a gentleman).

Refuting Bonny's allegation that the terrible decline of the rear column was Barttelot's fault, Quilter tells his readers that:

> there was that most bitter of personal grudges, the grudge due to social inequality, existing between Major Barttelot and Mr. Bonny, who had been only a corporal (I am now informed, not sergeant), and with whom Major Barttelot rightly or wrongly, would not associate on terms of intimacy.[52]

The (inaccurate) parenthetic gibe is just one ostentatious clue as to the direction of Quilter's sympathies. He evidently feels that the superior officer's narrative is the one to be believed, and this has consequences for cultural representation as much as for self-expression. It is worth saying, incidentally, that Bonny too had his reservations, commenting with wonderful pungency that Barttelot's being made second-in-command of the expedition must have been because he was 'the son of his father – it cannot be on account of his ability because he has none'.[53] I am beginning to suggest here that the plurality of voices generated by the expedition enforces a choice upon the auditor and that the reasons advanced for making the choice pose a fragmentation or contestation of what had before been taken (sincerely or otherwise) to be a basically unified audience. The character and composition of the expedition made this inevitable, and the subsequent stances that were taken are indicative of class allegiances and class values more generally.

Quilter complains that 'there was good *a priori* reason to believe that the real objects of the Emin Pasha expedition were not philanthropic, but political and commercial'.[54] Quilter's worry, and one shared by others, was that the acts committed as a result of deceit or hypocrisy sullied personal and national honour because they opened up a gap between stated and actual motive and therefore, critically, between deed and word. It was the latter divergence which provoked anxiety for it rendered problematic and potentially self-alienating the reading of the travel narrative and of the national narrative. The expedition and its aftermath caused a large degree of self-questioning about the processes of identification and of reading (and here I use reading in the widest sense to include the deciphering of cultural as well as literary texts). Of course, the multiplicity of accounts made this possible, but their existence was engendered by the social conditions of the time.

Stanley's donning of the cloak of philanthropy was for Quilter and others a social presumption, so that in this view the disparity between word and deed, which invites a more general scrutiny, has a class basis. For Quilter, reassessments had to be made when Stanley moved from simple vulgar boasting to neglecting the safety of his officers when they were alive and attacking their reputation when they were dead. What was more:

> when it became a matter of public suspicion whether he had not misled the entire English public by gaining their assistance and applause for one philanthropic enterprise when he was chiefly concerned for projects commercial, political and personal . . . I think there were few of us who did not feel inclined to let our judgments go by default, so unworthy of a gentleman and an honest man did such conduct appear.[55]

It is partly a matter of style, of presentation, that bothers Quilter, but this discomfort involves a concern with social mores too. Beneath the doubts over Stanley's conduct and its record is the observation that the clothes do not fit. Noting the Relief Committee's plans to secure its share of any ivory, Quilter proclaims:

> In view of the high-toned and altogether elevating philanthropy of Mr. Stanley's expedition, as described by its leader, these little commercial touches, appropriate to a nation of shopkeepers, are inexpressibly refreshing; they bring us down, as it were from that empyrean in which so

few of us can long breathe comfortably, and supply us with an intelligible motive for, and a proper commercial view of actions and their fitting recompense, which before seemed almost too chivalrous to be profitable, and too unselfish to be real.[56]

So the costume must be appropriate. The language and presentation have to be suitable. Quilter's criticism has him accepting the commercial character of the times. It is a grudging acceptance perhaps but all the same it has him so aware of its unavoidability that his quibble is with the arch-constructedness of what he regards as a false dress. It seems, for example, that his complaint is not so much about the lack of chivalry as about the pretence that chivalry was an object of the expedition. It was an ideal which had been held up both by Stanley himself and by the public which had supported the adventure in wanting to assuage guilt over the death of Gordon. On 3 September 1889 Stanley wrote to Marston of some of the obstacles he had faced and declared with characteristic reserve that 'A Sir Perceval in search of the Holy Grail could not have met with hotter opposition',[57] while Fox-Bourne, secretary of the Aborigines Protection Society, wrote of Jameson and Jephson as having travelled as 'modern knights-errant, in search of adventures'.[58] And A. J. Wauters, Chief Editor of the *Mouvement Géographique*, Brussels, demanded:

> Who shall say that the age of knight-errantry has passed away? Other ages have had their Xenophon, Godfrey de Bouillon, Marco Polo, Colombus, Vasco, and Magellan; the nineteenth century can boast of Stanley. The race of heroes is not yet extinct.[59]

A result of the expedition was the questioning of concepts of heroism; the asking, as early modernist writers were beginning to do, what capacity for heroism existed in the contemporary world and what form it might take. Even though Quilter disliked in Stanley his brashness and immodesty, he conceded that they were in keeping with the age, a manoeuvre which allowed both acceptance and detachment at the same time:

> The records of African travel, which happily is only another name for African heroism, were pretty full before Mr. Stanley's arrival, and have been continued since by many another intrepid and self-sacrificing explorer; but the story of such achievements has never, to the best of our belief, been told in such King Cambyses' vein, nor have the explorers demanded so persistently rewards so great, or advertised their achievements in so exhaustive a manner. However, the age is one of self-advertisement, and not too fastidious a taste.[60]

Accordingly, towards the end of one of his articles, Quilter calculates

Stanley's profits from the undertaking, which he puts at £50,000, including £20,000 from Sampson Low for *In Darkest Africa*, £1,000 from *Harper's Magazine* for an article, £10,000 for a lecture series in America, and £20,000 as the added value to his reputation and journalistic work.[61] It is charged that private gain has detracted from heroism and this allegation is used to indict Stanley and save Britain's honour. The nation is justified as it morally expels the explorer who has returned to its midst. Quilter assures his readers that Stanley will have to answer at the bar of public opinion,[62] a posture that apparently re-establishes authority in the people and seeks to make something positive out of the profusion of discordant voices by lining them up to speak, listen, and pass judgement. Democracy and justice are paraded.

The same strategy is apparent in a piece written by R. Bosworth Smith who turns everything to the nation's advantage:

> In all Imperial races . . . there is an element of the wild beast. . . . It seems almost like a law of Nature that civilised men, when thrown amongst uncivilised, should assimilate themselves to their surroundings, and should catch something, and at times . . . a double measure of their ferocity and their barbarism. Great Britain is no exception to the rule. . . . as a nation, we are so self-reliant, so self-contained, so conscious of our own superiority . . . that we need to be saved from our baser, and recalled to our nobler selves, by every engine at our command.
>
> And what engine can be compared, with this end in view, with Public Opinion?[63]

The author, a classics master at Harrow, hopes that public opinion will decide against violence and for the humanitarianism of a Livingstone so that Africa can be helped forward for its own people and not for the reward of great commercial companies.

A similar appeal to the populace was made in an anonymous article in the *Contemporary Review* which, in attempting to delineate the controversy, forms a strained effort to offer the nation as a fair-minded court. This is essentially a conservative ploy as is revealed in the silly sententiousness of the following proposition: 'Now that we have seen after all our hero has feet of clay, that in all respects he is like other men, we risk being blind to the head of gold with which only the great few are endowed'.[64] The safe, anodyne line is continued throughout. Barttelot's is deemed an essentially cruel nature and Jameson is thought to have condemned himself out of his own mouth (a most unhappy turn of phrase in the circumstances), but the latter's crime is seen as probably due to the atavistic qualities of the surroundings (an influence of Darwinist and naturalistic thought which of course later has its expression in Conrad), and the former, as an individual, ingrained trait, finds

Stanley and his backers culpable only in so far as they placed Barttelot in a position of responsibility. Prevarication, mistakes, and misunderstandings are admitted but the summing-up amounts to a slap on the wrist for behaving out of character:

> We do well to hang our heads at the thought that such deeds should have been done by Englishmen; but we may find some consolation in the fact that it is because of their very unwontedness in the records of modern British enterprise that all the world is ringing with them.[65]

Meanwhile, J. Scott Keltie, Librarian to and Secretary of the Royal Geographical Society, appealed to biblical authority to justify both the militaristic character of Stanley's expedition and the leader's martial spirit:

> Stanley's God, characteristically, is the God of the fighting-men of the Old Testament, the God of Battles, who leads his chosen people on to victory against all their enemies. No wonder, then, that he invoked such supernatural aid in the dire straits in which he so frequently found himself in the oppressive gloom of the terrible forest.[66]

The supernatural aid assists the promotion of Stanley as a man who manifests qualities that will, like the return of King Arthur, symbolise and achieve a national unity. Thus Scott Keltie praises the 'heroic spirit of courage, self-denial, and devotion to duty' shown by Stanley and his companions, and expresses the hope that such virtues are as much in evidence as in Elizabethan times. This image is used quite deliberately as a political balm:

> So long as our country has men like these at her service she need fear no evil. It is this spirit which has called forth the wild enthusiasm; it is this aspect of the expedition which has appealed to the nation, which, throwing all casuistry aside, has with one voice shouted 'Well done!' Some of the results may be disappointing, but that does not at all affect the conduct of the expedition.[67]

If, in his last sentence, Keltie sounds like an early England team manager of almost any sport, the relevance of such a posture is the solace it finds in the 'how' rather than the 'what' or 'why' of the adventure. To value manner over outcome – to make manner *the* outcome – is to reaffirm a faith in appearance. In this context the appearance is the language and form in which the stories are told.

Whether he be hailed an Old Testament type or labelled a sham explorer, Stanley excited in his audience a debate about old worth that in the former view he preserved, and in the latter could not hope to match. In each case the question of heroism in the late nineteenth century is posed, and I want now to return to the idea of mass production and the culture of commerce in order to address the issue specifically in terms of individuality and authenticity.

Stanley and the Market

Marston refers to the direct effects on employment and the market of *In Darkest Africa*, but there were gains in other forms for entrepreneurs similarly profiting from the climate of controversy whilst working to efface the troublesome elements. Stanley's publishers were able to bring out before the appearance of *In Darkest Africa* a cheap edition of his letters, and offered this as being 'in compliance with the urgent desire of correspondents', one of whom they quote as having followed with much interest the course of the expedition:

> I am much mixed up with men of the working class — mechanics, lace-makers, laborers, etc.; and I am of opinion that if you could issue a *small book* of Stanley's travels and varied experiences in the rescue of Emin Pasha ... you would be conferring a boon upon 'the masses' of this country.... [sic] There is at the present time a huge craving after anything and everything relating to Central Africa, and with the strong interest created by Mr. Stanley's thrilling adventures, I'm sure a *shilling book* would be a great success.[68]

The book supported Stanley, would make money for the publishers, and was presented as a response to the wants of the working class.

Another example of enterprise associated with the commoditisation of Stanley was 'Stanley in Africa', a kind of jig saw puzzle, which was published by Dean & Son to accompany a 'toy-book'.[69] The picture captions to the puzzle read: 'Departure of Mr. Stanley at Day-break from Major Barttelot's Camp at Yambuya'; 'During this period we lost 69 men from starvation and sickness'; 'Camp fire at night, Stanley talking with his men'; 'Female Water Carriers from Emin Pasha's Camp'; 'Fight with Mazambari's people'; 'Reception of Mr. H. M. Stanley on board H.M.S. Turquoise'; 'Meeting of Stanley and Emin Pasha at Kalvation on Lake Albert, Nyanza'. The captions do not include 'Mr. Jameson witnessing a cannibalistic murder'; 'Major Barttelot shot dead' or 'Emin Pasha falling from the window'. The choice of scenes makes possible the restructuring of the consumer's image of the expedition, whilst the workings of the puzzle literally restructure the narratives involved.

Reconstruction in the interest of politics and commerce is witnessed in the impact of the expedition on another sphere, that of the tradition of songs and music on an imperial heroic theme. There was, for instance, 'Stanley's Rescue' by J. Adelberg Lawson, containing headings such as 'leaving home and friends to rescue Emin Pasha', 'On the river',

'Pushing through the gloomy forest' and 'Triumphant meeting of Stanley and Emin Pasha'; as well as 'The Victor's Return' with words by Thomas Ward and music by Edward Slater, which included the lines:

On, Stanley, on! were the words of yore:
On, Stanley, on, let them ring once more.[70]

The songs and the jig saw are an indication of the absorption of manufactured images of the expedition into popular culture, an ideological process complementing the simultaneous movement into the market economy. Perhaps the interrelatedness of these spheres is best exemplified by the advertising of brand-name products that followed the expedition. John MacKenzie notes that 'Leibig's Extract of Meat Company seized upon the Emin Pasha expedition . . . issuing posters and adverts of members of the relief party revived by its product'.[71] And I have discussed in my earlier chapter on food and eating the United Kingdom Tea Company's advert showing Stanley and Emin supping its product.

The power of advertisements to provide narratives that will offer a balm is poignantly illustrated in Herbert Ward's recollection of Christmas at Yambuya. Against the backdrop of deaths from hunger and disease, and of waiting helplessly for porters from Tippu-Tib as the year goes out, the men look through old scraps of newspapers. Ward exclaims: 'What a fund of material for imagination and suggestion the advertisement column supplied us with!'[72] They wonder about the maid advertising for a post, the widow wanting a partner (is she young and with a taste for African adventurers?), the quack-medicine vendor, and the agony column advertisement placed by Regie. They wonder if Regie is 'still waiting outside St. James's Park Station for the faithless Lil?'.[73] Most interestingly, however, Ward communicates a suspicion of Regie's intentions that complements the very questions that were being asked (and would yet be asked) by many about the correspondence of language to truth:

What a wealth of love was his! Was it, though? The young man seemed to be pretty well up in phrasing his messages. There was the suggestion of an old master about his literary workmanship. How often had he written *via* the agony column to another Lil before? Faithless Regie! And Lil? Did she frequently use the St. James's Park Station as a meeting-place?[74]

This scepticism is unconvincingly relieved by an appeal to the men to forget their troubles. The identity of the man who is to provide the entertainment that will do the job is very revealing. He is the expedition's class-equivalent to Regie: 'To-day let us eat, drink, and be merry, for we know not what to-morrow may bring. Let us ask Bonny for a song'.[75]

Advertisements depend upon the commoditisation process and are the arena in which language and commerce are drawn together. They now furnish their own stories which can be a welcome distraction from the problems and complexities of one's true situation. They romanticise and stabilise their subjects, and so are as welcome to the troubled society as they are to Ward at Yambuya.

More closely bound up with the question of technology and power is the symbiotic relationship between the expedition and its medical suppliers, Burroughs & Wellcome. Each endorses the other, testifying to its efficacy in overcoming the attacks and obstructions of nature. Stanley wrote to Wellcome on 19 January 1890:

> We have been all delighted with your medicines and Dr. Parke is of opinion that we are more indebted to your medicines than to anything else for our preservation from climatic influences, this may however be due to Parke's modesty. Parke's skill combined with your medicines may probably explain the wonderful immunity we have enjoyed.[76]

A few days earlier Wellcome had assured Stanley 'We have hung unbounded confidence on your invincible character and unlimited resources and experience'.[77]

The more public exchange of confidence can, for the present purposes, be viewed straightforwardly as the introduction of commodity by brand-name into the narrative of exploration and the appearance of the discourse of exploration within that of advertising. At the end of Marston's book, for example, there is an advert for Burroughs & Wellcome's 'Tabloids', citing Stanley's approval of them in *In Darkest Africa*. The relevant passage from the book reads:

> Messrs. Burroughs, Wellcome & Co., of Snow Hill Buildings, London, the well-known chemists, furnished gratis nine beautiful chests replete with every medicament necessary to combat the endemic diseases peculiar to Africa. Every drug was in tabloids mixed with quick solvents, every compartment was well stocked with essentials for the doctor and surgeon. Nothing was omitted, and we all owe a deep debt of gratitude to these gentlemen.[78]

On the same pages Stanley also praises Edgington's tents, Fortnum & Mason's provisions and the Maxim Automatic Gun. Of course the mention of specific articles isn't new in these narratives – Baker, for example, mentions Bryant & May, and Crosse & Blackwell, as well as Reilly's guns[79] – but the Emin Pasha Relief Expedition does certainly seem to consolidate the principal features of this relationship. The listing of such products by name further imbues the narratives with the characteristics of the culture from which the explorer is journeying and gives him a highly visible commercial support, whilst the incorporation into the market economy and popular consciousness of figures and tropes from the expedition helps reinforce the connection between the adventurers and the public.

The crucial element of the adverts is the recognition that both the product they advertise and the traveller who has used them have returned tried, tested, and successful. Underlying the mutually supportive relationship is the working of the ideology to which they subscribe and which they help carry. Thus Parke, the expedition's medical officer, published in his narrative the following commendation in describing his administrations:

> These medicines are all contained in Burroughs & Welcome's [sic] tabloids, which I have found extremely satisfactory; as they are very soluble, while they occupy very little space, and have never lost their strength. I have never used any therapeutic preparations at all so convenient or so reliable. The medical departments of the services should abandon the present clumsy and inconvenient system of carrying fluids, pills, powders, &c., and adopt this mode of administering medicines: as it is safer, the dose is more reliable, and transport so much easier – they occupy less than quarter the space and weight; also one medical officer could attend to four times the number of patients.[80]

The saving in space and labour, which capitalism quantifies, should, then, recommend the tabloids to the services, and so we see quite clearly science in the aid of imperialism.

A wonderfully apt illustration of the process of validation may be seen in the case of Wellcome's medicine chests. The company's catalogue lists The 'Livingstone' Medicine Chest, The 'Congo' Medicine Chest (as supplied to Stanley, missionaries, and other travellers), and, in 1895, The 'Stevens' Raw Hide Medicine Chest. This could be seen as a direct attempt to attach an experiential reference to the article. Additional use of the travellers to authenticate and help market the items comes with the inclusion in the catalogue of extracts from their narratives. The catalogue for June 1895 has on its inside front cover passages from Stanley's In Darkest Africa and The Founding of the Congo Free State, as well as Parke's book, and on the inside back cover a similar recommendation of Burroughs & Wellcome's products from Stevens's Scouting for Stanley in East Africa.[81] The ideological importance of these juxtapositions lies in the metonymic use of the specific brandname for the larger culture.

The crisis of authority witnessed in the aftermath of the expedition saw an attempted resolution by the vesting of power and the effacing or containment of differences in commodities.

Fredric Jameson has expressed an anxiety that we should see mass culture:

> not as empty distraction or 'mere' false consciousness, but rather as a transformational work on social and political anxieties and fantasies which must then have some effective presence in the mass cultural text in order subsequently to be 'managed' or repressed. . . . Both modernism and mass culture entertain relations of repression with the fundamental social anxieties and concerns, hopes and blind spots, ideological antinomies and fantasies of disaster, which are their raw material; only where modernism tends to handle this material by producing compensatory structures of various kinds, mass culture represses them by the narrative construction of imaginary resolutions and by the projection of an optical illusion of social harmony.[82]

This is precisely what happens with the artefacts of the Emin Pasha Relief Expedition. The social and political tensions are present in the texts and I have shown some of them. Their presence, however, has them managed. One may depart from Jameson slightly and say that they are managed in the literature by a deceptive, flattering appeal to the reader to manage them by judging and therefore apparently resolving them, but certainly in the commodification of the experience – in the advertisements, the games and puzzles, the shows, and within some of the individual texts – there are both imaginary resolutions and optical illusions of social harmony.

The textual locus of this commodified resolution is apparent in comments made by L. Monteith Fotheringham, an agent of the African Lakes Company, whose book of adventure was published in 1891. In his first remarks we see how Africa, the object, has undergone literary commodification in a way that encourages the pretence that differences of social class no longer matter. The market (for literature on Africa) works to smoothe over class divisions:

> There is no meeting the demand for literature on what is now no longer – geographically speaking – 'the dark continent.' Nearly every man who goes on a hunting expedition to the interior, must, on his return to civilization, publish an account of his travels or deliver a lecture on his experiences. In this, the least-known simply imitates the most cele-brated.[83]

Stanley's celebrated work is seen to have stimulated the demand. Fotheringham does not mention the controversy nor the debates between the officers but instead supplies a picture of an expanding market which offers opportunities to the most humble of travellers, bestowing upon them visibility and audibility. What is more, Fotheringham unwittingly provides evidence that the referent has become lost; that what is looked for is the mass reproduction or repetition of the commodified object. Thus Fotheringham comments that not to have read *In Darkest Africa* is to:

> confess yourself not in touch with the times. Immediately a whole host of minor books is announced, so that by the end of the year every subscriber to a lending library ought to be as well acquainted with an African negro as with his next-door neighbour. On that account I make no apology for adding my quota.[84]

Notes

1 Quoted in Anthony Fothergill, *Heart of Darkness* (Milton Keynes: Open University Press, 1989), p. 39.
2 De Winton to Blackwood, 7 May 1889, Blackwood Papers 4531, National Library of Scotland. (Hereafter BP.) Werner's solicitor, Richard Preston, wrote to de Winton defending his client's forthcoming title: Richard Preston to de Winton, 9 May 1889. Mackinnon Papers, Box 84, File 10, School of Oriental and African Studies, London. (Hereafter MP.) Werner's book was published as *A Visit to Stanley's Rear Guard at Major Barttelot's Camp on the Aruwimi with an Account of River Life on the Congo* (Edinburgh: Blackwood, 1891).
3 De Winton to Richard Preston, 11 May 1889, BP 4531.
4 See MP, Box 93, File 53.
5 Lt. Col. Grant to Emin Pasha Relief Committee, 31 March 1887, MP, Box 83, File 3.
6 Edwin Arnold to Mackinnon, 24 December 1888, MP, Box 83, File 8. Arnold was editor of the *Daily Telegraph*.
7 Buckle to de Winton, 2 April 1889, MP, Box 83, File 9.
8 MP, Box 83, File 9.
9 Charles A. Cooper to de Winton, 2 April 1889. MP, Box 84, File 10.
10 MP, Box 84, File 10. Alexander L. Bruce, of the Scottish Geographical Society, had subscribed to the Emin Relief Fund and was a friend of Stanley's. He was also Livingstone's son-in-law.
11 MP, Box 84, File 10.
12 Edwin Arnold to de Winton, 21 May 1889, MP, Box 84, File 10.
13 MP, Box 84, File 10.
14 MP, Box 84, File 11.
15 Edward Lloyd to Mackinnon, 25 November 1889, MP, Box 84, File 11.
16 Mackinnon to McDermott, 18 December 1889. MP, Box 84, File 11.
17 Letters written by Stanley netted the Committee £2,200. See MP, Box 87.
18 Edmund Gosse to Lord Wolseley, 9 April 1889. The letter was sent and recommended to Sir Francis de Winton by Wolseley the next day. MP, Box 84, File 10.
19 Mackinnon to de Winton, 6 July 1888, MP, Box 83, File 6.
20 De Winton to A. E. Kinnear, 23 March 1888, MP, Box 86, File 25; recommendation by Harwood & Stephenson, solicitors, to de Winton, Box 84, File 10.
21 *Daily Telegraph*, 10 November 1890. The files on the Emin Pasha Relief Expedition held at the Royal Geographical Society include newspaper cuttings on the expedition. See volumes I, IV, and V. I am grateful to the RGS for allowing me to consult these.
22 *Daily Telegraph*, 10 November, 1890.
23 For a discussion of this role see Tim Youngs, '"My footsteps on these pages": the

inscription of self and "race" in H. M. Stanley's *How I Found Livingstone'*, *Prose Studies* 13, 2 (September 1990), 230–49. For another man's contribution to the image of Livingstone see Dorothy O. Helly, *Livingstone's Legacy: Horace Waller and Victorian Mythmaking* (Athens, Ohio: Ohio University Press, 1987).

24 Quoted from a cutting in the Mackinnon Papers, Box 92, File 52. The interview was dated 29 October [1890?].

    See also E. Belfort Bax's letter in the *Star* for 2 October 1888: 'Every one that has gone into the question in the least knows well enough that the whole business of Stanley, Emin and Co. is being machined by a ring of capitalists greedy for cheap labor, cheap ivory, and markets in which to shoot cheap home-made goods'.

25 *The Times*, 8 November, 1890.

26 *The Times*, 10 November 1890.

27 A good example of this positioning is found in his comments on the alleged cannibalism: 'The statement that Mr. Jameson merely happened upon the feast of the cannibals, and drew nearly all of the sketches from the description of the natives, could hardly have been put forward by one acquainted with the Central African tribes. Cannibalism with them is not an habitual practice. When they fight they eat their dead enemies, but it is not their custom to kill little girls and eat them. Therefore it could have been only by some special inducement, or for some particular reason, that this act of cannibalism which Mr. Jameson witnessed was perpetrated'. *The Times*, 14 November 1890.

28 *The Times*, 10 November 1890.

29 On this and other aspects of the press at this time, see John Stokes, *In the Nineties* (New York: Harvester Wheatsheaf, 1989). Also see, especially for the connection between the press and exploration, Beau Riffenburgh, *The Myth of the Explorer: The Press, Sensationalism, and Geographical Discovery* (London: Belhaven Press, 1993). Riffenburgh's focus is mainly on the reporting of polar expeditions.

30 *The Times*, 24 December 1890.

31 The *Standard*, 14 September 1888; my emphasis.

32 The *Spectator*, 15 November 1890.

33 'Topics of the day; the African horrors', The *Spectator*, 15 November 1890.

34 The *New York Herald*, 16 November 1890.

35 *Liverpool Post*, 10 December 1890.

36 *Daily Graphic*, 7 November 1890.

37 The *Observer*, November 1890. Precise date not known; taken from a cutting in the Emin Pasha Relief Expedition files at the Royal Geographical Society, vol. V.

38 *Saturday Review*, 8 February 1891.

39 The *National Observer*, 22 November 1890.

40 A. E. Rodway, 'The last phase', in *The Pelican Guide to English Literature*, vol. 6: *From Dickens to Hardy* (Harmondsworth: Penguin Books, 1958), pp. 389; 401. Henley's anthology *Lyra Heroica*, published in 1891, was reprinted nine times up to 1908, by which time it had sold fifty-two thousand copies. Aiming, in Henley's own words, 'to set forth, as only art can, the beauty and the joy of living, the beauty and the blessedness of death, the glory of battle and adventure, the nobility of devotion, the dignity of resistance, the sacred quality of patriotism', its themes have been summarised by Jeffrey Richards as 'sacrifice, comradeship, heroism and death'. See Jeffrey Richards, 'Popular imperialism and the image of the army in juvenile literature', in *Popular Imperialism and the Military, 1850–1950*, ed. John M. MacKenzie (Manchester: Manchester University Press, 1992), p. 82, which also includes the above words from Henley.

41 From Sir Arthur Quiller-Couch, ed., *The Oxford Book of English Verse 1250–1918* new edition (Oxford: Oxford University Press, 1939).

42 The *Daily News*, 7 November 1890.

43 *Rare Bits*, 15 November 1890.

44 *John Bull*, 22 November 1890.

45 For a discussion of the image of John Bull before this period see Jeannine Surel, 'John Bull', in *Patriotism: The Making and Unmaking of British National Identity*, vol. III *National Fictions*, ed. Raphael Samuel (London: Routledge, 1989), pp. 3–25.

46 The *Agnostic Journal*, 20 December 1890.

47 *Truth*, 25 October 1888.

48 Harry Quilter, 'Mr. H. M. Stanley as leader and comrade', *Universal Review* 8, 31 (1890), 314.

49 Walter George Barttelot, ed., *The Life of Edmund Musgrave Barttelot*, 3rd ed. (London: Richard Bentley & Son, 1890), p. 8.

50 Mrs J. S. Jameson, ed., *Story of the Rear Column of the Emin Pasha Relief Expedition by the late James S. Jameson, Naturalist to the Expedition* (London: R. H. Porter, 1890), p. xxiii.

51 Quilter, 'An African bubble! and how it was blown', *Universal Review* 8, 32 (1890), 473.

52 Quilter, 'The African bubble!', 471.

53 Quoted in Gould, *In Limbo*, p. 28.

54 Quilter, 'The African bubble!', 472.

55 Quilter, 'Mr. H. M. Stanley', 315.

56 Quilter, 'Mr. H. M. Stanley', 333.

57 Quoted in Marston, *After Work*, 233.

58 H. R. Fox-Bourne, *The Other Side of the Emin Pasha Relief Expedition* (London: Chatto & Windus, 1891), p. 46.

59 A. J. Wauters, *Stanley's Emin Pasha Expedition* (London: John C. Nimmo, 1890), p. 312.

60 Quilter, 'Mr. H. M. Stanley', 314.

61 Quilter, 'An African bubble!', 480–1.

62 Quilter, 'Mr. H. M. Stanley', 365.

63 R. Bosworth Smith, 'Englishmen in Africa', *Contemporary Review* 59 (1891), 73–4. Smith had taught at Harrow since 1864. His publications included lectures on *Mohammed and Mohammedism* (1874), a biography of Lord Lawrence (1883), and letters to *The Times* in which he urged the permanent occupation of the Sudan by England (13 February 1885) and protested against the threat of evacuating Uganda which was not carried out (1892). This information is to be found in the *Dictionary of National Biography Supplement 1901–1911* (Oxford: Oxford University Press, 1920). Reginald Bosworth Smith's emphasis is very much on a paternalistic idea of 'helping' Africa 'forward'. His article on 'Englishmen in Africa' also evokes the spirit of Gordon as a (supposed) contrast to men like Jameson and Barttelot, and asks whether 'Africa is to be "exploited" by great commercial companies for their own benefit, or whether she is to be helped forward – Africa for the Africans – to a natural development of her own, redolent alike of the people and the soil' (p. 76).

64 Anonymous, 'Mr. Stanley and the rear column', *Contemporary Review* 58 (1890), 786.

65 Anonymous, 'Mr. Stanley and the rear column', 795.

66 J. Scott Keltie, 'Mr. Stanley's Expedition: its conduct and results', *Fortnightly Review* New Series 48 (July–December 1890), 79.

67 Keltie, 'Mr. Stanley's expedition', 76.

68 J. Scott Keltie, ed., *The Story of Emin's Rescue as Told in Stanley's Letters* (New York: Harper & Bros., 1890; reprint ed., New York: Negro Universities Press, 1969), p. 3.

69 'Stanley in Africa', Dean & Son, *c.* 1890. I am grateful to Caroline Goodfellow of the Bethnal Green Museum of Childhood for supplying me with information on this puzzle.

70 The information on these songs is taken from 'Variations on an imperial theme', *Royal Commonwealth Society Library Notes* New Series no. 100, (April 1965), p. 1.

71 John M. MacKenzie, *Propaganda and Empire: The Manipulation of British Public Opinion, 1880–1960* (Manchester: Manchester University Press, 1984), p. 26.

72 Herbert Ward, *My Life with Stanley's Rear Guard* (London: Chatto & Windus, 1891), p. 57.

73 Ward, *My Life*, pp. 57–8.

74 Ward, *My Life*, p. 58.

75 Ward, *My Life*, p. 58.

76 H. M. Stanley to Wellcome, 19 January 1890. Wellcome Foundation Archives. I am grateful to the Wellcome Foundation for granting me access to the Henry Wellcome Personal Papers in their Contemporary Medical Archives Centre.

77 Wellcome to Stanley, 10 January 1890. Wellcome Foundation Archives. I am grateful to the Trustee of the Wellcome Trust for allowing me to quote from this letter.

78 Stanley, *In Darkest Africa or the Quest Rescue, and Retreat of Emin Governor of Equatoria*, new edition (London: Sampson Low, Marston & Company, [1890] 1893), pp. 24–5.

79 Sir Samuel White Baker, *Ismailia: A Narrative of the Expedition to Central Africa for the Suppression of the Slave Trade Organized by Ismail, Khedive of Egypt*, 2 vols (London: Macmillan & Co., 1874), I, 533–4, and *The Nile Tributaries of Abyssinia and the Sword Hunters of the Hamran Arabs* (London: Macmillan, [1867] 1907), p. 199.

80 Thomas Heazle Parke, *My Personal Experiences in Equatorial Africa as Medical Officer of the Emin Pasha Relief Expedition* (London: Sampson Low, Marston & Company Limited, 1891), p. 202.

81 Wellcome Group Archives, London.

82 Fredric Jameson, 'Reification and Utopia in mass culture', *Social Text* 1 (winter 1979), 141.

83 L. Monteith Fotheringham, *Adventures in Nyassaland: A Two Years' Struggle with Arab Slave-Dealers in Central Africa* (London: Sampson Low, Marston, Searle & Rivington, 1891), p. 1.

84 L. Monteith Fotheringham, *Adventures in Nyassaland*, p. 2.

CHAPTER SIX

Vaporising Bula Matari:
Conrad's *Heart of Darkness*

Nine years after the controversy of the Emin Pasha Relief Expedition and nine years after Conrad's own journey to the Congo,[1] *Heart of Darkness* was published. This novella has been described as 'the most over-interpreted literary text of the last hundred years',[2] so a little more interpretation surely can't do much harm.

For the benefit of those of my readers who are unfamiliar with Conrad's story, the tale is told by an anonymous framing narrator who is one of a small number of men (the Accountant, the Lawyer, Charlie Marlow, and the Director of Companies, who is their host and captain) on board the *Nellie* on the River Thames. Marlow, a seaman, begins telling them of the adventure which takes up, with only very brief interruptions, the rest of the book. He recounts how hope of gaining work as a steamboat captain on the (unnamed) River Congo led him to an interview with a continental company in Brussels (named only as the 'sepulchral city'), whose professions of philanthropy he does not believe. Once in Africa he hears of the reputation of Kurtz, a first-class agent and chief of the Inner Station, who has been sending back from his station as much ivory as all the other agents put together. His success has embittered some of the Company's other employees, and Marlow recoils from the jealous reactions he encounters at the Central Station. When he arrives at the Central Station, after a two-hundred-mile march, Marlow finds his steamer has sunk in mysterious circumstances, causing a three months' wait. After repairs to the boat, Marlow travels towards the Inner Station with the General Manager of the Central Station who has begun to express concern about Kurtz's well-being. During the trip, Marlow admires the restraint of his cannibal crew. When he finally reaches Kurtz, after first meeting a disciple of his, whom he describes (because of his appearance) as a harlequin, Marlow gives us the picture of a European gone native. There is talk of Kurtz's having participated in unspeakable midnight rites, there are heads on poles around his compound, and we are left with the impression that he may have taken as a mistress an African woman who is described as savage and superb, wild-eyed and magnificent. It seems evident that Kurtz has exploited the Africans' rituals and (as Marlow's audience would see it) their superstitions in order to gain a position of power and influence over them. Marlow makes much of the fact that, away from civilisation and the restraining influence of neighbours and public opinion, there has been nothing to hold back Kurtz's desires.

Marlow intercepts the ailing Kurtz who is crawling back to the forest and forces him instead to come to the boat as the first stage of a journey back to civilisation. But Kurtz dies on the boat, his last words being 'The horror! The horror!'. Once back in Europe, Marlow, who visits Kurtz's fiancée, named only as the Intended, feels under an emotional pressure not to disillusion her. Instead of revealing the truth of Kurtz's conduct and character, Marlow (who has already told his listeners of his detestation of lying) lies to her and says that her fiancé's last words were her name. It is a lie which not only shields the civilised world from the essential truth of its uneradicated darkness, but which seems to identify the ignorance of that civilised world with the feminine. It is a lie which also marks the ultimate complicity of the initially sceptical and cynical Marlow with the illusions of civilisation.

It is difficult to give any summary of this densely symbolic work without also giving an interpretation and without omitting much of importance (particularly as how the action is narrated is as significant as what is narrated). I have nevertheless tried in this description of the plot (knowing I have left out some important matters) to indicate the basis of the following discussion, in which further details are also included.

A number of critics have, rightly in my view, suggested Stanley as one of the models for Kurtz. In an essay refreshingly attentive to the historical context, Molly Mahood has argued that Kurtz's godfathers include not only Stanley but also Jameson, Barttelot, and Charles Stokes.[3] In particular, she sees parallels between Kurtz's Intended, Barttelot's fiancée, and Jameson's wife, the latter of whom journeyed to Zanzibar in a futile effort to obtain information she hoped would clear her husband's name. The similarities would seem too close to put aside. Marlow's lie to the Intended (or what we take to be his lie, since we have only his and the framing narrator's version of events) preserves an illusion of Kurtz in a way that recalls the naive kind of belief in the virtue of the English gentleman which was shattered by the revelations of Jameson's and Barttelot's behaviour on the Emin Pasha expedition. For Ethel Jameson, especially, the public effort to maintain an unbroken faith in her husband's rectitude was so immense that our awareness of this makes us feel the awful weight of Marlow's dilemma. Our knowledge of the establishment's pained questioning of the rear guard officers' conduct makes us conscious that Marlow's lie is a social and a national one, while Marlow's description of Kurtz's hollow soul, '"avid of lying fame, and of sham distinction, of all the appearances of success and power"',[4] strikes deep into the sense of social and national crisis I have discussed in my previous two chapters. The language and sentiments match up with those applied to Stanley after the Emin Pasha Relief Expedition.

Most literary critics, however, seem ignorant of the Emin Pasha expedition and of its consequences. Norman Sherry, for example, whose work is seen as one of the principal sources for Conrad in the Congo, has five lines on the Emin Pasha Relief Expedition, noting simply that the expedition once more put Stanley and Africa in 'the public mind' and that in summer 1889 'news of his expedition continued to be published in the press'.[5] It is remiss of Sherry not to at least refer to the controversy which continued throughout 1890. This background is often ignored by critics who wish to concentrate on promoting the status of *Heart of Darkness* as an early modernist work and by others who simply proffer it as an illustration of nineteenth-century views of Africa. Despite the vast body of criticism on *Heart of Darkness* relatively few commentaries have considered in detail either its roots in the 1890s or its relationship to the travel narratives on which it draws. On the other hand, historians and biographers who do make a connection between the Emin Pasha Relief Expedition and *Heart of Darkness* do so on the basis of factual precedents for Kurtz. John Bierman, for example, takes seven lines to suggest Jameson as a model for Kurtz but, typically, pays no attention to literary structures or the broader social context.[6]

There is no question but that the scandal of the Emin Pasha Relief Expedition and the issues raised by it permeate *Heart of Darkness*. There is no doubting, as Mahood correctly observes, that it is Stanley who is meant when Conrad has Marlow refer to the man who '"desired to have kings meet him at railway-stations on his return from some ghastly Nowhere, where he intended to accomplish great things"' (p. 67). But there is also a limit to the usefulness of tracing the progenitors of literary characters. While Ian Watt sensibly detects the presence of Leopold and Stanley behind Kurtz, his brief mention of possible models for Kurtz, for example, includes a paragraph on Emin Pasha, another on Barttelot, and a footnote on Jameson in which he refers (citing Roger Jones's book on the expedition) to allegations 'falsely' made that he had been involved in the cannibalistic killing of a young girl.[7] An emphasis on biographical sources can be a distraction from the socio-cultural arena which is so important to an understanding of a text like Conrad's (or of any text, for that matter). After all, '"All Europe contributed to the making of Kurtz"' (p. 50), and so we must be alert to a range of influences. Brantlinger also seems to share this view, declaring that '*All of the white officers in charge of Leopold's empire were in essence Kurtzes*',[8] but even this statement is unnecessarily selective, once more ignoring the pervasive unease closer to home.

Held up by some as revealing profound moral truths about the human condition, Conrad's story has been famously attacked by Chinua Achebe who denounced the author as a 'thoroughgoing racist',[9] and complained about the use of:

> Africa as setting and backdrop which eliminates the African as human factor. Africa as a metaphysical battlefield devoid of all recognizable humanity, into which the wandering European enters at his peril.[10]

Achebe's point is that Africa is continually used in a negative way as the touchstone by which European identity is confirmed. Achebe is right in this, of course, and the process he identifies has been the subject of the present book.

But the extent to which Conrad challenges prevailing stereotypes is often overlooked. I have to admit that from Achebe's end the challenge may not seem particularly impressive, and I believe he is quite justified in taking the stance he did: a stance, which, it seems to me, was dictated as much by the way academics in America and Europe have talked of *Heart of Darkness* as by the novella itself.[11]

The critical line usually taken on *Heart of Darkness* is that Conrad attacks the excesses and greed of the new imperialism, and questions its moral basis, while having no real alternative to offer and is himself implicated in some of the racial attitudes which fed it. Many readers feel that Conrad is caught in a double-bind and ends up reinforcing the very images which lie behind the views he seems to question, but from which he cannot free himself. Anthony Fothergill has given a concise expression of such a reading:

> That 'civilised' behaviour may be just a veneer covering aggressive, passionate, incomprehensible energies was a fear too current to be comfortably dismissed. But in order to articulate it, Conrad needed to construct the black as an objectification of what it was they [white Europeans] were anxious about. Thus, both a radical critical and a racist reactionary force are engaged in this use of the stereotypical representation of the African Other, a representation which simultaneously confirms while undercutting the European cultural myth of the black as a contemporary ancestor.[12]

A similar line, voiced more tersely, is held by Brantlinger, who pronounces that '*Heart of Darkness* offers a powerful critique of at least some manifestations of imperialism and racism as it simultaneously presents that critique in ways that can be characterized only as imperialist and racist'.[13]

I shall return to this idea in a moment, but before I do so it is worth remembering that the ambiguities and paradoxes of *Heart of Darkness* are usually taken to be features characteristic of an early modernist text. In brief, these ambiguities include the title itself (does it refer to a dark heart or to the heart, the centre, of a darkness?), the instability of language, the complex and distancing layers of narrative, and the sense of futility or degeneracy in the journey, which is also a voyage within. Conrad's language encourages a range of readings (political, cultural, psychological, mythical)[14] but it can be taken as further stereotyping Africa and its people by relying on familiar images to question familiar attitudes. I shall be arguing that *Heart of Darkness* loses a good deal of its significance if we react to these ingredients principally from the standpoint of artistic modernism, and that they ought instead to be judged according to the preconceptions of the *fin de siècle* and the generic conventions of the African travel narrative (which, on one level, is what the tale presents itself as being).

The elements I have just listed and the multilayered quality of the text, contributing to its symbolic richness, have led many critics to pounce on the framing narrator's comments on Marlow's storytelling, just as I am about to do:

> The yarns of seamen have a direct simplicity, the whole meaning of which lies within the shell of a cracked nut. But Marlow was not typical (if his propensity to spin yarns be excepted) and to him the meaning of an episode was not inside like a kernel but outside, enveloping the tale which brought it out only as a glow brings out a haze, in the likeness of one of these misty halos that sometimes are made visible by the spectral illumination of moonshine. (p. 9)

This hints at a different way of telling a story and accounts for the importance of outline, of impressions, and for the lack of clarity in the tale. It asks us to look around, outside, at the edges. The narrator's remarks have formed the basis of many critical interpretations of the story. Among the most celebrated is Ian Watt's suggestion that Marlow's storytelling is symbolist and impressionist:

> the abstract geometry of the metaphor is symbolist because the meaning of the story, represented by the shell of the nut or the haze around the glow, is larger than its narrative vehicle, the kernel or the glow; but the sensory quality of the metaphor, the mist and haze, is essentially impressionist.[15]

Watt's remarks are characteristic of the concern of many literary critics with Conrad's artistic techniques. The trouble with such approaches, however much they have to offer, is that they drag the tale away from the genre to which it most closely belongs. And if one fails to see that, one misses what is most interesting in the story. There is not much point in grubbing around for Kurtz's human antecedents if one does not also compare the way his story is told with the way theirs was.

Since, therefore, we are told that to Marlow the meaning of an episode lay not inside the kernel but outside, I prefer to contrast his narrative with chapter thirty-eight of Stanley's *The Congo and the Founding of its Free State*. This chapter is titled 'The Kernel of the Argument' (a heading which appears with repetitive force in the margin at the top of each page), and constitutes a paean to the commercial potential of the Congo, as indeed does the whole two-volume work.

First, however, the entire book strikes one rightaway for its sober title, its emphasis on duty and effort (which is evident in the subtitle 'A Story of Work and Exploration' and throughout), and for demonstrating clearly and beyond refute the links between capitalism and image-formation. Early in the work, which is dedicated to Leopold and those who helped Stanley, the author asserts: 'The charge of Quixotism, being directed against my mission, deterred many noble men in Manchester from studying the question of new markets, and deepened unjustly their prejudices against Africa and African projects'.[16] The implied connection here between commercial opportunity and positive views of the country is quickly made more explicit as Stanley goes on. He figures himself as an energetic promoter of commerce whose activities and their written record should serve to make Africa attractive to manufacturers and traders.

The Congo and the Founding of its Free State reads like a tonic against enervation. It hums with energy, and Stanley's vigour is at its hub. Action is held up as morally and physically beneficial, to both the individual and the community. The book is a monument to the power of capital, with the narrator embodying those forces. Earlier in the century, Marx and Engels wrote of how:

> The bourgeoisie, during its rule of scarce one hundred years, has created more massive and more colossal productive forces than have all preceding generations together. Subjection of nature's forces to man, machinery, application of chemistry to industry and agriculture, steam-navigation, railways, electric telegraphs, clearing of whole continents for cultivation, canalisation of rivers, whole populations conjured out of the ground – what earlier century had even a presentiment that such productive forces slumbered in the lap of social history?[17]

Subjection of nature's forces to 'man' is probably the principal motif of Stanley's text, and we find an example in his account of the construction

Figure 8 First house built by Stanley, showing railway material.
Photographed by Moore in the 1880s

of his garden at Vivi, in the course of which he refers to his now famous
nickname:

> It is for this work of pulverisation of rock that the Vivi chiefs, wonderingly
> looking on while I taught my men how to wield a sledge-hammer
> effectively, bestowed on me the title of Bula Matari – Breaker of Rocks –
> with which, from the sea to Stanley Falls, all natives of the Congo are now
> so familiar.[18]

Stanley seems proud of his African name, and when he makes a
request for some land near Kintamo or somewhere near the river where
his boats can have safe passage, he reports the local chief, Makoko, who
has heard the name and of the man's deeds and is in awe of him, as
replying in the affirmative. The reasons Stanley gives for his doing so
furnish another example of the role of commodities in the expansion of
capitalism, and we are back to beads again:

> 'I want to see plenty of white men here. I have many things given me long
> ago from the white men's land, and I have often wished to see those who

could make such wonderful things. I am told you people make all the cloth, the beads, the guns, the powder, plates, and glasses. Ah! you must be great and good people. Be easy in your mind. You shall build in Kintamo.'[19]

It is worth comparing this self-serving imperialist ventriloquism practised by Stanley, whose bestowal of human language upon the Africans is designed to justify an exploitative presence in the Congo, with Conrad's portrayals of blacks, whose words '"resembled no sounds of human language"' and whose murmurs are like '"the responses of some satanic litany"' (p. 66). The latter are offensive and racist, of that there can be no doubt, but when we read back into the texts to which Conrad and his contemporaries had access, then the voicelessness of Conrad's Africans, about which Achebe has quite properly complained, can take on a different significance. To withhold a human voice from Africans isn't any better than making them speak on one's own terms, but it is too easy to mistake Conrad's representations of Africa and its people for typical late-nineteenth-century depictions. In fact Conrad's figures are quite different from those found in many travel narratives – and, I think, deliberately so. I shall develop this argument below, but it will do for now to give as an illustration of Conrad's potential subversiveness the picture of the railway in *Heart of Darkness*. This railway, completely unlike the one repeatedly called for by the bullish Stanley, seems to be going nowhere. Its condition symbolises the lack of purpose and loss of direction of Europe in Africa, and stands too for the debilitating effects of the country on westerners. Marlow sees:

'an undersized railway-truck lying there on its back with its wheels in the air. One was off. The thing looked as dead as the carcass of some animal. I came upon more pieces of decaying machinery, a stack of rusty rails. To the left a clump of trees made a shady spot where dark things seemed to stir feebly. I blinked, the path was steep. A horn tooted to the right and I saw the black people run. A heavy and dull detonation shook the ground, a puff of smoke came out of the cliff, and that was all. No change appeared on the face of the rock. They were building a railway. The cliff was not in the way or anything, but this objectless blasting was all the work going on.' (p. 19)

On one plane, this scene perpetuates the idea of Africa as a hostile environment against which one proves one's manhood in the service of capitalism, but on another level, the ineffectiveness of this blasting makes a mockery of Stanley as Bula Matari and shows the forces of capitalism unable to make an impression on nature. Conrad undermines the confidence with which the agents of capitalism assume their power to make use of the land.

[189]

Figure 9 Congo railway material photographed by Moore in the 1880s

Stanley admits quite openly that 'It is especially with a view to rouse the spirit of trade that I dilate upon the advantages possessed by the Congo basin', but he warns against the introduction of what he calls the 'pauper immigrant' since 'European pauperism planted among [the Africans] would soon degenerate to the level of aboriginal degradation'. It's worth noting here that Marlow has heard that Kurtz may have had as a reason for going to Africa his future in-laws' disapproval of his financial standing: '"And indeed I don't know whether he hadn't been a pauper all his life. He had given me some reason to infer that it was his impatience of comparative poverty that drove him out there"' (p. 74). The man who is needed, Stanley goes on, is the one who receives from the 'native' the raw produce of the region in exchange for the finished product; 'the European middleman who has his home in Europe but has his heart in Africa is the man who is wanted'.[20]

In chapter thirty-eight, where he proffers the kernel of his argument, Stanley answers the question he rhetorically poses to himself from the 'clever practical people of Manchester' enquiring what they can obtain from the Africans in exchange for Manchester cloth. Stanley says he has shown that:

> there are 5250 statute miles of uninterrupted navigable water, which may

by overcoming a little trouble at one rapid be increased to 6000 miles in the Upper Congo section of the Congo basin.

The area through which these navigable channels flow is over 1,000,000 square miles superficial extent, and is throughout a fertile region unsurpassed for the variety of its natural productions.[21]

Stanley estimates the area's population at 43,000,000 (which some contemporary commentators dismissed as ludicrously high). He plays up (again) their willingness to trade, and he strongly urges, as in many parts of the book, the construction of a railway, combined with steamboat navigation, to transport the produce of the country. He speaks of a million Africans waiting to be told what further produce is needed 'beyond ivory, palm-oil, palm kernels, ground-nuts, gum-copal, orchilla-weed, camwood, cola-nuts, gum tragacanth, myrrh, frankincense, furs, skins, hides, feathers, copper, india-rubber, fibre of grasses, beeswax, bark-cloth, nutmeg, ginger, castor-oil nuts, &c.'.[22] And he offers traders further temptation in the way of the estimated costs and profits of a railway.

Near the end of the chapter Stanley expresses his hope that: 'Of the 325,000,000 of people in civilised Europe there must be some surely to whom the gospel of enterprise preached in this book through the medium of eight languages will present a few items of fact worthy of retention in the memory, and capable of inspiring a certain amount of action'.[23]

If Stanley's emphasis on the detail of the potential for commercial exploitation of the Congo, with the cultivation of the Africans almost as a presentational by-product, forms the kernel of his argument, then one can only note that Marlow, for whom the meaning of a tale lies outside, spends little time on the specifics of commerce. It is as if for him, and probably for Conrad too, the meaning is to be found in that which surrounds the kernel. If we pursue this line then we could say that Marlow's and Conrad's narratives differ from Stanley's in their perspective on the material in which the kernel is enclosed; or, to put it more plainly, in their attention to discourses and actions surrounding the central fact of Europe's exploitation of Africa. That is to say, Marlow attempts to look critically at the language and image of Kurtz in relation to his actual behaviour, with Marlow's thoughts of Kurtz shifting throughout, and Conrad maintains a critical perspective on Marlow's perception of Kurtz. Stanley, on the other hand, aims to make his language completely in the service of commercial interests. He appropriates the Congo and its inhabitants textually, ventriloquising or silencing at will, as a prelude or accompaniment to the physical appropriation for which he calls in eight languages. Through Marlow, Conrad looks for and listens to the differences between the substance and its casing. For Stanley there is no difference. Yet no writer can escape altogether the values and ideas of his or her society, and in one sense, Conrad's own narrative replicates the processes I have just described in Stanley: for Conrad, like authors of travelogues, profits from the transformation of raw material (experiences in Africa) into finished product (the text as both art and commodity). While at work on *Heart of Darkness*, he wrote to Edward Garnett, 'I am at a short story for B'wood which I must get out for the sake of the shekels'.[24] And on another occasion he referred to *An Outpost of Progress* as 'the lightest part of the loot I carried off from Central Africa, the main portion of course being the *Heart of Darkness*'.[25] Admittedly, he goes on to comfort himself with the thought that it is a small amount of plunder and would not have been of much use to anyone else, but one should not ignore the material aspects of writing on Africa.

Conrad's suspicion and dislike of the language of commerce and sham philanthropy which, by the end of the century, was known to mask the vicious greed of European activity in the Congo, is closely linked with the social climate of 1890s Europe and its reflection in cultural practice. His own views on art are connected with these preoccupations. Watt asserts that Conrad's 'fierce independence and ferocious contempt for commercial activities made every concession to the tastes of the public stick in his throat'.[26] In the preface to *The Nigger of the 'Narcissus'* Conrad refers to the 'worker in prose', whose task it is to make one *see*.[27] This phrase, along with similar ones in his letters and other of his writings, signals his views on writing as industry.[28] In some of his pronouncements on art, Conrad chooses to use metaphors that combine a sense of adventure with the service of duty. In 1905 he proclaimed:

> Action in its essence, the creative art of a writer of fiction may be compared to rescue work carried out in darkness against cross gusts of wind swaying the action of a great multitude. It is rescue work, this snatching of vanishing phases of turbulence, disguised in fair words, out of the native obscurity into a light where the struggling forms may be seen, seized upon, endowed with the only possible form of permanence in this world of relative values – the permanence of memory. And the multitude feels it obscurely too; since the demand of the individual to the art is, in effect, the cry, 'Take me out of myself!' meaning really, out of my perishable activity into the light of imperishable consciousness. But everything is relative and the light of consciousness is only enduring, merely the most enduring of the things of this earth, imperishable only as against the short-lived work of our industrious hands.[29]

This image of rescue work posits the artist as an heroic battler against the elements engaged in a potentially self-sacrificing mission to save others who are in difficulties. Effort and service are uppermost. What he is really endeavouring to rescue is the idea of romance from the destructive self-interest of materialism.

Conrad's own pronouncement in a letter written in 1922 that 'explicitness is fatal to the glamour of all artistic work, robbing it of all suggestiveness, destroying all illusion',[30] has often been cited as offering a rationale for his own methods. Where *Heart of Darkness* is concerned, the latter statement is usually taken as an explanation for the paucity of direct autobiographical and geographical reference and for the presence of an impressionistic kind of style. I believe, however, that if one considers all these factors in relation to the Emin Pasha Relief Expedition and to Stanley's earlier and continuing promotional work on the Congo, then Marlow's interest in what surrounds the kernel – contrasted with Stanley's obsessive emphasis on the kernel itself – and the lack of explicitness in Conrad's novella complicates our response to the undeniably denigrating and negative images he uses.

When we recall that *Heart of Darkness* first appeared in *Blackwood's Magazine*, a journal which had published explorers' and travellers' accounts of journeys in Africa and elsewhere for several decades, we can begin to appreciate the potential for subversion which the text contains. (I use the latter word in the dual sense of including and managing.) Quite apart from the uncertainty of the title's reference, we are presented with impenetrable narrative complications. Like Wells's *The Time Machine*, which was published four years earlier and whose author was to become friends with Conrad, the auditors of the protagonist's story are representatives of the English establishment, embodying the commercial and the professional (in this case the Director of Companies, who is the Captain; the Lawyer, and the Accountant). In addition there is the framing narrator, who, despite the wishful elisions made by many critics, further distances Conrad the author from Marlow. Our lack of knowledge about this narrator invests his identity with a vagueness which is again in contrast with the practices of travel writing of Africa at the time. As I have shown, for most travellers and explorers, identity is actually constituted and circulated through their visible textual persona. It is not enough to say that this difference is due to the fact that *Heart of Darkness* is 'fiction' and travelogues are 'non-fiction'. Conrad is constantly encouraging readers to see parallels only to then unsettle them.

By suggesting the limitations to Europeans' self-knowledge, as he does, Conrad implicitly questions their comprehension of others. Seen in this way, the shadowy figures on the riverbank, however disparaging a representation of Africans, may actually be taken to signify the lack of clarity to the west's vision of Africa, undercutting the writings of travellers and explorers, which insisted on the definitiveness of their ascriptions. Even where an air of foreboding and of a thrilling sense of mystery were transmitted, it was a clear and certain depiction of the unknown, fulfilling a conventional and understood role. Conrad turns this around. Shadows and silences in *Heart of Darkness* hint at more than is known. Discomfort is bred because, unlike the travel narratives in which the unknown functions as a sure boundary marker and therefore a self-defining other, the more disturbing insubstantialness of Conrad's Africans (about which Achebe, I say it again, rightly complains) results in an instability of self.

The shadowiness extends from image to narrative. Again the full effect of this can be appreciated only through comparison with conventional travel writing. Marlow records that his experience '"seemed somehow to throw a kind of light on everything about me – and into my thoughts. It was sombre enough too – and pitiful – not extraordinary in any way – not very clear either. No. Not very clear. And yet it seemed to throw a kind of light"' (p. 11). This lack of definition contrasts with the established notions of storytelling and authority, let alone with the usual stance towards Africans where many characters would be sharply drawn and the plot progression would be clear, as would the moral purpose. The figures would be clearly mapped. Conrad suggests there are things which have not been mapped and that those who would shed light on the 'dark continent' lack the ability to do so. In his essay 'Geography and Some Explorers',[31] Conrad links the passing of heroic and romantic, adventurous geography to the ending of opportunities for discovery and the commencement of commercial exploitation. The latter applies to writing too as well as to imperialism as we see when Conrad describes – referring to, but not naming, Stanley – 'the unholy recollection of a prosaic newspaper "stunt" and the distasteful knowledge of the vilest scramble for loot that ever disfigured the history of human conscience and geographical exploration'.[32]

Similar sentiments are to be found in Conrad's 1923 essay, 'Travel', in which he laments that 'the days of heroic travel are gone; unless, of course, in the newspaper sense, in which heroism like everything else in the world becomes as common if not as nourishing as our daily bread'.[33] (This also, of course, mourns the loss of romantic individualism in the face of mass production.) At times Marlow shares this sense of disillusionment, and articulates it in a way which posits a conflict between the romance of imagination and the fact of scientific materialism:

'Now when I was a little chap I had a passion for maps. I would look for hours at South America, or Africa, or Australia, and lose myself in all the glories of exploration. At that time there were many blank spaces on the earth and when I saw one that looked particularly inviting on a map (but they all look like that) I would put my finger on it and say: When I grow up I will go there. The North Pole was one of these places, I remember. Well, I haven't been there yet, and shall not try now. The glamour's off. Other places were scattered about the Equator and in every sort of latitude all over the two hemispheres. I have been in some of them and . . . well, we won't talk about that. But there was one yet – the biggest, the most blank, so to speak – that I had a hankering after.

'True, by this time it was not a blank space any more. It had got filled since my boyhood with rivers and lakes and names. It had ceased to be a blank space of delightful mystery – a white patch for a boy to dream gloriously over. It had become a place of darkness. But there was in it one river especially, a mighty big river that you could see on the map, resembling an immense snake uncoiled, with its head in the sea, its body at rest curving afar over a vast country and its tail lost in the depths of the land. And as I looked at the map of it in a shop-window, it fascinated me as a snake would a bird – a silly little bird. Then I remembered there was a big concern, a Company for trade on that river. Dash it all, I thought to myself, they can't trade without using some kind of craft on that lot of fresh water – steamboats! Why shouldn't I try to get charge of one? I went on along Fleet Street, but could not shake off the idea. The snake had charmed me.'
(pp. 11–12)

The displacement of romantic adventure by commercial activity is not only stated explicitly here but is indicated more subtly too by the presence of the map in the shop-window, an image of the link between geography and commerce. The passage also sets up a tripartite structure comprising individual agency (Marlow), nature (the Congo as snake), and European trade. The first of these parties is evidently in a subordinate position to the other two, a situation sharply emblematic of a perceived loss of individual power characteristic of the 1890s.

Marlow articulates the paradox that the more that is known of Africa the more the blank space becomes a place of darkness. Stanley, on the other hand, was altogether more sanguine about the process which he enabled. In *Through the Dark Continent* he had himself telling his companion Frank Pocock:

'Now, look at this, the latest chart which Europeans have drawn of this region. It is a blank, perfectly white. . .

'I assure you, Frank, this enormous void is about to be filled up. Blank as it is, it has a singular fascination for me. Never has white paper possessed such a charm for me as this has, and I have already mentally peopled it, filled it with most wonderful pictures of towns, villages, rivers, countries, and tribes – all in the imagination – and I am burning to see whether I am correct or not. *Believe* [that we shall succeed]? I see us gliding down by tower and town, and my mind will not permit a shadow of doubt. Good-night, my boy! Good-night! and may happy dreams of the sea, and ships,

[195]

and pleasure, and comfort, and success attend you in your sleep! To-morrow, my lad, is the day we shall cry — "Victory or death!".'[34]

When Stanley cries 'Victory or death!' we know that to whomever death will come it won't be him. Stanley revels in the filling of the blank spaces that Conrad appears to regret. For Stanley physical adventure and discovery are the fulfilment of imaginative projection; for Conrad they may preclude it. Conrad was later to write of 'an explored earth in which the latitudes and longitudes having been recorded once for all have become things of no importance, in the sense that they can no longer appeal to the spirit of adventure, lead no one up to the very gates of mortal danger'.[35] Conrad, of course, is suspicious of the mission for which Stanley is a prime agent, but, quite apart from that, one feels that for the artist reflecting on imperialism, as opposed to the journalist and explorer in the service of it, there is a contradiction between imaginative possibility and actual realisation. For Stanley the one unavoidably and desirably leads to the other.

Stanley, and those like him, survey what they see, capturing it in cognitive and discursive terms. For example, the instalment of Edward Glave as chief of the Lukolela station on 22 September 1883 leads Stanley to cast a capitalist's eye over the forest thereabouts, whose trees, he says, range from sixty to one hundred and fifty feet in height:

> A little exploration I made through this forest, which is scarcely more difficult to penetrate than the Thiergarten of Berlin, enabled me to estimate the number of useful trees in the forest of Lukolela at 460,000, which, allowing only 40 cubic feet to the tree, would furnish over 18,000,000 cubic feet of timber. The plane-trees are numerous; they would furnish easily workable planks for flat-boats, wooden steamers, tables, doors, flooring, rafters, window frames, &c.; while of the splendid teak might be formed keels, stem and stern-posts, decking, and the mahogany, red-wood, and guaiacum for furniture. A steam saw-mill might enable us to furnish all the timber needed for trading houses for generations out of this one forest.[36]

Though Stanley proceeds to remark that this forest is unusual for the scarcity of its useless trees, and to observe that the soil is poor (the trees have apparently grown in cavities in the ironstone filled with alluvium), his vision of the finished products from the raw material nicely epitomises the travel writer's transforming eye. Conrad again modifies this process. The fact that the door of the Intended at which Marlow knocks is made of mahogany and that inside her home is a grand piano, the keys of which, one presumes, are made of ivory (p. 72), would be of some satisfaction to Stanley, promoter of commerce. The fact that it is in the context of an unsettling sense of the presence of Kurtz and the wilderness in the heart of civilisation would not have been of much comfort to Stanley for it suggests reverse colonisation or at least an inability to control and manufacture in the way that Stanley, as a good capitalist, unquestioningly advocates. It is when Marlow is about to ring the bell at the door of the Intended that he feels Kurtz:

> 'lived then before me, he lived as much as he had ever lived – a shadow insatiable of splendid appearances, of frightful realities, a shadow darker than the shadow of the night, and draped nobly in the folds of a gorgeous eloquence. The vision seemed to enter the house with me – the stretcher, the phantom-bearers, the wild crowd of obedient worshippers, the gloom of the forests, the glitter of the reach between the murky bends, the beat of the drum regular and muffled like the beating of a heart, the heart of a conquering darkness. It was a moment of triumph for the wilderness, an invading and vengeful rush which it seemed to me I would have to keep back alone for the salvation of another soul.' (p. 72)

This extraordinary juxtaposition of the natural and the wild against the civilised and the social places *Heart of Darkness* with those enduringly fascinating texts of the late 1880s and the 1890s which have nature threatening to invade and swamp the civilised. I am thinking for example of Stevenson's *Jekyll and Hyde* and Wells's 'The Time Machine'. In these texts and others of the period an unnerving vitality is associated with the 'lower' classes (those deemed closer to nature), and an entropic state with the enervated middle and upper classes. The impression in these narratives is of a society in danger of refining itself out of existence. So, Conrad's idea of unmaking and disrupting the west's productions of the African landscape is strongly bound up with pauper Kurtz's intrusion into respectable, moneyed society. Marlow's sense of responsibility, coupled with his confidence that his words to the Intended will give him the power to hold back the wilderness, testifies to the power of narrative to suppress that which it has raised.

The idea of reverse colonisation pervades *Heart of Darkness*,[37] but is downplayed in readings that see Kurtz simply as someone who has 'gone native', for his fate is more complicated than that. For example, critics have often commented on Kurtz's baldness but have not always remarked on the terms and context in which it is described. Marlow speaks thus:

> 'The wilderness had patted him on the head, and behold, it was like a ball – an ivory ball; it had caressed him, and – lo! – he had withered; it had taken him, loved him, embraced him, got into his veins, consumed his flesh, and sealed his soul to its own by the inconceivable ceremonies of some devilish initiation.' (p. 49)

Beyond the evident irony of Kurtz's being made by the wilderness to resemble the commodity he and others like him crave, there lies the deeper matter of Kurtz's being transformed or moulded by the wilderness. In short, he has been finished by the environment in an ironic reversal of the capitalist process of taking raw materials and returning manufactured goods. Kurtz is the raw stuff on which the wilderness acts. (He is also said by Marlow, when he sees him on his stretcher, to resemble '"an animated image of death carved out of old ivory"' (p. 59); and, later, to have an '"ivory face"' (p. 68).) He therefore fails the capitalist creed by succumbing to nature rather than subduing it. Critics have tended to concentrate on the internal psychological manifestation of this as Kurtz is taken over by his socially repressed instincts, but equally important is the external aspect of Kurtz's inability to operate on and 'finish' the natural produce around him.

Marlow further points up this irony when – again, as many critics have noted – he mentions Kurtz's overweening possessiveness, only then to undercut this too:

> 'You should have heard him say, "My ivory." Oh yes, I heard him. "My Intended, my ivory, my station, my river, my . . . " everything belonged to him. It made me hold my breath in expectation of hearing the wilderness burst into a prodigious peal of laughter that would shake the fixed stars in their places. Everything belonged to him – but that was a trifle. The thing was to know what he belonged to, how many powers of darkness claimed him for their own. That was the reflection that made you creepy all over. It was impossible – it was not good for one either – trying to imagine. He had taken a high seat amongst the devils of the land – I mean literally.' (p. 49)

Clearly here both Marlow and Conrad are serving a diminution order on Kurtz to counteract his monumental claims of proprietorship. But they can do so only by taking a metaphysical perspective on his activities. Roughly speaking, this posture asks us to see human endeavour (and in Africa it is commercial activity performed by Europeans) against a surround of nature which outlasts humanity. Conrad's efforts to use nature as the touchstone by which the limitations of science and materialism are suggested often lead him in this direction and circumscribe the radical possibilities of his text.

When Marlow is examined by the Company doctor prior to departing for (what we guess to be) Africa, the doctor tells him: '"I always ask leave, in the interests of science, to measure the crania of those going out there"', and then, after saying that he never sees any who come back, states: '"the changes take place inside, you know"' (p. 15). Conrad shares the interest in the changes that cannot be seen. Conventionally, travellers and explorers did not admit to such alteration, even if they experienced it, their concentration instead being on physical transformation through illness. Sickness, wounds, or exhaustion were portrayed as critical moments in which the threat of dissolution is eventually overcome (perhaps with God's aid) as the recording self is reconstituted or reconfirmed. Conrad's reference to the internal changes is in itself an unusual move because it suggests a transformation, be it psychological or ideological, rarely admitted. Marlow certainly interprets the doctor's words in the way I have done. He offers his recollection of them later: '"It would be interesting for science to watch the mental changes of individuals, on the spot"', and observes laconically: '"I felt I was becoming scientifically interesting"' (p. 24).

Another way in which the discourses of imperialism and science are shown by Conrad to be inadequate and inappropriate is through the disruption by that which cannot be quantified, the darkness itself. Conrad destabilises the bases of imperialism by insisting on the immeasurableness of the imperial object. Marlow relates the words of the Company's chief accountant: '"When one has got to make correct entries one comes to hate those savages – hate them to the death"' (p. 22). Conrad then quite consciously undercuts the operation of commerce in the service of civilisation. Through Marlow he suggests the human and moral costs of the imposition of civilised routine. When Marlow leaves the chief accountant Marlow observes the latter '"bent over his books"', '"making correct entries of perfectly correct transactions; and fifty feet below the doorstep I could see the still tree-tops of the grove of death"' (p. 22). The ironic tone created by the repetition of 'correct', quite apart from the direct reference to death, suggests that imperialist activity actually entails a lack or loss of knowledge; a blindness to the consequences. It may well be, as critical consensus has it, that Conrad is eventually reconciled to imperialism, though disapproving of some of the methods, but he surely wishes for those implicated in it ('all Europe') to have some awareness of what is involved.

Nevertheless, his questioning of the confident assumption of knowledge that supports the imperial project, his challenge to mapping, does further stereotype Africa as the following passage shows:

'We called at some more places with farcical names, where the merry dance of death and trade goes on in a still and earthy atmosphere as of an overheated catacomb; all along the formless coast bordered by dangerous surf, as if Nature herself had tried to ward off intruders; in and out of rivers, streams of death in life, whose banks were rotting into mud, whose waters, thickened into slime, invaded the contorted mangroves that seemed to writhe at us in the extremity of an impotent despair. Nowhere did we stop long enough to get a particularised impression, but the general sense of vague and oppressive wonder grew upon me. It was like a weary pilgrimage amongst hints for nightmares.' (p. 17)

[199]

That the places have farcical names is, I take it, a sign of the inappropriateness of European nomenclature (and thus language) to the region. I doubt that Conrad's intention is to flag the gap as a healthy one, but at the end of a century which, with one or two exceptions, had revelled in the bestowal of European names upon African features, this is a distinctive statement to be making. The 'merry dance of death and trade' supports a metaphysical interpretation which crosses into the mythical. The idea of the 'formless coast', with its Stanley-like suggestion of the primeval, nature not yet made, is an example of the ambiguity of Conrad's imagery: it perpetuates a view of Africa as primitive and yet counters it by implying the difficulties of reading it. The formless and the shadowy cannot be clearly discerned, and this points to limitations in the power and accuracy of the observer. The image of nature attempting to 'ward off intruders' is very much in the tradition of Africa as hostile, supplying a challenge to those who would explore and travel through the landscape, and prove their manhood in doing so. The final two sentences are emblematic of the story as a whole. Nowhere does it or Marlow stop long enough to get a particularised impression. The hints for nightmares, with which the passage concludes, consciously takes the west's cultural fear and denigration of the landscape and deals with it in psychological terms.

A similar process is evident in another passage:

> 'The steamer toiled along slowly on the edge of a black and incomprehensible frenzy. The prehistoric man was cursing us, praying to us, welcoming us – who could tell? We were cut off from the comprehension of our surroundings; we glided past like phantoms, wondering and secretly appalled, as sane men would be before an enthusiastic outbreak in a madhouse. We could not understand because we were too far and could not remember because we were travelling in the night of first ages, of those ages that are gone, leaving hardly a sign – and no memories.' (p. 37)

To admit to a lack of comprehension is quite a failure in a travel narrative. It is a different thing from feeling awestruck, for example. A failure of understanding suggests incongruity of place and observer and an inadequacy of cognitive structures and language. Although this sets up deep ironies – as Said says,[38] Marlow's success is his power to tell the story – it is fundamentally different from the conventions of travel narratives. The implication of Marlow's incomprehension is the unreadability of the African, of the signifier.

In other respects, as many critics have asserted, the text is conservative. The people and the surroundings may be unreadable but, Marlow opines, this is because we (the civilised) have come so far since our primitive days. Marlow may talk of the shock of recognition, but it is a shock precisely because of the residual presence of the primitive within us. In no sense at all is there the possibility that the Africans are as civilised or as cultured or as developed in any of their human faculties as 'we' are:

'It was unearthly, and the men were. . . . No, they were not inhuman. Well, you know that was the worst of it – this suspicion of their not being inhuman. It would come slowly to one. They howled and leaped and spun and made horrid faces, but what thrilled you was just the thought of their humanity – like yours – the thought of your remote kinship with this wild and passionate uproar. Ugly. Yes, it was ugly enough, but if you were man enough you would admit to yourself that there was in you just the faintest trace of a response to the terrible frankness of that noise, a dim suspicion of there being a meaning in it which you – you so remote from the night of first ages – could comprehend. And why not? The mind of man is capable of anything – because everything is in it, all the past as well as all the future. What was there after all? Joy, fear, sorrow, devotion, valour, rage – who can tell? – but truth – truth stripped of its cloak of time.' (pp. 37–8)

That Freud should use a similar image when discussing the human mind in civilised society underlines the strength of this ethnocentric, culturally-rooted idea. In a psychoanalytic model which in some ways parallels the social Darwinist fear, played up by naturalistic writers, of the beast surviving within civilised 'man',[39] Freud wrote that: 'In the realm of the mind ... what is primitive is ... commonly preserved alongside of the transformed version which has arisen from it'.[40]

Much of the ambivalence of Conrad's text is established by the tension between Marlow's tone and the familiar outline of the Africans. The black shadows of disease and starvation, the 'complete, deathlike indifference of unhappy savages' (p. 19), would be images well known to those who had read or knew about the accounts of Stanley's rear guard camp. But Marlow's capability of critical self-scrutiny – '"After all, I also was a part of the great cause of these high and just proceedings"' (p. 19) – invests his words with a degree of self-directed irony seldom encountered in explorer-travellers. Furthermore, Marlow has the ability and the preparedness to see things from another perspective. On being saluted by one of the 'reclaimed' he sees the logic behind this, '"white men being so much alike at a distance that he could not tell who I might be"' (p. 19); a statement which reverses the (still) common gibe about blacks all looking the same.

Marlow displays a curiosity that seems out of keeping with the agents of imperialism. He wonders about the white worsted around the neck of a dying black man; he sees the grove of death fifty feet below the doorstep of the chief accountant; he lists the rubbishy goods which are

sent into the interior in exchange for precious ivory; and when he sets
out with a caravan he realises that:

> 'if a lot of mysterious niggers armed with all kinds of fearful weapons
> suddenly took to travelling on the road between Deal and Gravesend
> catching the yokels right and left to carry heavy loads for them, I fancy
> every farm and cottage thereabouts would get empty very soon.' (p. 23)

The racist epithet though marks the extent of his and Conrad's
departure from the attitudes they question.

Another example of Marlow and Conrad's racism occurring in tension
with Conrad's rearrangement of Stanley's shop-window Congo may be
found in the following passage of Marlow's narration:

> 'Everything else in the Station was in a muddle – heads, things, buildings.
> Caravans. Strings of dusty niggers with splay feet arrived and departed; a
> stream of manufactured goods, rubbishy cottons, beads, and brass-wire set
> into the depths of darkness, and in return came a precious trickle of ivory.'
> (p. 21)

The offensive portrayal of the Africans, which manifests and does not
transcend racism, pours cold water over Stanley's promotional brochure
for the Congo Free State. At the same time Marlow's words deny
Europeans the luxury of feeling good about their self-proclaimed service
towards the Africans. The goods they send them are all but worthless,
and again, incidentally, one can see how the confused role of beads both
as commodity and currency helps define the narrator's view.

From early on we have seen Marlow as sceptical of European activity,
or at least of the claims for it. He talks of his cynicism before he set out
for the Congo:

> 'I was also one of the Workers, with a capital – you know. Something like
> an emissary of light, something like a lower sort of apostle. There had been
> a lot of such rot let loose in print and talk just about that time, and the
> excellent woman [his aunt] living right in the rush of all that humbug got
> carried off her feet. She talked about "weaning those ignorant millions
> from their horrid ways," till, upon my word, she made me quite uncom-
> fortable. I ventured to hint that the Company was run for profit.' (pp.
> 15–16)

'Workers', with a capital, conflates the concepts of labour and mission
activity, just as they were conflated in reality. The passage sharply
satirises the loud justifications for imperialism, which Marlow and
Conrad doubt.

The distance between Marlow and what we might call the official
discourse is further achieved by the fact that Marlow is an outsider, a
loner. He does not share the identification of most travellers with the

culture which has, as it were, sent them out. In most of the narratives I have mentioned travellers portray their individuality through close relationship to the home society, unless they are engaged in idiosyncratic but none the less highly formalised celebrations of the Noble Savage or of primitivism. Marlow, on the other hand, manifests for most of the narrative a linguistic and visual suspicion of the dominant discourses. That he moves towards complicity with them, to the extent of lying to the Intended (a lie which also attempts to resurrect a dying chivalry), is due to authorial recognition of the mastery (the gendered noun is deliberate) of imperialism and of the identification of commercial exploitativeness with civilisation. It also enacts the kind of denial Freud later saw as practised by society:

> it is impossible to overlook the extent to which civilization is built upon a renunciation of instinct, how much it presupposes precisely the non-satisfaction (by suppression, repression or some other means?) of powerful instincts. This 'cultural frustration' dominates the large field of social relationships between human beings. . . . it is the cause of the hostility against which all civilizations have to struggle.[41]

Conrad, like Freud, attempts to show the primitive truth and its suppression. The loss of closure this engenders in the narrative may be radical, with the civilised world supported by a lie, but it can also be reactionary. The method Conrad adopts to counter the materialism of Stanley and other travellers has dangers of its own. In those passages where the dream-like quality of Marlow's experience is expressed, there is a worrying dilution of the material into an abstruse metaphysics. The real sufferings of the blacks and the physical exploitation of their continent are thus transformed into the shadowy realm of a universe where specifics and actualities are broadened out to a general (western) view of spiritual and moral states. Marlow tells his audience:

> 'He [Kurtz] was just a word for me. I did not see the man in the name any more than you do. Do you see him? Do you see the story? Do you see anything? It seems to me I am trying to tell you a dream – making a vain attempt, because no relation of a dream can convey the dream-sensation, that commingling of absurdity, surprise, and bewilderment in a tremor of struggling revolt, that notion of being captured by the incredible which is the very essence of dreams. . . .'
> He was silent for a while.
> '. . . No, it is impossible; it is impossible to convey the life-sensation of any given epoch of one's existence – that which makes its truth its meaning – its subtle and penetrating essence. It is impossible. We live, as we dream – alone . . .' (pp. 29–30)

In effect, then, *Heart of Darkness* works to destabilise the values which are central to explorer-travellers like Stanley and to the society which they served by deliberately looking at a 'larger' picture. This is one of the reasons for the abstract symbolism of the novella and for its almost complete lack of specific references. By putting the actions of an agent like Kurtz or Stanley into 'proportion' – i.e. against the backdrop of a force or a presence which was there before they arrived and which will still be there when they have gone – Conrad and to a lesser extent Marlow rob such men of the scale of values they hold dear. The potential radicalism of Conrad's text flattens out as he moves from the greed of commercial expansion as the kernel and its justifying discourses as what surrounds it, to human endeavour and the urge to make an impression on the world as the kernel and the eternity of non-human nature as the outside. At the station, observing those whom he thinks of as 'faithless pilgrims' apparently praying to ivory, Marlow muses:

> 'I've never seen anything so unreal in my life. And outside, the silent wilderness surrounding this cleared speck on the earth struck me as something great and invincible, like evil or truth, waiting patiently for the passing away of this fantastic invasion.' (p. 26)

One can't have a much clearer image of humanity's existence within nature than this. It is a synecdoche for the history of settlement, domestication, and civilisation. But two things about this framework need to be said at once. First, the blacks, the Africans, are envisaged as a part of raw nature, more at home in the wilderness than whites, and are therefore drawn in accordance with the stereotypes born of prejudice. Secondly, to attempt a critique of imperial voraciousness by setting it against an asocial, atemporal world is not a particularly radical thing to do. After all, it hardly offers an alternative to current practice (which is probably one of the reasons why Marlow has to lie), substituting instead an ultimately quiescent view of 'our' activity – Europe's, the only one that matters – as grimly farcical in the face of the immensity of planetary time.

Marlow's ability to perceive the metaphysical frame is pronounced. His audience, he says, cannot understand:

> 'How could you? – with solid pavement under your feet, surrounded by kind neighbours ready to cheer you or to fall on you, stepping delicately between the butcher and the policeman, in the holy terror of scandal and gallows and lunatic asylums – how can you imagine what particular region of the first ages a man's untrammelled feet may take him into by the way of solitude – utter solitude without a policeman – by the way of silence – utter silence, where no warning voice of a kind neighbour can be heard whispering of public opinion?' (pp. 49–50)

The wonderful image of civilised humanity stepping delicately between the butcher and the policeman perfectly evokes the then widespread concern over the balance between natural instinct and social restraint. It is part of Conrad's achievement that he is able to take the form of the travel narrative – in particular the travel narrative of Africa – and manipulate its conventions to communicate his vision of the precariousness of European society's civilised existence. In being provoked by the deadly victory of commercialism over the romantic, the triumph of mass production and mass expression over the chances for individual heroism and the practice of personal craft, and the loss of faith in noble designs, disinterested deeds and honest words; in all these things, Conrad is a product of his age. The fact that he knows this gives his work a tremendous tension between social utterance and the effort to find an individual voice. Arguably, the latter is gained only in the form of his narrative. When the scope for heroism is reduced, when the explorer is a sham, making '"no end of coin by trade"' (p. 13) is the aim, and language cannot be trusted, then there are no places to go. The blank spaces have all been filled and the domestic spaces are of no interest to spinners and auditors of adventure yarns. Unmapping and unmaking turn one in on oneself when the desire is to discover something external. It could have been bold of Conrad to delineate not just the fragility of one's hold on civilisation (or civilisation's hold on one) when away from public opinion, but even in Europe's streets with their solid pavements. Yet he cannot face the implication of his tale and ends up naturalising the social. The hair-raising (or, rather, in Kurtz's case, hair-erasing) excitement and danger of reverse colonisation slides into an intellectually and narratively dull projection of 'our' mortality. The body of Fresleven, whom Marlow has heard was killed in desperation by the son of the chief he was beating mercilessly, has '"grass growing through his ribs"' that was '"tall enough to hide his bones"' (p. 13); and in Brussels Marlow finds '"grass sprouting between the stones"' (p. 13). Implicit criticism of European activity in the Congo becomes diluted then as the text moves towards the old theme of human endeavour against mortality and forgetting. Not only this, but Conrad and his narrators continue to travel in narrative, while the women and blacks – those objects from and to whom they travel, crossing their thresholds at will – remain static,[42] their representation determined by the white male storytellers, for whom coming and going may or may not be a crisis, but which they feel is none the less an experience to be passed on as being of universal significance as they await the turning of the tide.

Notes

1 On Conrad's own experiences in the Congo see his 'The Congo Diary' in Joseph Conrad, *Last Essays*, with an Introduction by Richard Curle (New York: Doubleday, Page & Company, 1926), pp. 155–71; and Norman Sherry, *Conrad's Western World* (Cambridge: Cambridge University Press, 1971), pp. 9–133.

2 Patrick Parrinder, '*Heart of Darkness*: Geography as Apocalypse', in John Stokes, ed., *Fin de Siècle/Fin du Globe: Fears and Fantasies of the Late Nineteenth Century* (Basingstoke: Macmillan, 1992), p. 85.

3 See the chapter on 'Idols of the tribe: Conrad's *Heart of Darkness*' in M. M. Mahood, *The Colonial Encounter: A Reading of Six Novels* (London: Rex Collings, 1977), pp. 4–36.

4 Joseph Conrad, *Heart of Darkness* ed. Robert Kimbrough (New York: Norton, 1988), 3rd ed., p. 67. All subsequent references to *Heart of Darkness* will be given parenthetically and are to this edition. The volume also contains a useful selection of background and critical material, though it has little or nothing on the air of crisis engendered or reflected by the exploits of Jameson, Barttelot and Stanley on the Emin Pasha Relief Expedition.

5 Sherry, *Conrad's Western World*, p. 14.

6 John Bierman, *Dark Safari: The Life behind the Legend of Henry Morton Stanley* (London: Hodder & Stoughton, 1991), p. 329.

7 See Ian Watt, *Conrad in the Nineteenth Century* (London: Chatto & Windus, 1980), pp. 141–5.

8 Patrick Brantlinger, *Rule of Darkness: British Literature and Imperialism, 1830–1914* (Ithaca: Cornell University Press, 1988), p. 268.

9 Chinua Achebe, 'An image of Africa: racism in Conrad's *Heart of Darkness*' in *Hopes and Impediments: Selected Essays 1965–1987* (Oxford: Heinemann International, 1988), p. 8. The essay first appeared in 1975. It is also to be found in Kimbrough's Norton edition of *Heart of Darkness*, pp. 251–62. My page references are to *Hopes and Impediments*.

10 Achebe, 'An image of Africa', p. 8.

11 Patrick Parrinder also feels that Achebe's charge 'may be better directed against the trend of Anglo-American criticism of *Heart of Darkness* than against the text itself'. Patrick Parrinder, '*Heart of Darkness*: geography as apocalypse', p. 85.

12 Anthony Fothergill, 'Of Conrad, cannibals and kin', in *Representing Others: White Views of Indigenous Peoples*, ed. Mick Gidley (Exeter: University of Exeter Press, 1992), p. 53.

13 Brantlinger, *Rule of Darkness*, p. 257.

14 Fothergill helpfully names these as the four broad categories into which readings of the text generally fall. Fothergill, *Heart of Darkness*, pp. 4–5.

15 Ian Watt, *Conrad in the Nineteenth Century*, p. 169.

16 Henry M. Stanley, *The Congo and the Founding of its Free State: A Story of Work and Exploration*, 2 vols, cheaper ed. (London: Sampson Low, Marston, Searle & Rivington, 1886), I, v.

17 Karl Marx and Frederick Engels, *Manifesto of the Communist Party* (Peking: Foreign Languages Press, 1975), p. 39.

18 Stanley, *The Congo*, I, 147–8.

19 Stanley, *The Congo* I, 330.

20 Henry M. Stanley, *The Congo and the Founding of its Free State: A Story of Work and Exploration*, 2 vols (London: Sampson Low, Marston, Searle, & Rivington, 1885), II, 376.

21 Stanley, *The Congo*, II, 366.

22 Stanley, *The Congo* II, 368.

23 Stanley, *The Congo* II, 377.

24 Quoted in Kimbrough, *Heart of Darkness*, p. 200.

25 Quoted in Kimbrough, *Heart of Darkness*, p. 192.

26 Watt, *Conrad in the Nineteenth Century*, p. 129.

27 Quoted in Kimbrough, *Heart of Darkness*, p. 225.
28 One more example among many is his statement that 'I have been quarrying my English out of a black night, working like a coal miner in his pit'. Quoted in Kimbrough, p. 235.
29 Quoted in Kimbrough, *Heart of Darkness*, p. 229.
30 This extract is quoted in, among other places, Watt, *Conrad in the Nineteenth Century*, p. 137.
31 In *Last Essays*, pp. 1–21.
32 Conrad, 'Geography and some explorers', p. 17.
33 Joseph Conrad, 'Travel', in *Last Essays*, p. 89.
34 Henry M. Stanley, *Through the Dark Continent: Or the Sources of the Nile around the Great Lakes of Equatorial Africa and down the Livingstone River to the Atlantic Ocean*, new edition (London: Sampson Low, Marston, Searle, & Rivington, [1878] 1890), p. 449.
35 Conrad, 'Travel', p. 90.
36 Stanley, *The Congo* II, 66–7.
37 For a suggestive discussion of reverse colonisation in texts at this time see Stephen D. Arata, 'The Occidental tourist: *Dracula* and the anxiety of reverse colonization', *Victorian Studies* 33, 4 (summer 1990), 621–45.
38 Edward Said, *Culture and Imperialism* (London: Chatto & Windus, 1993), pp. 25–6.
39 Albert J. Guerard is just one critic to have noted that Kurtz's fate fits closely with contemporary naturalistic treatments of the idea of man (I use the gendered noun advisedly) reverting to the beast. See his 'The journey within' in *Heart of Darkness*, ed. Kimbrough, p. 245.
40 Sigmund Freud, 'Civilization and its discontents', in *Civilization, Society and Religion*, The Penguin Freud Library, gen. ed. James Strachey, vol. 12, ed. Albert Dickson (London: Penguin Books, 1991), p. 256.
41 Freud, 'Civilization and its discontents', pp. 286–7.
42 On the question of gender in *Heart of Darkness*, particularly the idea of masculinity, see Joseph Bristow, *Empire Boys: Adventures in a Man's World* (London: HarperCollins*Academic*, 1991), pp. 153–66. Bristow also makes a number of interesting and intelligent comments about the structure of the novella.

CONCLUSION

The 'tragic story has nothing whatever to do with exploration',[1] wrote the author of a popular book on heroic travellers when the time came to offer an appraisal of the Emin Pasha Relief Expedition. And in a sense, of course, it never really was about that. The British exploration of Africa was largely about Britain and we are meant to pretend that it was not.

We are still meant to pretend that it was not. Craig Raine, in an article in the *London Review of Books* not so long ago, attacked Achebe's attack on Conrad. He was free to do so, but it was not wise of him to do it by quoting against Achebe the writings of Stanley and of Stanley's contemporary, the missionary W. Holman Bentley. Raine says that these two men wrote about what they saw, and that Achebe cannot deny that savagery and cannibalism existed. He quotes (at second hand) Holman Bentley's reported conversation with a Bangala cannibal, who allegedly told him '"Ah! I wish I could eat everybody on earth"'.[2] Raine seems easily convinced, but never mind that his essay is uninformed and full of misreadings; what is more important, and more alarming, is his conclusion that 'All minorities will treat representations of themselves as typical, whereas art deals with actualities, and not necessarily with truth and justice'.[3] Raine uses this idea to uphold (as he sees it) 'authorial independence', which he believes Achebe's propaganda to be opposing. I have tried to show that there is no such thing as authorial independence, least of all in people like Stanley and Bentley, or in people who use their currency of images; that it is not the 'minorities' who treat the representations of themselves as typical; and that the actualities are based on questionable constructions.

In his fine novel *Things Fall Apart*, published in 1958, Achebe spends most of the story telling the tale of Okonkwo and of the Igbo society from which he comes. After Okonkwo's death, Achebe's narrator comments on the white District Commissioner's thoughts:

Every day brought him some new material. The story of this man who had killed a messenger and hanged himself would make interesting reading. One could almost write a whole chapter on him. Perhaps not a whole chapter but a reasonable paragraph, at any rate. There was so much else to include, and one must be firm in cutting out details. He had already chosen the title of the book, after much thought: *The Pacification of the Primitive Tribes of the Lower Niger.*[4]

In a marvellous manoeuvre Achebe has done unto the District Commissioner as the District Commissioner would do unto him, for this is the final paragraph of Achebe's book, and, apart from a brief appearance earlier, is the most significant mention of the white official. All that has gone before shows the complete inadequacy of the work the District Commissioner will write. Even if we suspend our judgement until we can consult a missionary like the omniscient Holman Bentley about the truth of the matter, I think it would not be unfair to say that a comparison of a work like Achebe's with that of someone like Stanley shows the ideological and historical constructedness of representations of the other. And of course 'we' are similarly constituted as readers (or as non-readers). It is as well, therefore, to notice the perspectives which are not given, for they are often those of 'minorities' like non-Europeans and women.

Travellers do not simply record what they see. They travel with a purpose. They journey with preconceptions. They observe and write according to established models, having these in mind even when they wish to query or depart from them. No one who travels and writes of their experiences can be said to be writing purely as an individual. Descriptions and judgements reveal the values of class, gender, and nationality. One appeal of travel writing is in the textual and imaginary space it creates for its readers where ideas of the social and the natural, the civilised and the savage, may meet and the uncivilised be made to seem so strange and threatening that the artificial is naturalised. This space must, like the worlds of novels, be an imaginary one for the readers, for even if they have travelled to the physical place described, it is unlikely they have done so in the actual presence of the author. This is one reason – and another is the common structural use of travel as a metaphor for a variety of quests and explorations both in 'factual' and 'fictional' writing – why, like Dennis Porter, I am uneasy about attempts to define travel writing as a genre.[5] The fascination of travel writing lies in its yoking together of the familiar and the strange, allowing a safely distanced scrutiny of 'our' identity, questioning and reconfirming 'our' group subjectivities when they are placed under threat. The threat, moreover, is more than likely to be from within. Porter has usefully remarked that:

not only is travel typically fueled by desire, it also embodies powerful transgressive values. . . . something of such an attitude no doubt contributes to the frequent ambivalence to be found in so many works of travel literature. . . .

. . . If one learns anything from a close reading of a variety of travel writings . . . it is precisely that although there are both cultural and historically specific fantasies concerning our various Others, there are also markedly idiosyncratic ones.[6]

Porter, I think, plays up the idiosyncrasies too much, often resorting to biographical explanations for versions of the Oedipus complex that may, in his eyes, have affected travellers' desires, their attitudes to authority, and thereby their views of the other. I do not find this emphasis on the individual convincing, and would prefer to see any such idiosyncrasy as structural. Those things which strike us as individual peculiarities are often due either to specific contemporary preoccupations, now half-forgotten, or to the effects of the overlaps of dominant, residual, and emergent forms.[7] In these latter cases, that which is remarkable is usually the result of the continued influence of inherited forms at a time when newer social relations and cultural practices are occurring alongside shifts in perceptions of the other but before newer forms for their expression have fully evolved. In other words, what may be taken for highly individual features (noteworthy either in their presumed uniqueness or in their distinctive communication of the typical) may in fact reflect tensions between older and newer forms and visions. Melville, Stanley (in all his voraciousness and brutality), and Conrad are so interesting because of their recognition of the insufficiency of dominant literary forms for what they wished to present as the truth of imperial relationships and racial perceptions. But because of this any idiosyncrasy in their texts is also an idiosyncrasy of the age.

The textual models available for travellers' self-fashioning, for the structuring of their accounts of their experiences and impressions, must be acknowledged as having an important effect on representations. Stanley's reading, for instance, included Samuel Johnson's *Rasselas*, Marryat, Cowper, Dryden, Pope, Milton, Spenser, Shakespeare, Fenimore Cooper,[8] Gibbon, Plutarch,[9] the Bible,[10] and Carlyle.[11] Quite apart from his reading of other travellers' and explorers' narratives, and the influence, both direct and indirect, of Darwinism, these references alone are enough to suggest that Stanley's literary presentation of himself, of his journeys, his thoughts, his encounters with others, his quests, his setbacks and doubts, and his triumphs, are all going to be affected consciously and subliminally by these Biblical, classical, and romantic models. One of the remarkable features of Stanley's writing is his blending of these with the discourses of late nineteenth-century science and popular journalism so that his texts seem to carry multiple layers of authority. Because of this, however, there is even greater need to see him not as an autonomous individual with his own idiosyncrasies, but as supremely representative and highly reflective of his age. It is surely strange that so many recent works on imperial and colonial discourse which insist on the typicality of authors' constructions of the other, at the same time grant those authors extraordinary powers of individual creativity by neglecting to consider the social origins of the author, contemporary ideas of authorship, previous and existing literary models, dealings with publishers, the publishers' (or others') editorial interventions, the marketing of the text, the intended and actual audience, the commercial status of the text and of its knowledge, and so on. There are, in short, all sorts of social, technological, and cultural factors which affect any individual's production and consumption of representations, and these are (or should be) particularly noticeable in the second half of the nineteenth century as social movements, technological innovations, and developments in the forms of capitalism combine with intellectual currents to shape not just people's comprehension of one another (and of self and other), but to alter the production, circulation, and reception of texts. Thus John MacKenzie is quite right to assert that:

> The evidence for the construction, development and utilisation of myths [of empire] is not to be found in official documents . . . or in the products of the 'official mind' of imperialism. It is to be found in the surrounding culture. This cultural environment provides important keys to the understanding of late nineteenth-century empire.[12]

This surrounding culture is a complex one, and at no time does its complexity give more concern than at the end of the century. Two of the most enduring adventurers of the *fin de siècle*, Conrad's Marlow and Wells's Time Traveller, address the anxiety not only of travel, but of interpreting the traveller and the tale. Explaining the difficulty of describing and understanding what one has seen, Wells's character draws the following analogy:

> Conceive the tale of London which a negro, fresh from Central Africa, would take back to his tribe! What would he know of railway companies, of social movements, of telephone and telegraph wires, of the Parcels Delivery Company, and postal orders and the like? Yet we, at least, should be willing enough to explain these things to him! And even of what he knew, how much could he make his untravelled friend either apprehend or believe?[13]

The Time Traveller's constant and unsatisfactory oscillation between socialist and Darwinist theories of economic and biological determinism brings home (literally) the problems of accounting for what one has seen. But the Traveller's use of the 'negro' from Central Africa makes it quite clear that the preoccupation is with self-knowledge. The African, like the very idea of time travel, and like the uses of spatial travel, is made to perform a defamiliarising role by which 'we', through temporal, cultural, or physical distance attempt to see 'ourselves' anew. Wells's cannibal, ape-like Morlocks are, we are told, descendants of the proletariat.[14] They are also a reminder of the beasts from which, evolutionary theory tells us, we are all descended and above which, naturalism contended, we have failed essentially to rise. Dwelling underground, except for nocturnal expeditions, they stand too for the unconscious and the dangers of the return of the repressed. Wells's powerful symbol of the racially, socially, and psychologically repressed, threatening control, serves as just one example of how the 'primitive', the 'savage', the black inhabitants of the 'dark continent' in the travel narratives I have discussed are made to bear multiple signification. It is this use of a textual space in which to project, displace, and work out problems of identity and relationship in order to understand 'ourselves' better that makes it wise to follow Edward Said's advice on the analysis of Orientalist (and, I would add, Africanist) texts: 'The things to look at are style, figures of speech, setting, narrative devices, historical and social circumstances, *not* the correctness of the representation nor its fidelity to some great original'.[15]

In avoiding the problems of an alternative ideological and textual construction of 'Africa' against which to judge travellers' representations of that continent, I certainly wish to understate neither the physical manifestations and results of imperialism nor the continued promotion of the images which accompanied it, and I hope I have gone some way to examining both.[16] I have tried neither to idealise a prelapsarian Africa nor to imply that today's travel writing is any purer or fairer or less self-serving than that which has formed the subject of the present study. Indeed, there is a depressing tendency nowadays to use the other for confirmation of the spiritual emptiness of one's own existence,[17] and to take as a cue for one's wanderings the treks of those 'heroic' figures which 'our' allegedly respectable but cautiously wistful post-imperial age lacks.[18] Such wilful nostalgia can make us blind to continued forms of domination. This case-study may stop at 1900 but the textual and physical consequences of the travellers' narratives are still apparent and active.

'Imperialism is total: it has economic, political, military, cultural and psychological consequences for the people of the world today',[19] writes the Kenyan author Ngũgĩ in the same work in which he denies that the works of Achebe or of any African novelist composing in European languages can be considered to be African literature, and in the same work in which, having decried and aiming to counter the alienating effects of a colonial education, he announces his 'farewell to English as a vehicle for any of my writings. From now on it is Gikuyu and Kiswahili all the way',[20] yet having in the same work acknowledged his debt to Conrad:

> the shifting points of view in time and space; the multiplicity of narrative voices; the narrative-within-a-narration; the delayed information that helps the revision of a previous judgement so that only at the end with the full assemblage of evidence, information and points of view, can the reader make full judgement – these techniques had impressed me.[21]

They impressed Ngũgĩ even as he realised they assumed a reader familiar with the convention of reading modern European novels, and as he began to move beyond these to strive for the development of authentic African literary forms in African languages as part of the 'ceaseless struggles of African people to liberate their economy, politics and culture from that Euro-American-based stranglehold to usher a new era of true communal self-regulation and self-determination'.[22] It is a stranglehold which travellers and readers of their narratives have helped to place.

Notes

1 N. Bell [N. D'Anvers], *Heroes of Discovery in South Africa* (London: Walter Scott, [1899]), pp. 393–4.
2 Craig Raine, 'Conrad and prejudice', *London Review of Books* 22 June 1989, 17.
3 Raine, 'Conrad and prejudice', 18.
4 Chinua Achebe, *Things Fall Apart* (London: Heinemann, [1958] 1962), pp. 147–8.
5 See Dennis Porter, *Haunted Journeys: Desire and Transgression in European Travel Writing* (Princeton: Princeton University Press, 1991), p. 19, note 27. Porter's unease is over 'certain relatively recent efforts to isolate "literary travel" from other kinds, to define the characteristics of the genre, and to formulate a poetics'.
6 Porter, *Haunted Journeys*, p. 9.
7 See Raymond Williams, 'Forms of English fiction in 1848', in *Writing in Society* (London: Verso, [n.d.]), pp. 150–65; and 'Dominant, residual, and emergent', in *Marxism and Literature* (Oxford: Oxford University Press, 1977), pp. 121–7.
8 Frank McLynn, *Stanley: The Making of an African Explorer* (London: Constable, 1989), pp. 25, 74, 82, 98.
9 John Bierman, *Dark Safari: The Life behind the Legend of Henry Morton Stanley* (London: Hodder & Stoughton, 1991), pp. 21–2. Bierman also notes that the young Stanley's purchases included Spenser's *Faerie Queene*, Pope's *Iliad*, Dryden's *Odyssey*, and Milton's *Paradise Lost* (pp. 21–2).
10 See for example Henry M. Stanley, *In Darkest Africa or the Quest, Rescue, and Retreat of Emin Governor of Equatoria*, new edition (London: Sampson Low, Marston & Company, [1890] 1893), pp. 181–2.
11 Jephson, one of Stanley's fellow officers on the Emin Pasha Relief Expedition, records being lent a copy of Carlyle's *Sartor Resartus* by Stanley. Dorothy Middleton, ed., *The Diary of A. J. Mounteney-Jephson: Emin Pasha Relief Expedition 1887–1889* (Cambridge: for the Hakluyt Society, Cambridge University Press, 1969), p. 224.

12 John M. MacKenzie, 'Heroic myths of empire', in *Popular Imperialism and the Military, 1850–1950*, ed. John M. MacKenzie (Manchester: Manchester University Press, 1992), p. 109.

13 H. G. Wells, 'The Time Machine', in *Selected Short Stories* (Harmondsworth: Penguin Books, 1958), p. 40. The tale was first serialised in the *New Review* in 1894–95, and published in book form in 1895.

14 Wells, 'The Time Machine', p. 47.

15 Edward W. Said, *Orientalism* (Harmondsworth: Peregrine Books, 1985), p. 21.
    On the ideological function of textual spaces see, for example, Lennard J. Davis, *Resisting Novels: Ideology and Fiction* (New York: Methuen, 1987).

16 For a review of some recent travel books on Africa see for example Tim Youngs, 'Writing Africa in the 1980s: travels with the doctor, the film maker and the anthropologist's wife', *Africa* 59, 3 (1989), 391–7.

17 For example see Bruce Chatwin's neo-primitivist book on his travels in Australia, *The Songlines* (London: Pan Books, 1988). James Clifford's application to ethnography and 'salvage anthropology' of Raymond Williams's comments on cultural nostalgia for an assumed pre-urban, harmonious, authentic whole are useful here. James Clifford, 'On ethnographic allegory', in *Writing Culture: The Poetics and Politics of Ethnography*, eds James Clifford and George E. Marcus (Berkeley: University of California Press, 1986), pp. 98–121. See especially pp. 112–19.

18 For just two of many examples see Peter Hudson, *Two Rivers: Travels in West Africa on the Trail of Mungo Park* (London: Chapmans, 1991) and Caroline Alexander, *One Dry Season: In the Footsteps of Mary Kingsley* (London: Bloomsbury, 1989).

19 Ngũgĩ wa Thiong'o, *Decolonising the Mind: The Politics of Language in African Literature* (London: James Currey, 1986), p. 2.

20 Ngũgĩ, *Decolonising the Mind*, p. xiv.

21 Ngũgĩ, *Decolonising the Mind*, p. 76.

22 Ngũgĩ, *Decolonising the Mind*, p. 4.

SELECT BIBLIOGRAPHY

Primary

Archive collections

Blackwood Papers, National Library of Scotland, Edinburgh.
Jameson Papers, Pitt Rivers Museum, Oxford.
Mackinnon Papers, School of Oriental and African Studies, London.
John Murray Publishers, London.
Royal Geographical Society, London.
Wellcome Institute and Foundation, London.

Books and articles

[Hardman, Fredrick.] 'Abyssinian aberrations'. *Blackwood's Edinburgh Magazine* 75 (February 1854), 129–50.

Anonymous. 'The Emin Relief Expedition', *The Aborigines' Friend* New Series 4, 3 (May 1890), 89–100.

Anonymous. 'Mr. Stanley and the Rear Column', *Contemporary Review* 58 (1890), 785–95.

Anonymous. '"The relief of Emin Pacha". In Darkest Africa by Henry M. Stanley', *The London Quarterly* 75 New Series 15 (October 1890), 25–48.

Anonymous. *Stanley and Africa*. London: Walter Scott, Limited, [n.d.].

Anonymous. *Recent Travel and Adventure*. New Edition. London: W. & R. Chambers, [n.d.].

Arnot, Fred. S. *Garenganze; or, Seven Years' Pioneer Mission Work in Central Africa*. 3rd ed. Introduction by Dr A. T. Pierson. London: James E. Hawkins, [n.d.].

Baker, Anne. *Morning Star: Florence Baker's Diary of the Expedition to Put down the Slave Trade on the Nile 1870–1873*. Foreword by Sir Ronald Wingate. London: William Kimber, 1972.

Baker, Sir Samuel W. 'On Abyssinia, or Ethiopia', *Proceedings of the Royal Institute* 5, 48 (1868), 404–18.

— *Ismailia: A Narrative of the Expedition to Central Africa for the Suppression of the Slave Trade Organized by Ismail, Khedive of Egypt*. 2 vols. London: Macmillan & Co., 1874.

— *The Nile Tributaries of Abyssinia and the Sword Hunters of the Hamran Arabs*. London: Macmillan & Co., Limited, 1907.

Baldwin, William Charles. *African Hunting: From Natal to the Zambesi, including Lake Ngami, the Kalahari Desert, etc., from 1852 to 1860*. New York: Harper & Brothers, 1863.

Ballantyne, R. M. *Hunting the Lions or the Land of the Negro*. London: James Nisbet & Co. Limited., [n.d.].

— *The Gorilla Hunters*. London: Collins' Clear-Type Press, [n.d.].

Barttelot, Walter George, ed. *The Life of Edmund Musgrave Barttelot*. 3rd ed.

London: Richard Bentley & Son, 1890.

Beke, Charles T. *The British Captives in Abyssinia*. 2nd ed. London: Longmans, Green, Reader, & Dyer, 1867.

Bell, N. [N. D'Anvers]. *Heroes of Discovery in South Africa*. London: Walter Scott, 1899.

Brown, Robert. *The Story of Africa and Its Explorers*. 4 vols. London: Cassell, 1892–95.

Buel, J. W. *Heroes of the Dark Continent and How Stanley Found Emin Pasha: A Complete History of all the Great Explorations and Discoveries in Central Africa, from the Earliest Ages to the Present Time*. Denver: World Publishing Co., 1889.

Burton, Richard F. *The Lake Regions of Central Africa: A Picture of Exploration*. 2 vols. London: Longman, Green, Longman, & Roberts, 1860.

— *'The Nile Basin' and 'Captain Speke's Discovery of the Source of the Nile' by James Macqueen*. London: Tinsley Brothers, 1864; reprint ed. with Introduction by Robert O. Collins, London: Frank Cass & Co., 1967.

— *Two Trips to Gorilla Land and the Cataracts of the Congo*. 2 vols. London: Sampson Low, Marston, Low, & Searle, 1876.

— *A Mission to Gelele, King of Dahome*. Edited by Isabel Burton. 2 vols. London: Tylston & Edwards, 1893.

Caddick, Helen. *A White Woman in Central Africa*. London: T. Fisher Unwin, 1900.

Cameron, Verney Lovett. *Across Africa*. 2 vols. London: Daldy, Isbister & Co., 1877.

Casati, Gaetano. *Ten Years in Equatoria and the Return with Emin Pasha*. Translated by the Hon. Mrs. J. Randolph Clay and Walter Savage Landor. 2 vols. London: Frederick Warne & Co., 1891.

Chaillé Long, C. *Central Africa: Naked Truths of Naked People. An Account of Expeditions to the Lake Victoria Nyanza and the Makraka Niam-Niam, West of Bahr-el-Abiad (White Nile)*. London: Sampson Low, Marston, Searle, & Rivington, 1876.; reprint ed., Farnborough: Gregg International Publishers Limited, 1968.

Conrad, Joseph. *Heart of Darkness*. Edited by Robert Kimbrough. 3rd ed. New York: W. W. Norton & Company, 1988.

Dufton, Henry. *Narrative of a Journey through Abyssinia in 1862–3*. London: Chapman & Hall, 1867.

Evelyn, J. *A Warrior King: The Story of a Boy's Adventures in Africa*. London: Blackie & Son, [n.d.].

Fotheringham, L. Monteith. *Adventures in Nyassaland: A Two Years' Struggle with Arab Slave-Dealers in Central Africa*. London: Sampson Low, Marston, Searle & Rivington, 1891.

Fox-Bourne, H. R. *The Other Side of the Emin Pasha Relief Expedition*. London: Chatto & Windus, 1891.

Gobat, Samuel. *Journal of Three Years' Residence in Abyssinia*. M. W. Dowd, 1851; reprint ed., New York: Negro Universities Press, 1969.

Grant, James Augustus. *A Walk across Africa or Domestic Scenes from my Nile Journal*. Edinburgh: William Blackwood & Sons, 1864.

[216]

BIBLIOGRAPHY

Gregory, B. K. *The Story of David Livingstone: Weaver-Boy, Missionary, Explorer*. 11th ed. London: The Sunday School Union, [n.d.].

Haggard, Henry Rider. *King Solomon's Mines* [1885]. Introduction by Roger Lancelyn Green. London: Collins, 1955.

Henty, G. A. *The March to Coomassie*. 2nd ed. London: Tinsley Brothers, 1874.

Hinderer, Anna. *Seventeen Years in the Yoruba Country: Memorials of Anna Hinderer, wife of the Rev. David Hinderer, C. M. S. Missionary in Western Africa*. Introduction by Richard B. Hone. New Edition. London: The Religious Tract Society, [n.d.].

Hoffmann, William. *With Stanley in Africa*. London: Cassell & Company, 1938.

Hore, Annie B. *To Lake Tanganyika in a Bath Chair*. London: Sampson Low, Marston, Searle, & Rivington, 1886.

Hotten, John Camden, ed. *Abyssinia and its People; or, Life in the Land of Prester John*. London: John Camden Hotten, 1868; reprint ed., New York: Negro Universities Press, 1969.

Jameson, Mrs J. S., ed. *Story of the Rear Column of the Emin Pasha Relief Expedition by the Late James S. Jameson, Naturalist to the Expedition*. London: R. H. Porter, 1890.

Johnson, Harry. *Night and Morning in Dark Africa*. London: London Missionary Society, [n.d].

Johnston, James. *Reality versus Romance in South Central Africa* [1893]. 2nd ed. with a new introduction by James Hooker. London: Frank Cass & Co., 1969.

Keltie, J. Scott. 'Mr. Stanley's expedition: its conduct and results', *Fortnightly Review* New Series 48 (1890), 66–81.

Keltie, J. Scott, ed. *The Story of Emin's Rescue as Told in Stanley's Letters*. New York: Harper & Bros., 1890; reprint ed., New York: Negro Universities Press, 1969.

Kingsley, Mary H. *Travels in West Africa: Congo Français, Corisco and Cameroons* [1897]. 4th ed. Introduction by Elizabeth Claridge, London. Virago, 1982.

Livingstone, David. *Missionary Travels and Researches in South Africa*. London: John Murray, 1857.

Lubbock, Sir John. *The Origin of Civilisation and the Primitive Condition of Man: Mental and Social Condition of Savages*. 3rd ed. London: Longmans, Green, & Co., 1875.

MacDonald, E. A. *Alexander MacKay: Missionary Hero of Uganda*. London: The National Sunday School Union, [n.d.].

Markham, Clements R. *A History of the Abyssinian Expedition*. London: MacMillan & Co., 1869.

Marston, Edward. *How Stanley Wrote 'In Darkest Africa': A Trip to Cairo and Back*. London: Sampson Low, Marston, Searle & Rivington, 1890.

— *After Work: Fragments from the Workshop of an Old Publisher*. London: William Heinemann, 1904.

Maurice, Albert. *H. M. Stanley: Unpublished Letters*. With a Preface by Denzil M. Stanley. London: W. & R. Chambers Ltd, 1955.

[217]

Moir, Jane F. *A Lady's Letters from Central Africa, a Journey from Mandala, Shiré Highlands, to Ujiji, Lake Tanganyika, and Back*. Introduction by Rev. T. M. Lindsay. Glasgow: James Maclehose & Sons, 1891.

Montefiore, Arthur. *Henry M. Stanley: The African Explorer*. 7th ed. London: S. W. Partridge & Co., [n.d.].

Mounteney-Jephson, A. J. *Emin Pasha and the Rebellion at the Equator: A Story of Nine Months' Experiences in the Last of the Soudan Provinces*. With the revision and co-operation of H. M. Stanley. 3rd ed. London: Sampson Low, Marston, Searle & Rivington, 1890; reprint ed., New York: Negro Universities Press, 1969.

— *The Diary of A. J. Mounteney-Jephson: Emin Pasha Relief Expedition 1887–1889*. Edited by Dorothy Middleton. Cambridge: for the Hakluyt Society at the University Press, 1969.

Nicoll, D. J. *Stanley's Exploits; or, Civilizing Africa*. 2nd ed. Aberdeen: James Leatham, 1891.

Parke, Thomas Heazle. *My Personal Experiences in Equatorial Africa as Medical Officer of the Emin Pasha Relief Expedition*. London: Sampson Low, Marston & Company Limited, 1891.

Parkyns, Mansfield. *Life in Abyssinia: Being Notes Collected During Three Years' Residence in that Country*. 2 vols. London: John Murray, 1853.

Perham, Margery, and Simmons, J. *African Discovery: An Anthology of Exploration*. London: Faber & Faber, 1942.

Peters, Carl. 'Stanley and Emin Pasha', *Contemporary Review* 58 (1890), 634–8.

Portal, Gerald H. *My Mission to Abyssinia*. London: Edward Arnold, 1892; reprint ed., New York: Negro Universities Press, 1969.

— *The British Mission to Uganda in 1893*. Edited by Rennell Rodd. London: Edward Arnold, 1894.

Pringle, M. A. *A Journey in East Africa Towards the Mountains of the Moon*. New edition. Edinburgh: William Blackwood & Sons, 1886.

Proctor, L. J. 'Dr. Livingstone', *Fraser's Magazine*. Old Series 86. New Series 6 (November 1872), 614–27.

Quilter, Harry. 'Mr. H. M. Stanley as leader and comrade', *Universal Review* 8, 31 (1890), 313–65.

— 'An African bubble! and how it was blown', *Universal Review* 8, 32 (1890), 469–98.

Romero, Patricia W., ed. *Women's Voices on Africa: A Century of Travel Writings*. Princeton: Markus Wiener Publishing, 1992.

Sanderson, Edgar. *Africa in the Nineteenth Century*. London: Seeley & Co. Limited, 1898.

Selous, Frederick Courtney. *Travel and Adventure in South-East Africa: Being the Narrative of the Last Eleven Years Spent by the Author on the Zambesi and its Tributaries; with an Account of the Colonisation of Mashunaland and the Progress of the Gold Industry in that Country* [1893]. London: Century Hutchinson Publishing, 1984.

Smith, R. Bosworth. 'Englishmen in Africa', *Contemporary Review* 59 (1891), 69–76.

Speke, John Hanning. *Journal of the Discovery of the Source of the Nile* [1863].

London: J. M. Dent & Co., 1906.

— *What Led to the Discovery of the Source of the Nile*. Edinburgh: William Blackwood & Sons, 1864.

Stairs, Lieut. W. G. 'Shut up in the African Forest', *The Nineteenth Century* XXIX, 167 (January 1891), 45–62.

— 'From the Albert Nyanza to the Indian Ocean', *The Nineteenth Century* XXIX, 172 (June 1891), 953–68.

Stanley, Dorothy, ed. *The Autobiography of Sir Henry Morton Stanley*. London: Sampson, Marston & Co. Ltd., 1909.

Stanley, Henry M. *Coomassie and Magdala: The Story of Two British Campaigns in Africa* [1874]. London: Sampson Low, Marston & Company, [n.d.].

— *How I Found Livingstone: Travels, Adventures, and Discoveries in Central Africa; Including Four Months' Residence with Dr. Livingstone* [1872]. New edition. London: Sampson Low, Marston, Searle, & Rivington, 1887.

— *Through the Dark Continent: Or the Sources of the Nile around the Great Lakes of Equatorial Africa and down the Livingstone River to the Atlantic Ocean* [1878]. New edition. London: Sampson Low, Marston, Searle, & Rivington, 1890.

The Congo and the Founding of its Free State: A Story of Work and Exploration. 2 vols. Cheaper edition. London: Sampson Low, Marston, Searle, & Rivington, 1886. Vol. I.

— *The Congo and the Founding of its Free State: A Story of Work and Exploration*. 2 vols. London: Sampson Low, Marston, Searle, & Rivington, 1885. Vol. II.

In Darkest Africa or the Quest, Rescue, and Retreat of Emin Governor of Equatoria [1890]. New edition. London: Sampson Low, Marston & Company, 1893.

Stanley, Richard, and Neame, Alan, eds. *The Exploration Diaries of H. M. Stanley*. London: William Kimber and Co., 1961.

Stevens, Thomas. *Scouting for Stanley in East Africa*. London: Cassell & Company, [n.d.].

Thomson, Joseph, and Harris-Smith, Miss. *ULU: An African Romance*. 2 vols. London: Sampson Low, Marston, Searle, & Rivington, Ltd, 1888.

Troup, J. Rose. *With Stanley's Rear Column*. London: Chapman & Hall, 1890.

— 'Mr. Stanley's rear-guard', *The Fortnightly Review* New Series 48 (1 December 1890), 817–29.

Wallis, J. P. R., ed. *The Zambesi Journal of James Stewart 1862–1863: With a Selection from his Correspondence*. London: Chatto & Windus, 1952.

Ward, Herbert. *Five Years with the Congo Cannibals*. London: Chatto & Windus, 1890.

— *My Life with Stanley's Rear Guard*. London: Chatto & Windus, 1891.

— 'Life among the Congo savages', *Scribner's Magazine* VII, 2 (February 1890), 135–56.

Wauters, A. J. *Stanley's Emin Pasha Expedition*. London: John C. Nimmo, 1890.

Wells, H. G. 'The Time Machine'. In *Selected Short Stories*, pp. 7–83. Harmondsworth: Penguin Books, 1958.

Yarborough, J. Cooke, ed. *The Diary of a Working Man (William Bellingham) in*

Central Africa, December, 1884, to October, 1887. London: Society for Promoting Christian Knowledge, [n.d.].

Secondary

Achebe, Chinua. *Things Fall Apart* [1958]. London: Heinemann, 1962.
— *Hopes and Impediments: Selected Essays 1965–1987*. Oxford: Heinemann International, 1988.
Adewumi, Mary Fadeke. 'Racial attitudes in the European literature of Africa from H. Rider Haggard to Joyce Cary'. Ph.D. thesis, Arizona State University, 1977.
Altick, Richard D. *The English Common Reader: A Social History of the Mass Reading Public 1800–1900*. Chicago: Chicago University Press, 1957.
Anonymous. *The Romance of Exploration and Emergency First-Aid from Stanley to Byrd*. New York: Burroughs, Wellcome & Co., 1934.
Anstey, Roger. 'The Congo rubber atrocities: a case study', *African Historical Studies* 4, 1 (1971), 59–76.
Anstruther, Ian. *I Presume: H. M. Stanley's Triumph and Disaster*. New edition. Gloucester: Alan Sutton, 1988.
Appadurai, Arjun, ed. *The Social Life of Things: Commodities in Cultural Perspective*. Cambridge: Cambridge University Press, 1986.
Arata, Stephen D. 'The Occidental tourist: *Dracula* and the anxiety of reverse colonization', *Victorian Studies* 23, 4 (summer 1990), 621–45.
Arens, W. *The Man-Eating Myth: Anthropology & Anthropophagy*. Oxford: Oxford University Press, 1980.
Arnold, David, ed. *Imperial Medicine and Indigenous Societies*. Manchester: Manchester University Press, 1988.
Arnold, Percy. *Prelude to Magdala: Emperor Theodore of Ethiopia and British Diplomacy*. Edited by Richard Pankhurst. London: Bellew Publishing, 1991.
Asad, Talal, ed. *Anthropology & the Colonial Encounter*. London: Ithaca Press, 1973.
— 'Anthropology and the analysis of ideology', *Man* New Series 14, 4 (1979), 607–27.
Beachey, R. W. 'The East African ivory trade in the nineteenth century', *Journal of African History* 8, 2 (1967), 269–90.
Becker, Peter. *The Pathfinders: The Saga of Exploration in Southern Africa*. Harmondsworth: Penguin Books, 1987.
Beidelman, T. O. *Colonial Evangelism: A Socio-Historical Study of an East African Mission at the Grassroots*. Bloomington: Indiana University Press, 1982.
Benjamin, Walter. 'The work of art in the age of mechanical reproduction'. In *Illuminations*, pp. 219–53. Edited by Hannah Arendt. Translated by Harry Zohn. London: Fontana, 1973.
Bennett, Norman R., ed. *Stanley's Despatches to the New York Herald 1871–1872, 1874–1877*. Boston: Boston University Press, 1970.
Best, Geoffrey. *Mid-Victorian Britain 1851–1975*. London: Fontana Press, 1979.
Bhabha, Homi K. 'The other question: difference, discrimination and the

discourse of colonialism'. In *Literature, Politics and Theory: Papers from the Essex Conference*, pp. 148–72. Edited by Francis Barker, Peter Hulme, Margaret Iversen, and Diana Loxley. London: Methuen, 1986.

Bierman, John. *Dark Safari: The Life Behind the Legend of Henry Morton Stanley*. London: Hodder & Stoughton, 1991.

Bishop, Peter. 'Consuming Constable (Diet, Utopian Landscape & National Identity)', Working Paper, Department of Geography, University of Nottingham, July 1990.

Bitterli, Urs. *Cultures in Conflict: Encounters between European and Non-European Cultures, 1492–1800*. Translated by Ritchie Robertson. Oxford: Polity Press, 1989.

Blake, Susan L. 'A woman's trek: what difference does gender make?'. In *Western Women and Imperialism*, pp. 19–34. Edited by N. Chaudhuri and M. Strobel. Bloomington: Indiana University Press, 1992.

Bolt, Christine. *Victorian Attitudes to Race*. London: Routledge & Kegan Paul, 1971.

Bongie, Chris. *Exotic Memories: Literature, Colonialism, and the Fin de Siècle*. Stanford: Stanford University Press, 1991.

Boon, James A. *Other Tribes, Other Scribes: Symbolic Anthropology in the Comparative Study of Cultures, Histories, Religions and Texts*. Cambridge: Cambridge University Press, 1982.

Brantlinger, Patrick. *Rule of Darkness: British Literature and Imperialism, 1830–1914*. Ithaca: Cornell University Press, 1988.

Bridges, R. C. 'Sir John Speke and the Royal Geographical Society', *Uganda Journal* 26 (1962), 23–43.

— 'Explorers and East African history', *Proceedings of the East African Academy* 1 (1963), 69–73.

— 'John Hanning Speke: negotiating a way to the Nile'. In *Africa and Its Explorers: Motives, Methods, and Impact*, pp. 95–137. Edited by Robert I. Rotberg. Cambridge, Mass.: Harvard University Press, 1970.

— 'Europeans and East Africans in the age of exploration'. In *The Exploration of Africa in the Eighteenth and Nineteenth Centuries*, pp. 119–39. University of Edinburgh Seminar Proceedings, 1971.

— 'The historical role of British explorers in East Africa', *Terræ Incognitæ* 14 (1982), 1–21.

— 'Nineteenth-century East African travel records with an appendix on "armchair geographers" and cartography'. In *European Sources for Sub-Saharan Africa Before 1900: Use and Abuse*. Edited by Beatrix Heintze and Adam Jones, *Paideuma* 33 (1987), 179–96.

Briggs, Asa. *Victorian Cities*. Harmondsworth: Penguin Books, 1968.

— *Victorian Things*. Harmondsworth: Penguin Books, 1990.

Bristow, Joseph. *Empire Boys: Adventures in a Man's World*. London: HarperCollinsAcademic, 1991.

Brode, Dr Heinrich. *Tippoo Tib: The Story of his Career in Central Africa. Narrated from his Own Accounts by Dr. Heinrich Brode and Translated by H. Havelock with a preface by Sir Charles Eliot*. London: Edward Arnold, 1907.

[221]

Brodie, Fawn M. *The Devil Drives: A Life of Sir Richard Burton*. London: Eyre & Spottiswoode, 1967; reprint ed., London: Eland, 1986.

Burnett, John. *Plenty and Want: A Social History of Diet in England from 1815 to the Present Day*. London: Nelson, 1966.

Cairns, H. Alan C. *Prelude to Imperialism: British Reactions to Central African Society 1840–1890*. London: Routledge & Kegan Paul, 1965.

Cannadine, David. 'The context, performance and meaning of ritual: the British monarchy and the "invention of tradition", c. 1820–1977'. In *The Invention of Tradition*, pp. 101–64. Edited by Eric Hobsbawm and Terence Ranger. Cambridge: Cambridge University Press, 1983.

Carter, Paul. *The Road to Botany Bay: An Essay in Spatial History*. London: Faber & Faber, 1987.

Casada, James Allan. 'The imperialism of exploration: British explorers and East Africa, 1856–1890'. Ph.D. thesis, Vanderbilt University, 1972.

— 'The motivational underpinnings of the British exploration of East Africa', *Proceedings of the South Carolina Historical Association* (1973), pp. 58–68.

— 'Henry Morton Stanley: the explorer as journalist', *Southern Quarterly* 15 (1977), 357–69.

Chamberlain, M. E. *The Scramble for Africa*. London: Longman, 1974.

Chandler, D. G. 'The expedition to Abyssinia, 1867–8'. In *Victorian Military Campaigns*, pp. 105–59. Edited by Brian Bond. London: Hutchinson, 1967.

Chatwin, Bruce. *The Songlines*. London: Pan Books, 1988.

Chrisman, Laura. 'The imperial unconscious? Representations of imperial discourse', *Critical Quarterly* 32, 3 (autumn 1990), 38–58.

Clifford, James. *The Predicament of Culture: Twentieth-Century Ethnography, Literature, and Art*. Cambridge, Mass.: Harvard University Press, 1988.

Clifford, James, and Marcus, George, eds. *Writing Culture: The Poetics and Politics of Ethnography*. Berkeley: University of California Press, 1986.

Collins, Harold Reeves. 'His image in ebony: the African in British fiction during the age of imperialism'. Ph.D. thesis, Columbia University, 1951.

Collins, Robert O. 'Old wine, emu, and I. P. A.', *Victorian Studies* 12, 4 (June 1969), 441–7.

Coombes, Annie Elena Stuart. 'The representation of Africa and the African in England, 1890–1913'. Ph.D. thesis, University of East Anglia, 1987.

Conrad, Joseph. *Last Essays*. Introduction by Richard Curle. New York: Doubleday, Page & Company, 1926.

Coupland, Sir Reginald. *The Exploitation of East Africa 1856–1890: The Slave Trade and the Scramble*. 2nd ed. Introduction by Jack Simmons. London: Faber & Faber Limited, 1968.

Crapanzano, Vincent. 'On the writing of ethnography', *Dialectical Anthropology* 2, 1 (February 1977), 69–73.

Cumming, Duncan. *The Gentleman Savage: The Life of Mansfield Parkyns 1823–1894*. London: Century Hutchinson, 1987.

Curtin, Philip D. *The Image of Africa: British Ideas and Action, 1780–1850*. London: Macmillan & Co. Ltd., 1965.

Curtin, Philip D., ed. *Africa Remembered: Narratives by West Africans from the Era of the Slave Trade*. Madison, Wisconsin: The University of Wisconsin Press, 1968.

— Africa & the West: Intellectual Responses to European Culture. Madison, Wisconsin: The University of Wisconsin Press, 1972.

Davis, Lennard J. *Resisting Novels: Ideology and Fiction*. New York: Methuen, 1987.

Diamond, Stanley. *In Search of the Primitive: A Critique of Civilization*. Foreword by Eric Wolf. New Brunswick: Transaction Books, 1987.

Douglas, Mary. 'Deciphering a meal'. In *Implicit Meanings: Essays in Anthropology*, pp. 249–75. London: Routledge & Kegan Paul, 1975.

Driver, Felix. 'Henry Morton Stanley and his critics: geography, exploration and empire', *Past& Present* 133 (November 1991), 134–66.

— 'Geography's empire: histories of geographical knowledge', *Society and Space* 10 (1992), 23–40.

Dunae, Patrick A. 'British juvenile literature in an age of empire: 1880–1914'. Ph.D. thesis, Victoria University of Manchester, 1975.

Eagleton, Terry. *Criticism and Ideology: A Study in Marxist Literary Theory* [1976]. London: Verso, 1978.

Elias, Norbert. *The Civilizing Process: The History of Manners*. Translated by Edmund Jephcott. Oxford: Basil Blackwell, 1978.

Eliot, T. S. *Notes towards the Definition of Culture* [1948]. London: Faber, 1962.

Emery, Frank. *Marching over Africa: Letters from Victorian Soldiers*. London: Hodder & Stoughton, 1986.

Fabian, Johannes. *Time and the Other: How Anthropology Makes its Object*. New York: Columbia University Press, 1983.

Fancher, Raymond E. 'Francis Galton's African ethnography and its role in the development of his psychology', *British Journal for the History of Science* 16 (March 1983), 67–79.

Fanon, Frantz. *The Wretched of the Earth*. Preface by Jean-Paul Sartre. Translated by Constance Farrington. Harmondsworth: Penguin Books, 1967.

— *Black Skin, White Masks*. Translated by Charles Lam Markmann. London: Pluto Press, 1986.

Farb, Peter, and Armelagos, George. *Consuming Passions: The Anthropology of Eating*. Boston: Houghton Mifflin Company, 1980.

Fischler, Claude. 'Food habits, social change and the nature/culture dilemma', *Social Science Information* 19, 6 (1980), 937–53.

— 'Food, Self and Identity', *Social Science Information* 27, 2 (1988), 275–92.

Foran, W. Robert. *African Odyssey: The Life of Verney Lovett-Cameron*. London: Hutchinson & Co., 1937.

Forgacs, David, ed. *A Gramsci Reader: Selected Writings 1916–1935*. London: Lawrence & Wishart, 1988.

Forster, Imogen. 'Nature's outcast child: black people in children's books', *Race & Class* 31, 1 (1989), 59–77.

Fothergill, Anthony. *Heart of Darkness*. Milton Keynes: Open University Press, 1989.

— 'Of Conrad, cannibals, and kin'. In *Representing Others: White Views of Indigenous Peoples*, pp. 37–59. Edited by Mick Gidley. Exeter: The University of Exeter Press, 1992.

Fraser, W. Hamish. *The Coming of the Mass Market, 1850–1914*. London: Macmillan, 1981.

Freud, Sigmund. 'Civilization and its discontents'. In *Civilization, Society and Religion*, The Penguin Freud Library vol. 12, pp. 243–340. General Editor James Strachey. Editor of Vol. 12 Albert Dickson. London: Penguin, 1991.

Galbraith, John S. *Mackinnon and East Africa 1878–1895: A Study in the 'New Imperialism'*. Cambridge: Cambridge University Press, 1972.

Geary, Christraud M. 'Photographs as materials for African history: some methodological considerations', *History in Africa* 13 (1986), 89–116.

Geertz, Clifford. *Works and Lives: The Anthropologist as Author*. Oxford: Polity Press, 1988.

George, Katherine. 'The civilized west looks at primitive Africa: 1400–1800: a study in ethnocentrism', *Isis* 49 (1958), 62–72.

Girouard, Mark. *The Return to Camelot: Chivalry and the English Gentleman*. New Haven: Yale University Press, 1981.

Goode, John. 'The decadent writer as producer'. In *Decadence and the 1890s*, pp. 109–29. Edited by Ian Fletcher. London: Edward Arnold, 1979.

Goody, Jack. *Cooking, Cuisine and Class: A Study in Comparative Sociology*. Cambridge: Cambridge University Press, 1982.

Gordon, Jan B. '"Decadent spaces": notes for a phenomenology of the fin de siècle'. In *Decadence and the 1890s*, pp. 31–58. Edited by Ian Fletcher. London: Edward Arnold, 1979.

Gould, Tony. *In Limbo: The Story of Stanley's Rear Column*. London: Hamish Hamilton, 1979.

Greene, Graham. *Journey Without Maps*. London: Pan Books, 1957.

Hall, Richard. *Stanley: An Adventurer Explored*. London: Collins, 1974.

— *Lovers on the Nile*. London: Collins, 1980.

Hammond, Dorothy, and Jablow, Alta. *The Africa that Never Was: Four Centuries of British Writing about Africa*. New York: Twayne Publishers, 1970.

Harcourt, Freda. 'Disraeli's imperialism, 1866–68: a question of timing', *The Historical Journal* 23, 1 (1980), 87–109.

Hardy, Barbara. *The Moral Art of Dickens*. London: Athlone, 1970.

Harman, Nicholas. *Bwana Stokesi and his African Conquests*. London: Jonathan Cape, 1986.

Harms, Robert. 'Slave systems in Africa', *History in Africa* 5 (1978), 327–35.

Harrison, J. F. C. *Early Victorian Britain, 1832–51*. London: Fontana Press, 1979.

— *Late Victorian Britain 1870–1901*. London: Fontana Press, 1990.

Hawthorn, Jeremy. *Joseph Conrad: Language and Fictional Self-Consciousness*. London: Edward Arnold, 1979.

Headrick, Daniel R. *The Tools of Empire: Technology and European Imperialism in the Nineteenth Century*. New York: Oxford University Press, 1981.

Helly, Dorothy O. '"Informed" Opinion on Tropical Africa in Great Britain 1860–1890', *African Affairs* 68 (1969), 195–217.

— *Livingstone's Legacy: Horace Waller and Victorian Mythmaking*. Athens, Ohio: Ohio University Press, 1987.

Herbert, Christopher. *Culture and Anomie: Ethnographic Imagination in the Nineteenth Century*. Chicago: The University of Chicago Press, 1991.

Himmelfarb, Gertrude. *The Idea of Poverty: England in the Early Industrial Age*. London: Faber & Faber, 1984.

Hobsbawm, E. J. *The Age of Empire 1875–1914*. London: Cardinal, 1989.

Hooker, James R. 'Verney Lovett Cameron: a sailor in Central Africa'. In *Africa and Its Explorers: Motives, Methods, and Impact*, pp. 255–94. Edited by Robert I. Rotberg. Cambridge, Mass.: Harvard University Press, 1970.

Houghton, Walter E. *The Victorian Frame of Mind 1830–1870*. New Haven: Yale University Press, 1957.

Hsu, Francis L. K. 'Rethinking the concept "primitive"', *Current Anthropology* 5 (1964), 169–78.

Hulme, Peter. *Colonial Encounters: Europe and the Native Caribbean, 1492–1797*. London: Methuen, 1986.

Humphries, Reynold. 'The discourse of colonialism: its meaning and relevance for Conrad's fiction', *Conradiana* 21, 2 (1989), 107–33.

Ingham, K. 'John Hanning Speke: a Victorian and his inspiration', *Tanganyika Notes and Records* 49 (1957), 301–11.

— *A History of East Africa*. 3rd ed. London: Longman, 1965.

Jameson, Fredric. 'Of islands and trenches: naturalization and the production of Utopian discourse', *Diacritics* 7, 2 (1977), 2–21.

— 'Reification and Utopia in mass culture', *Social Text* 1 (winter 1979), 130–48.

— *The Political Unconscious: Narrative as a Socially Symbolic Act*. London: Methuen, 1981.

Jones, Roger. *The Rescue of Emin Pasha: The Story of Henry M. Stanley and the Emin Pasha Relief Expedition, 1887–1889*. London: History Book Club, 1972.

Joyce, Elisabeth. 'White man's burden: white woman's lark. Mary Kingsley and the myth of the explorer hero', *Trent Papers in Communication* 2 (1984), 99–116.

Kiernan, V. G. *The Lords of Human Kind: European Attitudes Towards the Outside World in the Imperial Age*. Harmondsworth: Penguin Books, 1972.

Killam, G. D. *Africa in English Fiction 1874–1939*. Ibadan: Ibadan University Press, 1968.

Klein, Martin A. 'Slavery, the slave trade, and legitimate commerce in late nineteenth-century Africa', *Etudes d'Histoire Africaine* 2 (1971), 5–28.

Knox-Shaw, Peter. 'The explorer, and views of creation', *English Studies in Africa* 27, 1 (1984), 1–26.

— *The Explorer in English Fiction*. Basingstoke: Macmillan, 1987.

Konczacki, Janina. 'The Emin Pasha Relief Expedition (1887–1889): some comments on disease and hygiene', *Canadian Journal of African Studies* 19, 3 (1985), 615–25.

Kramer, Fritz W. 'The otherness of the European', *Culture and History* 6 (1989), 107–23.

Kuklick, Henrika. *The Savage Within: The Social History of British Anthropology, 1885–1945*. Cambridge: Cambridge University Press, 1991.

Lamb, Patricia Anne Frazer. 'The life and writing of Mary Kingsley: mirrors of the self'. Ph.D. thesis, Cornell University, 1977.

Lamden, S. C. 'Some aspects of porterage in East Africa', *Tanganyika Notes and Records* 61 (1963), 155–64.

Langlands, B. W. 'Early travellers to Uganda, 1860–1914', *Uganda Journal* 26 (1962), 55–71.

Lévi-Strauss, Claude. *Tristes Tropiques*. Translated by John and Doreen Weightman. Harmondsworth: Penguin Books, 1976.

Livingston, Judith Hochstein. 'The impact of Africa upon major British literary figures, 1787–1902'. Ph.D. thesis, University of Wisconsin-Madison, 1977.

Lorimer, Douglas. *Colour, Class and the Victorians: English Attitudes to the Negro in the Mid-Nineteenth Century*. Leicester: Leicester University Press, 1978.

— 'Theoretical racism in late-Victorian anthropology, 1870–1900', *Victorian Studies* 31, 3 (spring 1988), 405–30.

Lucas, John. *Modern English Poetry: From Hardy to Hughes*. London: B. T. Batsford, 1986.

— 'Love of England: the Victorians and patriotism', *Browning Society Notes* 17, 1–3 (1987–8), 63–76.

Luck, Anne. *Charles Stokes in Africa*. Foreword by H. B. Thomas. Nairobi: East African Publishing House, 1972.

MacKenzie, John M. *Propaganda and Empire: The Manipulation of British Public Opinion, 1880–1960*. Manchester: Manchester University Press, 1984.

— *The Empire of Nature: Hunting, Conservation and British Imperialism*. Manchester: Manchester University Press, 1988.

MacKenzie, John M., ed. *Imperialism and Popular Culture*. Manchester: Manchester University Press, 1986.

— *Popular Imperialism and the Military, 1850–1950*. Manchester: Manchester University Press, 1992.

McLellan, David. *Marx's Grundrisse*. London: Granada Publishing, 1971.

McLynn, Frank. *Stanley: The Making of an African Explorer*. London: Constable, 1989.

— *Burton: Snow upon the Desert*. London: John Murray, 1990.

— *Stanley: Sorcerer's Apprentice*. London: Constable, 1991.

— *Hearts of Darkness: The European Exploration of Africa*. London: Hutchinson, 1992.

Mahood, M. M. *The Colonial Encounter: A Reading of Six Novels*. London: Rex Collings, 1977.

Maitland, Alexander. *Speke* [1971]. Newton Abbot: Victorian (& Modern History) Book Club, 1973.

Manning, Patrick. *Francophone Sub-Saharan Africa 1880–1985*. Cambridge: Cambridge University Press, 1988.

Marcus, George E., and Cushman, Dick. 'Ethnographies as texts', *Annual Review of Anthropology* 11 (1982), 25–69.

Marx, Karl, and Engels, Frederick. *Manifesto of the Communist Party*. Peking: Foreign Languages Press, 1975.

Mazrui, Ali A. 'European exploration and Africa's self-discovery', *Journal of Modern African Studies* 7, 4 (1969), 661–76.

Memmi, Albert. *The Colonizer and the Colonized*. London: Souvenir Press

(Educational & Academic) Ltd, 1974.

Mills, Sara. 'Alternative voices to Orientalism', *LTP: Journal of Literature Teaching Politics* 5 (1986), 78–91.

— *Discourses of Difference: An Analysis of Women's Travel Writing and Colonialism*. London: Routledge, 1991.

Mintz, Sidney W. *Sweetness and Power: The Place of Sugar in Modern History*. New York: Viking, 1985.

Moorehead, Alan. *The Blue Nile*. London: Hamish Hamilton, 1962.

— *The White Nile*. Harmondsworth: Penguin Books, 1963.

Murcott, Anne, ed. *The Sociology of Food and Eating: Essays on the Sociological Significance of Food*. Aldershot: Gower, 1983.

Myatt, Frederick. *The March to Magdala: The Abyssinian War of 1868*. London: Leo Cooper, 1970.

Nash, Dennison, and Wintrob, Ronald. 'The emergence of self-consciousness in ethnography', *Current Anthropology* 13, 5 (December 1972), 527–42.

Nederveen Pieterse, Jan. *White on Black: Images of Africa and Blacks in Western Popular Culture*. New Haven: Yale University Press, 1992.

Neetens, Wim. *Writing and Democracy: Literature, Politics and Culture in Transition*. London: Harvester Wheatsheaf, 1991.

Ngũgĩ wa Thiong'o. *Petals of Blood* [1977]. Oxford: Heinemann, 1986.

— *Decolonising the Mind: The Politics of Language in African Literature*. London: James Currey, 1986.

Nichols, Ashton. 'Silencing the other: the discourse of domination in nine-teenth-century exploration narratives', *Nineteenth Century Studies* 3 (1989), 1–22.

Oakes, Katherine Beverley. 'Social theory in the early literature of voyage and exploration in Africa'. Ph.D. thesis, University of California, 1944.

O'Connor, Erin. '"A pleasure to be indulged with caution": gender and prophylaxis in Mary Kingsley's *Travels in West Africa*', paper delivered to the 1993 INCS Conference at Arizona State University.

Oliver, Roland. *The Missionary Factor in East Africa*. London: Longmans, Green & Co., 1952.

Owusu, Maxwell. 'Ethnography of Africa: the usefulness of the useless', *American Anthropologist* 80, 2 (June 1978), 310–34.

Parrinder, Patrick. '*Heart of Darkness*: geography as apocalypse'. In *Fin de Siècle/Fin du Globe: Fears and Fantasies of the Late Nineteenth Century*, pp. 85–101. Edited by John Stokes. Basingstoke: Macmillan, 1992.

Parry, Benita. 'Problems in current theories of colonial discourse', *The Oxford Literary Review* 9, 1–2 (1987), 27–58.

— *Conrad and Imperialism: Ideological Boundaries and Visionary Frontiers*. London: Macmillan, 1983.

Porter, Dennis. *Haunted Journeys: Desire and Transgression in European Travel Writing*. Princeton, N.J.: Princeton University Press, 1991.

Pratt, Mary Louise. *Imperial Eyes: Travel Writing and Transculturation*. London: Routledge, 1992.

Raine, Craig. 'Conrad and prejudice', *London Review of Books*, 22 June 1989, 16–18.

Ranger, Terence. 'The invention of tradition in Colonial Africa'. In *The Invention of Tradition*, pp. 211–62. Edited by Eric Hobsbawm and Terence Ranger. Cambridge: Cambridge University Press, 1984.

Ransford, Oliver. *'Bid the Sickness Cease': Disease in the History of Black Africa*. London: John Murray, 1983.

Richards, Thomas. *The Commodity Culture of Victorian England: Advertising and Spectacle, 1851–1914*. Stanford, California: California University Press, 1990.

Riffenburgh, Beau, *The Myth of the Explorer: The Press, Sensationalism, and Geographical Discovery* (London: Belhaven Press, 1993).

Robinson, Ronald; Gallagher, John; and Denny, Alice. *Africa and the Victorians: The Official Mind of Imperialism*. 2nd ed. Basingstoke: Macmillan, 1981.

Rodway, A. E. 'The last phase'. In *The Pelican Guide to English Literature*. Vol. 6: *From Dickens to Hardy*, pp. 385–405. Edited by Boris Ford. Harmondsworth: Penguin Books, 1958.

Rogers, Alfred Henderson. 'Racial and cultural values of three Victorian explorers in Africa'. Ph.D. thesis, University of Mississippi, 1970.

Rotberg, Robert I., ed. *Africa and Its Explorers: Motives, Methods, and Impact*. Cambridge, Mass.: Harvard University Press, 1970.

Said, Edward. *Orientalism* [1978]. Harmondsworth: Peregrine, 1985.

— 'Representing the colonized: anthropology's interlocutors', *Critical Inquiry* 15, 2 (1989), 205–25.

— *Culture and Imperialism*. London: Chatto & Windus, 1993.

Sams, Henry W. 'Malinowski and the novel; or, cultural anthropology', *The Journal of General Education* 26, 2 (1974), 125–38.

Shannon, Richard. *The Crisis of Imperialism 1865–1915*. London: Paladin, 1976.

Sherry, Norman. *Conrad's Western World*. Cambridge: Cambridge University Press, 1971.

Simpson, Donald. *Dark Companions: The African Contribution to the European Exploration of East Africa*. London: Paul Elek, 1975.

Sinfield, Alan. *Alfred Tennyson*. Oxford: Basil Blackwell, 1986.

Smith, Iain R. *The Emin Pasha Relief Expedition 1886–1890*. Oxford at the Clarendon Press, 1972.

Spidle, Jake W. 'Victorian juvenilia and the image of the black African', *Journal of Popular Culture* 9, 1 (summer 1975), 51–65.

Stocking, George., Jr. *Victorian Anthropology*. New York: The Free Press, 1987.

Stokes, John. *In the Nineties*. New York: Harvester Wheatsheaf, 1989.

Street, Brian. *The Savage in Literature: Representations of 'Primitive' Society in English Fiction 1858–1920*. London: Routledge & Kegan Paul, 1975.

Surel, Jeannine. 'John Bull'. In *Patriotism: The Making and Unmaking of British National Identity*. Vol. III: *National Fictions*, pp. 3–25. Edited by Raphael Samuel. London: Routledge, 1989.

Tannahill, Reay. *Food in History*. London: Eyre Methuen, 1973.

Tanner, Tony. '"Gnawed bones and artless tales" – eating and narrative in Conrad'. In *Joseph Conrad: A Commemoration. Papers from the 1974 Inter-*

national Conference on Conrad, pp. 17–36. Edited by Norman Sherry. London: Macmillan, 1976.

Tennyson, Alfred Lord. The Works of Alfred Lord Tennyson Poet Laureate. London: Macmillan, 1893.

Tessore, Alberto. 'Different approaches to other cultures by foreign travellers in Ethiopia', Quaderni di Studi Etiopia 3–4 (1982–3), 5–25.

Thompson, E. P. 'Time, work-discipline, and industrial capitalism', Past and Present 38 (1967), 56–97.

Thompson, John B. Ideology and Modern Culture: Critical Social Theory in the Era of Mass Communication. Oxford: Polity Press, 1990.

Thornton, Robert. 'Narrative ethnography in Africa, 1850–1920: the creation and capture of an appropriate domain for anthropology', Man New Series 18, 3 (1983), 502–20.

Torgovnick, Marianna. Gone Primitive: Savage Intellects, Modern Lives. Chicago: The University of Chicago Press, 1990.

Turner, Brian. 'The discourse of diet', Theory, Culture & Society 1 (1982), 23–32.

Wassermann, Jacob. Bula Matari: Stanley, Conqueror of a Continent. Translated by Eden and Cedar Paul. New York: Liveright, Inc., 1933.

Watt, Ian. Conrad in the Nineteenth Century. London: Chatto & Windus, 1980.

Welbourn, F. B. 'Speke and Stanley at the court of Mutesa', Uganda Journal 25 (1961), 220–3.

White, Hayden. Tropics of Discourse: Essays in Cultural Criticism. Baltimore: The Johns Hopkins University Press, 1978.

Williams, Raymond. Marxism and Literature. Oxford: Oxford University Press, 1977.

— The Country and the City. London: The Hogarth Press, 1985.

— Keywords: A Vocabulary of Culture and Society. London: Fontana Press, 1988.

— Writing in Society. London: Verso, [n.d.].

Wyk Smith, M. van 'The origins of some Victorian images of Africa', English in Africa 6, 1 (1979), 12–32.

— '"Waters flowing from darkness": the two Ethiopias in the early European image of Africa', Theoria 68 (1986), 67–77.

Wyllie, R. W. 'Some contradictions in missionizing Africa', Africa 46 (1976), 196–204.

Young, Robert. White Mythologies: Writing History and the West. London: Routledge, 1990.

Youngs, Tim. 'Writing Africa in the 1980s: travels with the doctor, the film maker and the anthropologist's wife', Africa 59, 3 (1989), 391–7.

— '"My footsteps on these pages": the inscription of self and "race" in H. M. Stanley's How I Found Livingstone', Prose Studies 13, 2 (September 1990), 230–49.

— Review-essay on Clifford Geertz, Works and Lives: The Anthropologist as Author. In Theory and Society 19 (1990), 382–6.

— 'Victorian Britain and "primitive" Africa: figures and tools of imperialism', Africa 61, 1 (1991), 118–27.

[229]

— 'The medical officer's diary: travel and travail with the self in Africa'. In *Representing Others: White Views of Indigenous Peoples*, pp. 25–36. Edited by Mick Gidley. Exeter: The University of Exeter Press, 1992.

— 'Buttons and souls: some thoughts on nineteenth-century women travellers to Africa'. Paper given at the 1992 Sociology of Literature Symposium, 'Writing Travels', University of Essex.

INDEX

Note: Page references in *italics* refer to figures

Abyssinia 14–50
Achebe, Chinua 185, 189, 194, 208, 212
   Things Fall Apart 208–9
Adulteration of Foods Act
   (1860) 56
   (1872) 57
Agnostic Journal 165
Allen, Charles 114
American Civil War 24, 31
Anglo-Belgian Katanga Company 105, 125
Anthropological Society 24
Appadurai, Arjun 82
Armelagos, George 67
Arnold, Edwin 120, 152, 167
Aroghee, battle of 27–8
Assize of Bread 56
Austin, Alfred 42, 43

Baker, Sir Samuel White 29, 67, 82
Baldwin, William 71, 72
Barttelot, Major Edmund Musgrave 141, 155
   cruelty of 156–9
   death 116, 131
   public opinion of 167, 168, 171–2
   racism of 121–2
   role in Emin Pasha Relief
      Expedition 116–17, 119–20, 121–2, 122–7, 128
   social class 124, 134
   on Stanley 119–20, 122, 123, 126, 127
   Ward on 139
Barttelot, Walter George 122, 123, 124, 126
Beke, Charles 30, 37–9
Bennett, James Gordon Jr 30
Bennett, Norman 74

Bentley, W. Holman 208, 209
Bhabha, Homi 3, 4, 81
Bierman, John 184
Bismarck 24
Blackwood, John 84, 85–7
Bonny, Sergeant William 117, 118, 127, 133, 138, 147, 157, 158, 168, 175
Bradshaw, Captain 104
Brantlinger, Patrick 9, 10, 184, 185
Bridges, Roy 5, 6, 87–8, 90
Bright, John 24
Brontë, Emily: *Wuthering Heights* 7
Bruce, James 14, 56, 58–9, 62, 64, 65, 152, 153
Burnett, John 55, 56, 68
Burroughs & Wellcome 175, 176
Burton, Richard, Sir 74, 87, 92–3, 95–8, 105, 135, 157
   criticism of Speke 82–3
   on food 67–70
   on gifts 96–8
   Lake Regions of Central Africa, The 95
   Nile Basin, The 92

Cameron, Captain Verney Lovett 26, 83, 99–105, 125
   Across Africa 101, 104
Campanhia da Zambesia 105
Cannadine, David 31
cannibalism 77, 129, 130, 208
Casada, James 81, 82
Casati, Major Gaetano 73
Cobden, Richard 24
commoditisation 173–8
Conrad, Joseph 2, 11, 119, 171, 211
   'Geography and Some Explorers' 194

Heart of Darkness 77, 105, 106, 182–205
Nigger of the 'Narcissus', The 192
Outpost of Progress, An 192
'Travel' 194
Consuming Passions 77
Contemporary Review 171
Cooper, Charles 152, 153
Cracroft, Bernard 24
Crapanzano, Vincent 22
Crimean War 24
Cromer, Lord 46, 47
cruelty 128–9, 156–9
Cumming, Duncan 36–7
Gentleman Savage, The 22

Daily Chronicle 154
Daily Graphic 161
Daily News 152, 163
Daily Telegraph 152, 153, 155, 156
De Gama, Vasco 96
de Noailles, Countess 117
de Winton, Sir Francis 151, 152, 153, 154
Dickens, Charles 44
Bleak House 20
Great Expectations 57
Dillon, W.E. 99
Disraeli, Benjamin 25
Driver, Felix 6
Dufton, Henry 28–9

Eagleton, Terry 119
East India Company 95
Eliot, T.S. 58
Emin Pasha Relief Expedition 66, 76, 113–47, 151
Barttelot on 122–7
commoditisation of 173–8
connection with Conrad's *Heart of Darkness* 183–5
Jameson on 127–31
Jephson on 131–5
Parke on 135–7
press claims on proprietorship 151–4
press comments on 155–67

public opinion of 167–73
Stanley on 140–7
Troup on 121–2
Ward on 137–40
Engels, F. 187
Essays on Reform 24
Eyre, Governor 24, 25

Farb, Peter 67
Felkin, R.W. 114
Fischler, Claude 58, 62, 70
food and eating
adulteration 56–7
and bestiality 68
cannibalism 77, 129, 130, 208
eating habits in Britain 54–6
food, commodity and identity 75–8
hierarchical eating habits 61–2
raw 58–72
and sex 64–5
and the town 54–8
and writing 72–5
Foran, W. Robert 104–5
Fothergill, Anthony 1, 185
Fotheringham, L. Monteith 177–8
Fox-Bourne, H.R. 170
Freud, Sigmund 201, 203

Garnett, Edward 192
Glave, Edward 196
Godman, Mabel 119, 120
Goody, Jack 55, 64–5, 75
Gordon, General 114
Gordon, Jan 120
Gosse, Edmund 154
Gramsci, A. 6
Grant, James Augustus 83, 85, 87, 90, 93–5, 106
Great Exhibition (1851) 7, 15–16
Greene, Graham 1

Hammond, Dorothy 83
Harcourt, Freda 25
Hardman, Frederick: 'Abyssinian Aberrations' 23
Hardy, Barbara 57
Hardy, Thomas 145

Hassall, Dr Arthur 56
Hawthorn, Jeremy 2
Henley, W.E. 162
Henry, John 157–8
Henty, G.A. 30, 145
Hewett, Admiral Sir William 41
Hoffmann, William 118
Homer: *Odyssey* 15
Hooker, James R. 104
Hotten, John Camden 39
Hulme, Peter 4, 70
Hunt, James 24
Hutchisson (servant) 42, 43

Imperial British East Africa Company
    126
Indian Mutiny 24

Jablow, Alta 83
Jameson, Andrew 127, 168
Jameson, Ethel 128, 183
Jameson, Fredric 177
Jameson, James Sligo 116, 117,
    127–31, 140, 158, 159–60, 170
    Story of the Rear Column 127
Jameson, John 117
Jephson, James Mounteney 66, 117,
    118, 126, 131–5, 147, 170
    *Emin Pasha and the Rebellion at
    the Equator* 131
Johannis, King 41, 42, 48, 49, 50
John Bull 163, 166
Johnson, Samuel: *Rasselas* 17
Jones, Roger 118, 184
Juma (cook), hanging of 141
Jumah (servant) 100

Kamrasi, King of Unyoro 91–2
Kasongo, Chief 101
Kassa, Prince of Tigré 41
Keltie, J. Scott 172
Kipling, Rudyard 162
Knox-Shaw, Peter 142

Lawson, J. Adelberg: 'Stanley's rescue'
    173

Leopold, King of Belgium 114, 115,
    151, 184
Leslie, Dr R. 118
Lévi-Strauss, Claude 67
Liverpool Post 161
Livingstone, David 8, 30, 32, 82, 83,
    99, 106, 156, 171
Lloyd, Edward 153
Lorimer, Douglas 25
Low, Sampson 171
Lubbock, Sir John: *Origin of
    Civilisation and the Primitive
    Condition of Man* 74
Lucas, John 42, 43

M'Kate (servant) 95
Mackenzie, John 174, 211
Mackinnon, William 114–15, 140,
    152, 153, 154
Macqueen, James 92, 93, 98, 135
Mahood, Molly 183, 184
Maitland, Alexander 87
Makoko, Chief 188
Manchester Guardian 153
Markham, Sir Clements 99
marriages between Europeans and
    Africans 18–19
Marston, Edward 120, 167, 170, 175
    *How Stanley Wrote 'In Darkest
    Africa': A Trip to Cairo and Back*
    144
Marx, Karl 67, 187
McLynn, Frank 118
Melville, Herman 210
Menelek, King of Shoa 49
Mill, Stuart 45
Moorehead, Alan 54, 93
Mouvement Géographique 170
'Mr. Portal's Mission to Abyssinia' 49
Mtésa 91, 94
Murabo, Chief 134
Murphy, Lieutenant Cecil 99
Mussolini, B. 50
Myatt, Frederick 36

Napier, Sir Robert 26, 28–30, 39, 41,
    44, 54

National Observer 162–3
Neetens, Wim 119
Nelson, Captain Robert 117, 132, 133, 136, 147
New York Herald 152, 160
Ngũgĩ wa Thiong'o 212
  Petals of Blood 78
Nile, sources of 11, 82–3, 93
Noble Savage, idea of 14, 23–4, 35, 46, 62, 89, 96

Palmerston, Lord 24, 37, 94
Paris Geographical Society 83
Parke, Dr Thomas Heazle 66, 117, 132, 135–7, 147, 175, 176
Parkyns, Mansfield 15–24, 25, 28–30, 36, 39, 43, 45, 87, 102
  on food 59–62, 66, 75
  Life in Abyssinia 16, 17, 20
Pasha, Emin 76, 114–16, 131, 134, 143–4
Pasha, General Hicks 41
Pieterse, Jan Nederveen 7
Pocock, Frank 195
Portal, Gerald H. 39–42, *40*, 44–50
  My Mission to Abyssinia 39
Porter, Dennis 209, 210
Pringle, M. A. 74

Quilter, Harry 167, 168–71

race fetish 81
Raine, Craig 208
Ranger, Terence 70
Rare Bits 163, *164*
Ras Alula, Chief 41, 46, 47
Rashid, Chief 141
Rawlinson, Sir Henry 33
Reform Act
  (1867) 24, 25
  (1884) 119
Report on the Sanitary Condition of the Labouring Population of Great Britain 55
Richards, Thomas 75
Ripon, Earl of 83
Rodd, R. 47

Royal Geographical Society 82, 83, 87–8, 93, 99
Rumanika, King 90

Said, Edward 2–3, 10, 11, 200, 212
  Orientalism 1
Sale of Food and Drugs Act (1875) 57
Samuel (steward) 30
Sanderson, Edgar 26, 28
Sanga (porter) 123, 127
Saturday Review 161–2
Schnitzer, Edouard see Pasha, Emin
Scotsman, The 152
sex 18, 20, 64–5
Shakespeare, William
  Othello 127
  Tempest, The 70–1
Sherry, Norman 184
Slater, Edward 174
slavery 103
Smith, Adam 45
Smith, Iain 115, 116, 117
Smith, R. Bosworth 171
social class, importance of 118, 124, 134
Spectator 160
Speke, John 67, 82–93, *84*, 99, 102, 106, 135, 136, 157
  criticism by Burton 92–3
  Journal of the Discovery of the Source of the Nile 84, 88, 92
  parentage 87
Spencer, Herbert 67
Stairs, Lieutenant William 118, 125, 126, 132, 136, 147
Standard, The 152
Stanley, Henry Morton 82, 83, 105–10, 131
  on Abyssinia 30–7
  on Africans and writing 73–4
  Autobiography 146
  Barttelot on 119–20, 122, 123, 126, 127
  cartoons of 163–5, *164*, *166*
  commoditisation 76, 173–8
  Congo and the Founding of its Free State, The 133, 176, 187

Emin Pasha and 115–16
Emin Pasha Relief Expedition and
  115–22, 140–7
on exploitation of Congo 187–91,
  195–6
on food 54, 66
How I Found Livingstone 31, 65
In Darkest Africa 118, 140, 145,
  146–7, 175, 176
Jameson on 130
Jephson on 134–5
Parke on 136–7
press reaction to 155–6, 160
on power of money 32–3
public opinion on 167–73
reading 210
Through the Dark Continent 83,
  105, 109, 120, 154
Troup on 121, 156–7
Staveley, Sir Charles 26
Stern (missionary) 26
Stevens, Thomas: *Scouting for
  Stanley in East Africa* 176
Stevenson, R.L.: *Jekyll and Hyde* 197
Stocking, George 89, 90
  Victorian Anthropology 67
Stoker, Bram 145
Suez Canal 83

Tannahill, Reay 61, 64
tea 76–7, 174
Tennyson, Alfred Lord 42, 119
Theodore, King of Abyssinia 25–7, 29,
  31, 38, 41, 42, 45
  house at Magdala 27
  suicide 28, 35–6
Thompson, John 2
Thomson, Joseph: *Ulu* 10

Times, The 152, 153, 158
Times Weekly Edition 156
Tippu-Tib 102, 116, 117, 122, 123,
  130, 174
Travers, R.L. 165
Troup, John Rose 117, 118, 136, 154,
  156, 162, 163
  With Stanley's Rear Column 121
Truth 165
Tures 18, 37
Tylor, E.B. 67

Uledi (coxswain) 106–7
United Kingdom Tea Company 76,
  174
Universal Review 167

Victoria, Queen 26, 30, 36, 91–2, 99

Wakley, Thomas 56
Walker, John 133
Ward, Herbert 117, 136, 137–40, 154,
  174, 175
  *Five Years with the Congo
    Cannibals* 137
  My Life with Stanley's Rear Guard
    137
Ward, Thomas 174
Watt, Ian 184, 186, 192
Wauters, A.J. 170
Wells, H.G. 211–12
  Time Machine, The 77, 193, 197
Werner J. R. 151–2
Williams, Raymond 7, 10, 47
Wolseley, Lord 153
writing, Africans and 72–5

Yorkshire Post 153